ELASTIC EMPIRE

Stanford Studies in Middle Eastern and
Islamic Societies and Cultures

ELASTIC EMPIRE

Refashioning War through Aid in Palestine

Lisa Bhungalia

STANFORD UNIVERSITY PRESS

Stanford, California

Stanford University Press
Stanford, California

Printed in the United States of America on acid-free, archival-quality paper

Library of Congress Cataloging-in-Publication Data
Names: Bhungalia, Lisa, author.
Title: Elastic empire : refashioning war through aid in Palestine / Lisa Bhungalia.
Other titles: Stanford studies in Middle Eastern and Islamic societies and cultures.
Description: Stanford, California : Stanford University Press, [2024] | Series:
   Stanford studies in Middle Eastern and Islamic societies and cultures | Includes
   bibliographical references and index.
Identifiers: LCCN 2023010840 (print) | LCCN 2023010841 (ebook) | ISBN 9781503634527
   (cloth) | ISBN 9781503637511 (paperback) | ISBN 9781503637528 (ebook)
Subjects: LCSH: Economic assistance, American—Political aspects—Palestine.
   | Terrorism—Law and legislation—United States. | Terrorism—Palestine—
   Prevention. | United States—Foreign relations—Palestine. | Palestine—Foreign
   relations—United States.
Classification: LCC E183.8.P19 B48 2024 (print) | LCC E183.8.P19 (ebook) |
   DDC 338.91/7305694—dc23/eng/20230503
LC record available at https://lccn.loc.gov/2023010840
LC ebook record available at https://lccn.loc.gov/2023010841

Cover design: Sandra Rosales
Cover photo: Lisa Bhungalia

Contents

ELASTIC EMPIRE

Introduction

THE WALLS WERE LINED WITH PHOTOS OF THE DISAPPEARED, MANY held without charge in administrative detention, their sentences renewed every six months, indefinitely. Others had been released. It was a hot July, even for here. Fans blew Post-it notes marking important sections of case files. There were binders upon binders.

I had landed here via a chain of phone calls. This was one among a handful of visits to organizations on "the list." The list came from a report I had been carrying around since landing in Palestine earlier that summer. Published by Israel's Ministry of Strategic Affairs (MSA), the seventy-six-page document features a split-image cover containing half a clean-shaven, suit-wearing professional and half a keffiyeh-wrapped gun-flaunting terrorist—a hybrid terrorist-executive. Leaving little to the imagination, the report, entitled "Terrorists in Suits," purports to expose deep links between terror groups and Palestinian nongovernmental organizations (NGOs). "Just go down the list of organizations featured in this report," an analyst with a Palestinian think tank had told me a few months back, "and you have a sense of who will be hit next."[1] I was now in the office of one such organization included in the report, Addameer, a prisoner support and human rights association. "Come on back," a senior-level staffer said to me. She apologized for the delay. I would thank her too much for taking the time to meet with me. These were not *normal* times even in the long arc of settler colonial dispossession.

We were three years into the Trump presidency, and US policy in the region was "on steroids" as Middle East analyst Mouin Rabbani would describe it.[2] Washington was waging a series of heightened pressure policies on the Palestinians while directly facilitating Israel's most maximalist claims. In May 2018, the United States recognized Jerusalem as the capital of Israel and Israeli sovereignty over the occupied Syrian Golan Heights. Soon thereafter, it closed the Palestine Liberation Organization (PLO) mission in Washington and the US consulate in East Jerusalem, establishing instead a Palestinian Affairs Unit within the US embassy to Israel, thereby subsuming US–Palestinian relations within, and as subordinate to, its bilateral relationship with Israel.[3] Washington furthermore ordered US agencies, such as the State Department, to cease referring to the West Bank and Gaza Strip as "occupied territory" and asserted that Israel had the right to annex West Bank territory. Alongside these diplomatic maneuvers, Washington terminated US aid to the Palestinians, thereby dispensing with any pretense of measured liberalism from US interventionism in the region.[4] Accordingly, Washington shuttered its bilateral aid mission—the US Agency for International Development (USAID) in the West Bank and Gaza—and ended its contributions to the United Nations Relief and Works Agency (UNRWA), formerly the agency's largest contributor, directly jeopardizing the ability of the agency to provide for Palestinian refugees. Meanwhile the decade-long siege on Gaza remained in place, and the settler movement, emboldened by the political environment created by a Trump–Netanyahu alliance, gained strength. Amid these currents, aggressive measures undertaken by Israel and affiliated organizations further restricted the ability of Palestinian civil organizations to administer critically needed services to the Palestinian population and advocate on behalf of Palestinian political and human rights in a time of heightened aggression. Palestinians were undergoing, as Ilana Feldman describes it, a "full spectrum assault."[5]

Founded during the first Palestinian *intifada* to provide support to Palestinian political prisoners held in Israeli prisons, Addameer had been targeted by Israeli authorities for some time and had, in recent years, been subjected to mounting aggressions on multiple fronts. As with other organizations included on the MSA list, Addameer had been raided earlier that year by the Israel Defense Forces (IDF). On September 19, 2019, the IDF broke into Addameer's Ramallah office at 2:00 a.m., seizing computers, hard drives, files, and equipment. Two years later, Addameer, along with five other Palestinian NGOs, would be labeled "terrorist organizations" by Israel's Ministry of Defense, raided soon thereafter, and shut down by Israeli military order. Listing is, of course, an antecedent to more spectacular forms of violence, whether designating bodies for arrest (no-fly lists) or death (kill lists) or scripting territories as "terrorist havens" or regimes as "hostile entities" as a precursor for war. Throughout the course of my visit, however, we would not talk about the raid. Instead, my interlocutor would share what she considered to be a more ominous development.

In recent months, she recounted, Palestinian NGOs had been receiving notices from their European funders that enhanced "anti-terrorism" infrastructures and protocols would be integrated into their aid contracts. European Union (EU) Article 1.5 bis, included in EU grant contracts beginning in July 2019, introduced an "anti-terrorism" clause into European funding streams stipulating that recipients ensure EU assistance is not transferred to EU-designated terrorist entities. It also mandated that civil society organizations screen potential beneficiaries and partners against EU sanctions lists and ensure compliance with EU restrictive measures. The EU claimed these enhanced measures were consistent with EU policy since 2001. Many Palestinian NGOs argued otherwise—saying that the integration of the heightened counterterrorism measures imposed new obligations on them to police and surveil their recipients, further embroiling them in the reproduction of a security regime that criminalizes the Palestinian struggle for self-determination.[6] As we reviewed documents of various terrorism protocols received from European donors, my interlocutor duly underscored how this most recent development, while worrisome, was not new; rather it marked the escalation of a process that had been underway for nearly two decades. "All the terrorism regulations and policies developed since September 11th are now the norm," she said.[7] This sentiment was echoed by many Palestinians within the NGO sector. The director of another NGO in the West Bank remarked that while counterterrorism laws and terrorist databases predate 9/11, heavily securitized aid practices did not become common until recent decades. The "global war on terror," he emphasized, has given rise to infrastructures of surveillance that are fundamental to the way aid works in Palestine today. "This is now normalized," he underscored, and "the US paved the way for this trend."[8] During the early years of the global war on terror, the United States introduced, and subsequently intensified, a counterterrorism paradigm into its aid flows in the West Bank and Gaza Strip. Some two decades later, this heavily securitized model of aid has become normalized throughout foreign donor intervention in Palestine. This book tells the story of how aid also became war.

AID AND WAR

Processes of dispossession spanning over half a century have rendered the Palestinian population in the West Bank and Gaza Strip nearly entirely aid dependent.[9] Foreign assistance—primarily from the United States, European Union, United Nations, and other Western bilateral and multilateral agencies, alongside Arab donors such as Qatar and Saudi Arabia—provides much-needed assistance for basic infrastructural and development needs, public services, and emergency relief (especially in the Gaza Strip). At the same time, foreign aid governance in the Palestinian territories is shaped foremost by the foreign policy and security regimes of donor states, bound up as these are with Israel, which maintains a military occupation over the Palestinian population. These security logics are particularly influential in the structuring of US aid programs administered to the Palestinians.

A strong ally of the United States, Israel receives over $3 billion per year in US bilateral military aid.[10] It is moreover the largest cumulative recipient of US foreign assistance since World War II, totaling over $150 billion.[11] The scope and parameters of the US–Israel relationship have a profound impact on US policies toward the Palestinians, manifesting perhaps most evidently in America's adoption of Israeli definitions of the conflict and diplomatic support of its negotiating position.[12] American civilian aid programs to the Palestinians are not exempt from this larger framing. The primary objectives underpinning US assistance to the Palestinians are thus shaped foremost by Israel's geopolitical interests, security prerogatives, and counterinsurgency aims. Other objectives can and do factor into the allocation of American aid to the Palestinians so long as they do not diminish or threaten these larger security goals. Aid thus serves as a key site for the production of national security projects, while simultaneously serving as a lifeline for a population living under conditions of ongoing dispossession and war.

The US–Israel security relationship is reflected through a host of US federal laws, executive orders, and national security mandates that shape and constrain US aid programs to the Palestinians. US terrorism law—or material support legislation, which bans tangible and intangible assistance to US-designated foreign terrorist organizations—plays a particularly influential role. Today the US government classifies thousands of individuals, groups, and entities, including a number of Palestinian political parties, factions, and organizations, as "foreign terrorist organizations" (FTOs), Specially Designated Global Terrorists, or Specially Designated Nationals and Blocked Persons. Among the Palestinian groups so classified are some better-known movements and parties such as Hamas, which has governed the Gaza Strip since 2007, but also various factions associated with the PLO. As per US terrorism financing law, American aid to the Palestinians cannot be diverted to or support (directly or indirectly) any group, individual, or activity bearing this classification.

Given the deep entanglement of the security apparatuses of the United States and Israel, this classification is assigned to those groups and individuals Israel deems threatening to its geopolitical and military dominance over the Palestinian population. The practices of aid governance, this book demonstrates, are themselves part and parcel of an ever-more sophisticated regime of colonial management.[13] It is this securitized model that has been normed across donor practice in Palestine. Tracing how the infrastructures of aid on which Palestinians are largely reliant are bound up with the security and counterterrorism regimes of capitals and institutions oceans away, *Elastic Empire* exhibits how the foreign aid regime that has emerged in Palestine to purportedly manage the most deleterious effects of ongoing settler–colonial dispossession and rule—whether through the provision of vital foodstuffs, medical care, or repair of destroyed infrastructure and homes—has simultaneously proliferated the sites and means through which Palestinian life is regulated, surveilled, and policed. Aid serves as a key site through which a relation of war is mitigated and maintained. The United States has played a pivotal role in shaping this aid–war dynamic.

US SHADOW WARS

The United States has been at war for over two decades—though this war has been waged largely in the shadows, in the concealed spaces of black sites, extraordinary renditions, sweeping and secret global surveillance, drone assassination programs, and "small footprint" operations carried out by special operations forces.[14] The secret military Joint Special Operations Command (JSOC), for instance, which operates parallel to but separate from the CIA, has grown tenfold over the last decade. Currently operational in over a hundred countries, JSOC carries out an increasing number of US counterterrorism operations from intelligence-gathering missions and lethal raids to interrogations and torture in secret prisons around the world. It also runs a parallel drone-assassination program to the CIA and has authorization from the president to select individuals for its kill list. Over the course of the global war on terror, the US covert drone war, wherein "targets" are selected by classified intelligence for assassination without indictment or trial, has supplanted interrogation and detention and boot-heavy counterinsurgency operations to become a cornerstone of its counterterrorism warfare.

Notably, the Obama administration played a key role in expanding this covert, territorially boundless war, its legal regimes of authorization and attendant global surveillance architectures, to an unprecedented degree.[15] Indeed, one of the key legacies left behind by the Obama administration is that it set the precedent for and normed the seemingly endless expansion of US secret wars—relying in large part on "state secrets privilege"—even as it touted its intention, as has the Biden administration after it, to scale back US wars, close Guantanamo, and withdraw US troops from Iraq and Afghanistan.[16]

Much war-making, we could say, has happened in the shadows cast by the repeal of highly visible and spectacular modes of warfare.[17] So, too, as the US soldier is removed and perhaps, at some point, Guantanamo closed, US proxy regimes and private contractors will continue to carry out the *work* of war with less accountability, visibility, and knowledge of its existence. Even as US wars are proliferating, they are increasingly in the shadows. This book tracks a little-known but ever-expanding war, one that manifests not through spectacular modes and modalities of military warfare and violence, in covert assassinations, or in the archipelago of US-proxy black sites, but rather one that travels in and through an expanding body of US counter-terrorism law tethered to aid flows and monetary transactions around the world.

WAR THROUGH LAW

"Good morning," President Bush announced on September 24, 2001. "At 12:01 a.m. this morning, a major thrust of our war on terrorism began with the stroke of a pen. Today, we have launched a strike on the financial foundation of the global terror network."[18] With these words, Bush signed into force Executive Order (EO) 13224, an emergency declaration that allowed the president to put in place an extensive program to attack terrorist financing that would have reverberations across the globe. "[T]his war on terrorism," Bush declared, "will be fought on a variety of fronts, in different ways." While the US military would remain on guard, Bush promised the American people, "the front lines [of this war] will look different from the wars of the past." EO 13244, merely one legal instrument within a broader legal-war complex, created a list of Specially Designated Global Terrorists, froze their assets, and banned all transactions with them. "This list is just a beginning," Bush warned.

Connected to a larger legal-war apparatus with roots in the 1990s, EO 13224 conferred especially broad powers on the US Treasury to target the financial support infrastructure of global terror networks, casting an ever-expanding net on who and what could be prosecuted by the US security state.[19] NGOs and humanitarian institutions were rendered part and parcel of the global terrorist infrastructure on which the United States had just declared war. As Bush warned in his speech on September 24, the newly administered order would target not only US-declared terrorist organizations and leaders but also "nongovernmental organizations [that serve] as fronts for their activities." The civilian realm was effectively folded into the center of this war; and in this way, a broad array of civilian agencies—including NGO personnel, humanitarian and relief workers, and development contractors—were conscripted into carrying out the work of the US security state. Bush's order, and the financial war on terror more broadly, collapsed any clean division between civilian and military, humanitarianism and war.

The workings of the US war state through humanitarian aid flows transgresses normative categories of war. We cannot make sense of it solely or primarily through the analytic of territoriality.[20] It also does not necessarily fit within contemporary debates on asymmetric and small wars, which have tended to foreground the military and kinetic dimensions of contemporary warfare, with critical liberal counterinsurgency theorists being the exception.[21] Nor can it fully be understood vis-à-vis the analytic of "humanitarian war"—there is nothing liberal or humanitarian about US terrorism law, and the war on terror more broadly from which it springs.[22] There is no recuperation, no "civilizing mission," no reform. The US global war on terror, and its attendant legal-war architecture, is intended to punish, isolate, and eliminate "targets" conscripted outside the bounds of the human. At the same time this law lives, breathes, and animates itself within the realm of humanitarianism, within the civilian sphere. Here we see the re-strategization of war through the civil realm.[23] This accounting of the US war state, as it proliferates through global aid flows—re-embedding and animating itself in putatively nonmilitary institutions of care, relief, and aid—tells us something significant about the evolving character, spatialities, and modalities of war, its realignments and reformulations, and its increasingly concealed and shadowy forms.[24] Accordingly, the story of US war chronicled here is not one of tanks, grenades, and guns. It is instead one of a more silent war waged through the interlacing of aid and law.

A TURN TO THE TOPOLOGICAL

Bush's little-known order, an appendage of the broader counterterrorism regime to which EO 13224 is connected, presented itself everywhere in Palestine: it sowed division between universities and the municipalities in which they were situated; it disrupted the contiguous development of water infrastructure and roads; it punctuated Gaza's greenhouses; it prohibited collaboration among Palestinian health providers; it stymied youth democracy projects; it spurred boycotts—it produced particular kinds of landscapes while preempting and disallowing others. It sowed contractual relationships. I would first bump up against Bush's order while sitting in a café in the West Bank city of Nablus in conversation with a friend of a friend who had recently left his job in a UNRWA-administered refugee camp to work for a development contractor on a "rule of law" project. It pays well, he said, "but we have to sign 'the paper.' " "The paper"—or anti-terrorism certification (ATC)—that is connected to EO 13224 stipulates that recipients of US monies certify that they do not provide support for terrorist acts or to designated foreign terrorist organizations identified on the US Office of Foreign Assets Control (OFAC) list. The OFAC database contains a number of Palestinian parties, groups, and individuals that are prohibited from receiving US monies. Banned parties also include those "otherwise associated" with designated entities. The paper is one component of a more complex national security infrastructure that transposes a regime of surveillance, sanction, and punishment far beyond the sites and domains where the US claims jurisdiction. Some 6,000 miles from US territorial borders, the US national security state is intimately *here*.

The paper—and the broader legal-war regime to which it is connected—proffers insight into the topological relations at play in contemporary imperial formations, which rely, in large part, on mobile technologies, mediated arrangements of power, proxies, and blurred genres of rule that link far-flung places in intimate and often indeterminate ways. A turn to the topological opens up crucial analytical terrain for thinking about relations of presence and absence as this is measured not necessarily by metrics or physical distance, but rather by the modes of interconnectivity, exchanges, and relationships involved.[25]

Topological approaches to space and power have gained considerable traction in critical theory,[26] across the social sciences,[27] and in human geography specifically.[28] With roots in nineteenth-century mathematics, topology has gained broader appeal in critical social theory for the promise it holds of a "post-Euclidean spatial theory, a way of thinking about relationality, space, and movement beyond metrics, mapping, and calculation."[29] It is, as Michel Serres puts it, a "science of proximities."[30] Dispensing with metric and linear conceptualizations of space (and time), a topological approach attunes us to how spatialities of power are constituted through "social relations across spaces and distances, rather than merely radiating from certain locations."[31] A key insight of topology, as Anna Secor suggests, is that "some spatial problems depend not on the exact shapes of the objects involved" but on "the ways that they are put together,"[32] on their relationalities, connectivities, cuts, and fracturings.[33] Drawing insight from the Deleuzian emphasis on how technologies fold together places, actors, and actants,[34] topology attunes us to look for modes of connection and disconnection and to relations of presence and absence within different kinds of socio-spatial formations.[35] The linkages and circulations of distributed activities do not predetermine what happens, but rather make certain kinds of relations and events possible.[36] In the case of Palestine, for instance, the very presence of a securitized aid infrastructure is made possible by the global expanse of US war-making on the one hand, and by the very condition of aid dependency (itself a product of decades-long project of settler colonial dispossession) on the other.

The spatiality at play in a topological arrangement is one that, like the figure of the Möbius strip, blends insides and outsides while also keeping them in relation to each other. Such a relation figures centrally in Agamben's work on sovereignty and the exception wherein the banishment of certain bodies from political life constitutes a more complex topological relation than one of simply inclusion/exclusion vis-à-vis the juridical order.[37] The state of exception is not necessarily a space of void, but one of a field of forces conjoined on a threshold, wherein inside and out, norm and anomie, anomie and law remain in relational proximity.

Finding topology generative for theorizing relations between interiority and exteriority, geographers have turned to the topological to make sense of the refashioning of sovereignty regimes as states bend and flex across extra-territorial domains producing regimes of enforcement and exclusion through a mosaic of sites and proxy authorities far from the formal border per se, while dually internalizing regimes of exclusion within domestic space.[38] Mat Coleman, for one, charts the interlacing of different political spaces across territorial boundaries, coining what he calls a "proxy geography" of state immigration enforcement to account for how US border policing is reproduced in sites far afield from the border proper through a kind of double move: the outsourcing of US immigration policing to authorities in source and transit countries, on the one hand, and the devolution of immigration policing to sub-state proxy forces, on the other.[39] In this topological reworking, the US border and the regime of exclusion on which it is predicated are spatially reproduced through a mosaic of sites and mediated arrangements of power that reproduce US enforcement apparatuses in sites and through authorities far afield from the formal border per se.

Similar trends can be seen with the European Union, as EU states expand their border enforcement regimes offshore—on islands, at sea, and through

mediated arrangements with transnational and private actors—to interdict migrants bound for European shores. Alison Mountz's work on islands
as sites of a broader "enforcement archipelago" of detention is particularly
instructive here.[40] Mountz traces how offshore islands serve as "key sites
of territorial struggle where nation-states use distance, invisibility, and
sub-national jurisdictional status" to deter would-be asylum seekers from
reaching sovereign territory. Crucially, as Mountz shows, these sites are connected "not only to one another but to the detention of migrants *internal* to
sovereign territory as well," creating lines of continuity between so-called
internal/domestic and external/foreign realms.[41] Luiza Bialasiewicz too has
pointed to how the Mediterranean has long served as a key arena for Europe's
"border work" (as well as "Europe's graveyard") whereby it conscripts other
authorities and states, such as Libya, to disrupt migratory flows inbound to
Europe and "secure the external."[42] Indeed, state geographies of immigration
enforcement in Europe and beyond have enlisted an "extended 'playing field'
of local, transnational, and private actors."[43] Topology thus offers a spatial
grammar for the refashioning of sovereignty and border regimes, as lines between internal and external, what is proximate and afar, blend and enfold
into one another.[44]

Yet even as a turn to the topological offers a particularly useful conceptual language—a spatial lexicon for how borders and sovereignty regimes
are being reworked, interlaced, and embedded across space and time—less
attended to is how the topological helps us make sense of spatialities of
power underwriting contemporary imperial formations and complexes of
empire. Topologies, as Chris Harker shows in his work on debt in Palestine,
are "a particular type of spatial relations, which tie indebted residents to
people and institutions that have lent them money. They are like an invisible
bit of string that can stretch quite far."[45] These ties may be, most obviously,
to banks but also to other relations, including familial and friendship ties
that span disparate sites and spaces. The string, as Harker suggests, "becomes twisted in increasingly complex figurations. Each strand retains its
specificity, but the whole becomes elaborately interconnected." I use Harker's conceptualization of indebtedness, applied to aid assemblages, as a set
of topological relations that string or bind entities together across disparate
spaces, but also retain a certain kind of specificity. A turn to the topological
opens up crucial analytical terrain for thinking about the different modes of

connectivity and relationalities that render, in this case, Washington's punitive counterterrorism regime intimate and embedded in the lifeworlds of those afar. More broadly, a topological analysis of the US security state tells us something significant about the workings of late modern imperial power, its global mechanisms, array of techniques, and flexible technologies of rule.

THINKING EMPIRE TOPOLOGICALLY

Scholars of late modern empire and imperial sovereignty have long been attuned to the topological workings of power, even if they have not employed the terminology as such.[46] US imperial power, as these scholars underscore, operates most often through various modes of connection and disconnection, proxies and client regimes, informal dependencies, partial sovereignties, transnational arrangements, and aid flows mediated through asymmetrical relations of power.[47] Put differently, the contemporary workings of US empire most often do not take shape through direct modes of domination and territorial acquisition—some obvious examples notwithstanding, including the originary settler colonial violence and territorial usurpation on which the United States is founded. Indeed, much of the challenge in studying US imperial formations resides specifically in their ability to shape-shift, to blend and merge into the political and institutional infrastructure of foreign sites and territories. Abdullah al-Arian, for one, has traced the embedding of the US sanctions regime in the Lebanese banking and financial sector, which resulted in the banning of one of Lebanon's key political actors in the 2017 election. US empire, as al-Arian argues, manifests largely through a "deterritorialized set of institutions and practices that have become so deeply entrenched in the global order that they no longer rely exclusively on the active projection of US power."[48] It is only when we start to conceive of US global power this way, as al-Arian suggests, that we can begin to understand how Lebanon's "first fully home-grown electoral law," which banned one of Lebanon's key political actors, "could so seamlessly integrate an international legal norm conceived in Washington."[49]

Scholars of detention and torture have similarly pointed to modes of obscuration central to US-directed torture operations undertaken across a range of black sites stretching from Diego Garcia to Morocco, Poland to Yemen, and Thailand to Afghanistan.[50] The offshoring of torture to "other sovereigns" as Darryl Li has demonstrated, enables US-directed torture to continue apace while responsibility is offloaded to other political authorities.[51] Indeed, as Li suggests, much work of "US hegemony is about calibrating the relationship between authority and responsibility, with the goal of satisfying strategic goals while displacing burdens onto client regimes."[52] The construction of plausible deniability is central to the workings of liberal empire: as the US offloads the "dirty work" of torture, counterinsurgency, and empire management to pliant regimes and proxies, it maintains a veneer of adherence to legal norms and regulatory and ethical compliance. An enduring feature of US empire is its ability to transmogrify, to embed and configure in new constellations at multiple scales, through various technologies and in heterogeneous forms. Indeed, as Ann Stoler suggests, it is precisely through the deployment of flexible technologies and "blurred genres of rule" that US power takes hold while dually enabling the United States to evade responsibility for the territories and populations over which it exercises control.[53] This is how late modern US empire works: through proxies and indirect control, unclarified sovereignties and blurred genres of rule, ambiguity, and specters.[54]

If we understand US empire this way, Palestine emerges as an archetypal example of the workings of American empire. It is one where the presence of the United States, despite having no de jure claim to sovereignty or territory, is nevertheless viscerally felt, most notably through its military aid and weapons contracts, its exertion of diplomatic pressure via supranational bodies, and the projection of regimes of sanction and punishment through financial and transnational aid flows. If indeed US empire evades any kind of classical, territorial notion as such, as is commonly used to characterize nineteenth- and twentieth-century European empires, we might be better attuned to track the workings of US empire not only "in the details," as Catherine Lutz has suggested,[55] but also in the hazy, liminal, and undeclared spaces in and through which US power takes hold. Accordingly, *Elastic Empire* applies a topological analytic to US imperiality, tracing how Washington's counterterrorism regime embeds, bundles, and blends into civilian aid flows, stitching geographically disparate sites—in this case Washington to Palestine—in intimate and at times in the most unsuspecting of ways. This constitutes what I call the elastic workings of US empire. Elasticity provides a useful analytic for considering how the US security state embeds into the lifeworlds of those far away, at once stitching Palestine to Washington in at times exceedingly intimate ways, while at the same time creating vast distances between geographically proximate sites.

ELASTIC EMPIRE

This book examines the shape-shifting nature of sovereignty and enforcement regimes as states, and in this case, the United States, distend into global space, folding geographically distant populations into their ambit of power while dually exempting them from political life (they remain subjects, not citizens).[56] The concept of elasticity, even if not termed as such, has captured the attention of geographers and border scholars alike to theorize the creative refashioning of state jurisdiction and shape-shifting border regimes as states bend and flex across extraterritorial domains, de-linking legal and territorial borders to creatively refashion jurisdiction and excise certain bodies from political space.[57] Here we see a double move: the casting out of enforcement regimes across transnational sites and domains and the production of spaces of enforcement " 'on the inside' absent the law."[58] The border moves, collapses, extends, and proliferates with different bodies and to different ends.[59] The borders of heavily securitized states, such as the United States and Israel for instance, travel and attach to immigration control officials stationed in other sovereign spaces to strategically intercept populations en route. The sea and the movement of authorities across it, as Alison Mountz and Nancy Hiemstra have shown, constitute a key site of border enforcement: US authorities carry out operations in the Caribbean and the Pacific, Australia intercepts boats in the Pacific and Indian Oceans, and the European Union member states intercept boats in the Mediterranean.[60] Equally, borders move inward domestically to capture and remove certain subjects (usually racialized, working class, and from the Global South) from within. In the United States for instance, noncitizen subjects located within 100 miles of any physical US border—the Amtrak train station in Syracuse, New York, as but one example—are deemed never-to-have-arrived in the United States and are thus rendered deportable.

The twin processes of externalization and internalization function to incorporate certain subjects located beyond territorial boundaries into rules and laws governing the "domestic" while dually excluding racialized subjects within domestic space from protections and rights afforded by domestic law. The net effect of these processes, as Coleman demonstrates, is the state capture and deportation of noncitizens who, having reached US domestic space, are deemed "here enough" to be arrested but not "here enough" to address their detention in the courts.[61] The production of legal bans "do not map onto discrete spaces but rather are generalized across populations of immigrants regardless of location."[62] In this topological formulation, sovereign power attaches to bodies differentially, blending insides and outsides.

In a similar vein, Pauline Maillet, Alison Mountz, and Kira Williams demonstrate how the internalization of regimes of exclusion parallels the externalization of state enforcement regimes as they distend into global space to interdict bodies (i.e., the asylum seeker) and place them outside the scope of law and protections in "nowhere" sites such as the airport, at sea, or on excised territory.[63] Drawing on the concept of elasticity at the US–Canada border, Emily Gilbert[64] likewise traces how borders are stretched and distended but also how they "snap back into place" so as to limit state accountability and access to rights.[65] Gilbert's analysis centers heterogeneous processes of "geographical illocalization,"[66] as these occur vis-à-vis migrants, but also in relation to authorities responsible for border enforcement. The expansion of preclearance facilities in Canada, which allow travelers to clear customs before embarking on flights to the United States, enacts a new legal apparatus that "dramatically affect[s] the rights of travelers, but also limit[s] the accountability of US border agents who will receive immunity while at work in Canada."[67] The border, Gilbert argues, "ebbs and flows for different populations in different ways and with different effects."[68]

Eyal Weizman's conceptualization of elastic geography in Palestine/Israel echoes Gilbert's analysis of the ways sovereign power blends insides and outsides to creatively refashion political-legal geographies.[69] For Weizman, elasticity captures the persistent and constant transformation of Israel's frontier in the Occupied Territories. Far from a linear frontier, Israel's "border" with Palestinians is one of "constant transformation"—one consisting of a "temporary, transportable, deployable and removable border [technologies]," including flying and permanent checkpoints, separation walls, closed military and security zones, military bases, settlements and outposts, and "killing zones" (i.e., Gaza)—that "shrink and expand the territory at will."[70] The architectures of Israel's occupation, Weizman contends, "are dynamic, constantly shifting, ebbing and flowing; they creep along, stealthily surrounding Palestinian villages and roads. They may even erupt into Palestinian living rooms, bursting in through the house walls," as seen in the case of Nablus during the second *intifada*. One could indeed incorporate the Palestinian Authority into this accounting of the constant transformation and transmutation of Israel's settler colonial regime, in this case through a putatively Palestinian governing body. The "dynamic morphology of Israel's elastic frontier," Weizman contends, "resembles an incessant sea dotted with multiplying archipelagos of externally alienated and internally homogenous ethno-national enclaves—under a blanket of aerial Israeli surveillance."[71] Weizman's accounting of elasticity is helpful as it reminds us of the power hierarchies at play even as Israel's frontier shape-shifts, blends, and morphs. Israel retains power and control as the occupying authority even as this power relationship can be obfuscated within the matrix of control, a dizzying array of civilian and state actors therein, and by tactics of "constructive blurring." Part of the insidious work elastic geographies do, Weizman suggests, is to obfuscate "facts of domination."[72]

The concept of elastic empire, as I develop it here, draws on and expands in new directions an analysis of the elasticity of state and imperial power as it manifests in global counterterrorism and enforcement regimes (and their uneven application) rather than through an analysis of the border as it relates to state immigration and enforcement regimes per se.[73] The main protagonist in this story is US terrorism law, its transnational workings and intimate embeddings into the material, social, and political worlds of those afar through contractual relationships of aid. The descriptor "elastic" is utilized to hold at the fore of analysis relations of connectivity that remain across global space, even if transmogrified through different institutional forms and administrative and civilian constellations.

Following the law, *Elastic Empire* traces how the tethering of US terrorism law to civilian aid flows and monetary transactions around the world gives rise to a highly flexible and versatile mode of sovereign power, or what I call the elastic workings of sovereignty, that bends and fixes in particular sites and onto certain bodies.[74] Here jurisdiction exceeds territory, akin to Stuart Elden's *imperio*[75]—a boundless, limitless power containing no spatial boundary—that offers a useful entry point for considering how imperial power tethers and affixes to mobile subjects scattered across global space.[76] Equally, it is important to qualify that *imperio* does not operate in a limitless and even-handed manner across space. Rather it manifests in a highly uneven fashion: at times the security state projects a hyper-intensified presence (and regime of punishment) vis-à-vis hypervisible subjects;[77] other times it is entirely absent. The workings of the security state ebb and flow differentially. This differential, punctuated, uneven presence and absence pivots on and is correlated to the racialized coding of particular subject populations as suspect/safe, dangerous/trustworthy, familiar/queer. The accounting of elastic imperiality undertaken in this book tracks the sovereignty configurations and constellations produced through *imperio* or imperial geographies of US war-making, militarization, and encounter[78] and informed by racial economies of threat and disorder resulting less in an "everywhere war"[79] and more a punctuated mode of warfare and imperial presence.

In foregrounding these quieter articulations of imperiality, *Elastic Empire* tells a story of US empire not often told. It is not one of spectacular, episodic displays of military force and violence as exhibited so forcefully in the early aughts. Rather, this is a quieter accounting of US power but nevertheless one that indelibly transfigures the lives of those subjects caught in the crosshairs; it is one that emerges in the interstices and infrastructures of daily life, in a library, a greenhouse, in the halls of foreign municipal councils, in local elections and in Gaza-bound milk and biscuits. US empire, I argue, is not only "in the details," à la Lutz, but also in the hazy, liminal, and in this case "humanitarian" spaces in and through which US power often takes hold.[80] This constructive blurring is at the heart of elastic sovereignty. The insidious work elastic geographies do is to obfuscate the "facts of domination."[81] This is the story, my book contends, of how late modern empire works. Tracking the work of the US security state from within Palestine over the course of nearly a decade, *Elastic Empire* constructs a different theoretical apparatus of war and empire—it tells us something significant about the shape-shifting nature of imperial formations, their realignments and reformulations, their haunted sites, and their obscured but intimate forms.

Equally, *Elastic Empire* moves beyond a singular focus on the topological workings of the US security state, and US aid specifically, to make a broader claim about evolving techniques of population management under conditions of late modern settler–colonial rule and evolutionary tactics of late modern war.[82] The Oslo Accords (1993–2001) introduced significant changes to the political and economic structures governing Palestinians' lives in the West Bank and Gaza Strip. While the trappings of a "self-rule" government were set up in the form of the Palestinian Authority (PA), on the one hand, a nongovernmental sector boomed on the other, with the work of both sustained by foreign aid flows subject to Israeli political calculation. Even though the Oslo peace process has officially collapsed, the political arrangement it enacted remains. Accordingly, questions of who rules and how governing power is asserted over the Palestinian population today do not yield easy answers. Power and authority blend and merge: a Palestinian police uniform signals Israeli coordination; a newly paved USAID road likely means a settlement has been accommodated; and a development expert in Ramallah is a reminder of the foreign imprint on the making of Palestine.[83]

Thus, the predicaments facing Palestinians today are exceedingly complex. The post-Oslo period has seen the growth of a governance apparatus that has extended the reach of Israel's security regime through institutions of "self-rule," development, and humanitarian relief, while undermining and obstructing collective modes of politics and political mobilization through, among other things, the production of new kinds of individualized, professionalized, self-regulating colonial subjects. Perhaps most disconcerting for many in Palestine, and indeed the subject of much internal discussion, are the ways that Palestinians have themselves come to participate in the reproduction of a regime of governance that has done little to alter their status as subjects under protracted settler–colonial rule and indeed much to sustain it.[84]

Palestine, then, speaks more broadly to evolutionary tactics of late modern warfare and liberal counterinsurgency, which aim to reshape, reconstitute, and pacify populations through various war, policing, and interventionary practices "geared at governing the political aspirations of target societies."[85] In the transition from colonial modernity to the postcolonial era, as Vivienne Jabri argues, the postcolonial subject has, in each moment she has made a claim to politics, come "face to face with global operations of power that seek to control and govern."[86] Such is true of the Palestinian colonial condition. An expansive foreign aid regime has developed over the course of three decades in Palestine to build the institutional foundation for a putative Palestinian state, on the one hand, and provide critical humanitarian relief for a population besieged on the other. That regime is itself, as Jabri might argue, part and parcel of a war infrastructure that has banished politics. Not lost on Palestinians is how almost any activity, behavior, or act of speech that challenges their subjugated position within the current political order is scripted as a security threat and equated to terrorism. Put differently, Palestinians have suffered a double dispossession not only in terms of the ongoing loss of material resources (land, territory, water, homes), but so too of capacity for politics and political subjectivity. As subjects targeted by liberal interventionary forces, Palestinians are reduced, per Jabri, to a "division between culprits and victims, where the former come to be defined as the enemy [here those imbued with the terrorist moniker] while the latter constitute . . . a mass to be protected or rescued."[87] Within this schema, as Jabri suggests, there is not a "right to politics, which assumes agency and distinct subjectivity framed in the contingencies of social and political life, but a life lived as mass, simply one element in a category inscribed elsewhere and by others."[88]

The deepening securitization of aid, this book demonstrates, is part and parcel of the refinement and evolution of liberal warfare and counterinsurgency.[89] Here we see not only the exercise of a brutal sovereign power—although this certainly persists—but so too the calibration of Palestinian life and the delimiting of Palestinian political capacities through the infrastructures of aid on which Palestinians are largely reliant. The various processes traced throughout this book—the collection of personal information, mapping of coordinates of land plots, development of internal policing and reporting systems, intelligence gathering and the forging of alliances and divisions between various social groups—are all involved in ever-more sophisticated methods of identification, mapping, controlling, dividing, and making legible this population that has time and time again refused wholesale defeat.[90]

In tracing these developments, *Elastic Empire* illustrates how strategies of population control and management do not only extend to the prison or the checkpoint or take shape exclusively in the form of separation walls and settlements; they are also being worked through the moral technologies, humanitarian infrastructures, and systems of monitoring that have become the means for administering a population living under protracted military rule.[91] As such, war can and should be understood as occurring not simply in the meeting of two adversaries on a battlefield but, perhaps more sinisterly, through the humanitarian regimes that have become the means for governing the displaced, the refugee, the poor, and the "vulnerable."[92] Accordingly, *Elastic Empire* demonstrates how regimes of war and violence are reproduced through mechanisms, infrastructures, and institutions purportedly designed to promote stability and peace. More broadly, it lends insight into the multiple forms of violence that exist within our concept of war— not only the spectacular and the crisis-laden, but also the mundane, bureaucratic, routinized, and largely concealed.[93]

Accordingly, this book situates Palestine within a broader discussion of what historians Hew Strachan and Sibylle Scheipers call "the changing character of war"[94] in conversation with a range scholarly works on the shifting spatialities and modalities of late modern war,[95] critical humanitarian studies,[96] and contemporary colonialisms, including Palestine in particular.[97] The logics, politics, and practices underwriting contemporary liberal warfare and intervention have no doubt given rise to new forms of interventionary power in zones of war and conflict in the quest to "stabilize" and reconstruct societies deemed problematic and dangerous. As Laleh Khalili's seminal work on counterinsurgencies of the twentieth century demonstrates, tactics of war have shifted beyond wholesale slaughter to incorporate more elaborate systems of population control, confinement, and regulation; these tactics, while no less lethal or dangerous to populations in sites of intervention, are nonetheless marketed as more "humane" techniques for violent processes of social engineering.[98] A key contribution of *Elastic Empire* is its fine-grained analysis of the securitized modes of administration emergent within war and conflict zones as the lines between humanitarianism and counterterrorism are increasingly blurred.

Humanitarianism has become an increasingly central feature of global politics in light of mass displacements, environmental crises, low-grade counterinsurgencies, and overt military interventions of the twenty-first century;[99] so too is humanitarian relief increasingly governed by a counterterrorism framework. The tethering of counterterrorism laws to global aid flows, increasing prohibitions on foreign assistance to civilian populations living in "terrorist-controlled" territories, and the increased bombings of hospitals and medical facilities in war zones are but some ways in which humanitarianism, as Jonathan Whittall contends, has "faded into an enemy landscape."[100] This book sits in such landscapes where the lines between humanitarianism and the global war on terror are increasingly indeterminate. Tracing how humanitarian and development complexes are coming up against a growing counterterrorism legal infrastructure that criminalizes a broad notion of "material support for terrorism," it demonstrates how the architectures of care and relief on which populations across the Global South are increasingly reliant become sites for the punitive regulation, policing, and surveillance of lives deemed simultaneously suspicious and in need of help. Tracing these securitized aid dynamics from the ground up and the racialized anxieties that underwrite them, this book brings into view how transnational projects of security and counterterrorism stitch together heterogeneous actors dispersed globally while producing intimate insecurities and precarity for racialized populations at the receiving end of transnational aid flows. In analyzing the modes of social regulation being produced through the increasing drive towards securitization, it becomes clear that aid is both relief and racialized warfare.

METHODOLOGY, MOVEMENT, IDENTITY

Elastic Empire is an ethnographic exploration of the world that foreign aid is making and unmaking in Palestine, with attention to the multiple and at times contradictory strategies being adopted by Palestinians to realize life and dignity under overlapping regimes of authority, domination, and rule. It draws on research spanning over a decade (2009–2021), including over two years of cumulative fieldwork conducted in Palestine, as well as research trips to Amman, Jordan, where the UNRWA headquarters are situated, and Washington, DC, where I interviewed congressional policy analysts and US foreign policy, legal, and Israel–Palestine experts.[101] Research conducted in Palestine included ethnographic research, semi-structured interviews, and participant observation. For the greater part of my fieldwork, I was based in Ramallah and traveled frequently throughout the West Bank and at times to Tel Aviv to speak with USAID officials.

Throughout the duration of this research, I conducted over 150 semi-structured interviews with various sectors that comprise a transnational aid network, including USAID officials, bureaucrats, and lawyers; UN officials; private contractors and firms; US and international NGOs; Palestinian Authority and municipal officials; Palestinian NGOs (including Palestinian organizations placed under investigation for terrorism financing and designated as "terrorist organizations" by Israel); community-based organizations, coalitions, and Palestinian scholars and grassroots organizers. I also conducted participant observation in 2010 with two organizations: the Dalia Association, a grassroots organization working to decrease dependency on external aid, and the Center for Development Studies at Birzeit University. I served as a volunteer at Dalia for a year and worked as a development consultant at Birzeit where I contributed to research for a UN-administered report on development under conflict. Additionally, in the summer of 2015 I provided research support to Aid Watch, which develops policy analyses grounded in the experiences of Palestinian aid-receiving communities.

I also reviewed and analyzed primary source legal and policy materials, including US material support laws and executive orders, congressional documents, and US State and Treasury Department terrorism and sanctions lists on a regular basis to track changes in federal laws that directly affect institutions through which US funds are channeled. The majority of these documents are available through the US National Archives, US Treasury, and US State Department sites. US congressional reports on foreign aid to the Palestinians made available through Congressional Research Service were reviewed on a regular basis to keep abreast of changes in US federal law and policy and to track recommendations made to congress by Middle East experts. Classified US embassy cables released by Wikileaks were also reviewed, as were US agreements made with multilateral aid institutions, including the Framework for Cooperation Between the United Nations Relief and Works Agency for Palestine Refugees in the Near East and the United States, 2021–2022. Additionally, I examined relevant texts from various negotiations conducted between Israel and the Palestinian leadership, including the Declaration of Principles on Interim Self-Government Agreements (1993), the Camp David Summit (2000), the Road Map for Peace (2003), and guiding documents for the Palestinian Authority, including the Palestinian Reform and Development Plan (PRDP) (2008–2010). The Abraham Accords, the Peace to Prosperity plan, and reports from Israel's Ministry of Strategic Affairs were also reviewed. Reports, figures, and other materials made available through the Israeli Civil Administration, and specifically statements from the Coordinator of Government Activities in the Territories (COGAT), pertaining to changes in official Israeli policy regarding donor activity in the occupied Palestinian territories were also periodically reviewed, as were World Bank technical reports and analysis. Lastly, statements and reports in English and Arabic from Palestinian human rights groups, NGOs, and grassroots organizations including Al-Shabaka, Al-Haq, the Boycott, Divestment and Sanctions (BDS) movement, the Palestinian NGO Network (PNGO), BADIL, and the Dalia Association, among others were consulted, as were employment ads placed in local newspapers for Palestinian staff in USAID-funded organizations.

As with any research conducted in Israel/Palestine, one's identity directly influences what kind of research can be done, where, and how. There were numerous ways in which my identity afforded me greater mobility, as well as closed some avenues down. An elaborate system of checkpoints, walls, settlements, apartheid roads, and permits severely limits and often entirely arrests the movement of Palestinians across borders. As a US citizen, I was not subject to the same restrictions as a Palestinian living in the West Bank or Gaza, nor did I face the same restrictions as a Palestinian with foreign citizenship.[102] Thus, I was thus able to travel freely throughout Israel to visit USAID headquarters in Tel Aviv, conduct interviews with contractors and NGOs based in Jerusalem, and attend lectures and meetings throughout Israel.[103] Had I been subject to the mobility restrictions imposed on Palestinians, I would not have been able to trace the articulations of the USAID network across these various geopolitical zones, nor would I have gained access in the same way to debates circulating among Palestinians living inside Israel (and Jerusalem in particular). This book, as any, is the product of the researcher. While I was fortunate to have had the opportunity to live and research in Palestine for years, I hold no illusions that the conversations I had, the information I was given, the circles into which I was admitted, and the insights I present here are not deeply inflected by my positioning as a foreigner, and in particular, a US citizen. What I present in the pages that follow reflects my positionality as well as the relationships built over the course of nearly twelve years traveling to and residing within Palestine.

Taken together, the experiences and opportunities accrued over the course of a decade afforded insight into a range of debates circulating within Palestine on foreign aid intervention and helped me develop a more nuanced understanding of the manifold ways Palestinians are negotiating an increasingly securitized aid regime that has become a central feature of political, economic, and material life in post-Oslo Palestine. In so doing, this book joins a growing body of critical work on the role of foreign aid within evolving techniques of late modern settler–colonial rule through fine-grained attention to how counterterrorism has come to govern humanitarianism.[104]

SHAPE OF THE BOOK

The book reflects the story that I am to tell—one of the silent wars waged through a globally expansive legal-war architecture that indelibly shapes the lives of those caught in its crosshairs. To tell this story, we must begin a decade before the official start of the global war on terror. It was during the 1990s, as Chapter 1 traces, that the legal infrastructure for US terrorism financing law was consolidated—and Palestine, it shows, is central to this story. More broadly, Chapter 1 argues that the material support ban has codified into legal practice a preemptive model of punitive governance that authorizes state violence on bodies conscripted as threats-in-waiting, and in so doing, significantly expands the scope and reach of the prosecutorial web of the US security state, which has implications far beyond terrorism prosecutions, Israel, the United States, and Palestine.

Chapter 2 further develops an analysis of the topological arrangements that underwrite contemporary imperial formations and war regimes in a putatively postcolonial world broadly and the concept of elastic imperiality specifically. In tracing the highly flexible and versatile operations of the US security state in Palestine and the blurred genres of rule to which it gives rise, Palestine, it argues, emerges as an archetypal example of the workings of American empire. It is one where the presence of the United States, despite having no de jure claim to sovereignty or territory, is nevertheless indelibly felt. This chapter shows how Palestinians are objects of empire, though in ways often unrecognized, while at the same time holding open the promise and possibility of how the topological ties that bind can, and often do, come undone.

Chapter 3 homes in on the political work of terrorism lists, delving further into their political and material implications for the racialized bodies and landscapes on which they touch down. Chapter 3 examines how the technology of the terrorism list in Palestine is part and parcel of the amalgam of counterinsurgency forces that work on and through Palestinians to fragment, pacify, and render them more easily governable in the long arc of dispossession. Drawing on extensive ethnographic work, this chapter centers on the punitive regimes of policing and surveillance terrorism lists inaugurate in Palestine, but also on how Palestinians refuse the security logics they impose.

Chapter 4 examines a different iteration of US empire in Palestine—its afterlives and reverberations in the wake of the official end of US aid to Palestinians during the Trump era. Rather than ameliorating pressure, this period saw the intensification of the counterterrorism paradigm across donor aid practice more broadly. The chapter shows how the securitized practices, technologies, and norms the United States has long promoted and normalized in Palestine have lived on, metastasized, and, perhaps most significantly, established a new aid-governing norm for Western-aligned donor intervention in Palestine. It considers what remains living and breathing in absence—what kind of violence is embedded in a world that cannot be returned.

Finally, Chapter 5 tracks a culminating moment in the long war traced in this book through the "point of the list." It chronicles the story of six Palestinian organizations designated as terrorist organizations by Israel's Ministry of Defense in October 2021 and subsequently shut down by Israeli military order roughly a year later. Drawing on interviews and visits to the organizations shortly following the ministry's designation, this chapter examines how Israel's classification enacts what I call *asphyxiatory violence:* a modality of violence that realizes its destructive effects through less spectacular means than a bomb or tank, but through a quieter, temporally stretched process of constriction, one that progressively erodes conditions of livability through forced disconnection and isolation. The chapter moreover argues that the slow, debilitating processes of violence that the terrorism classification inaugurates present us with a different temporality of war—one wherein violence is stretched over time—and a different optics of violence—there is no bomb to condemn nor troops to demand come home. It is arguably precisely because of the visual and temporal registers that slow, debilitating processes of asphyxiation evade that make blacklisting practices, sanctions regimes, and seemingly mundane financial restrictions an increasingly preferred method of warfare, most notably for liberal imperial and settler–colonial powers that seek to manage the field of visibility for their crimes.

The Conclusion returns us to questions regarding the optics and redistributions of contemporary warfare and late modern empire. The counterterrorism regime examined in this book, it argues, constitutes a key architecture through which the United States has redistributed its capacities for war-making and violence. Shrouded in secrecy and mundane in its application, the violence this regime inflicts takes place in a shadow world unknown to most of us. *Elastic Empire* seeks to put this war—or these distributions of war—ongoing in Palestine and elsewhere back on the map, most notably because their very "unknowability" is precisely the point.

One

WAR THROUGH LAW

MUHAMMAD SALAH

In January of 1993, Muhammad Salah, a Palestinian American citizen and Chicago resident, traveled to the Gaza Strip. At the Erez checkpoint on the Gaza border, he was blindfolded, shackled, and thrown into an Israeli military jeep. Hours later he was deposited at the Shin Bet (Israel Security Agency) interrogation center in Ramallah. Salah was held for nearly five years in military prison, during which time a confession was extracted under torture.[1] Israel alleged he was a Hamas operative carrying funds to be distributed to the organization. Salah and his lawyers maintained he was delivering humanitarian aid to the Gaza Strip. The timing of Salah's arrest was not insignificant. Five weeks earlier, Israel had deported 415 Palestinians to South Lebanon, many of them involved in local charities, resulting in a disruption of relief services in the West Bank and Gaza Strip.[2]

Days after Salah's arrest, Israel announced that it had captured a "top Hamas military commander" and further declared that the Hamas leadership had moved its military command center to the United States.[3] Urging US officials to take a more aggressive stance against Hamas, Israeli officials distributed a chart displaying Hamas activity in Iran, Jordan, Syria, Lebanon, and Sudan with lines feeding to a central leadership in the United States.[4] "The point," as one security official stated, was to demonstrate that "this organization is your problem, too," and in so doing link together, at least rhetorically, US and Israeli security interests.[5] Presenting Salah as proof of its charge, Israel pressured the US to outlaw Hamas and criminalize transnational networks of support to it.[6] The US government, however, found no evidence to corroborate the claim that Salah had in fact been at the head of a US-based Hamas cell or anything close to it, and at least initially offered meager support to Salah during his first months of detention. This support would soon dwindle, and the US position would change course entirely with the onset of the global war on terror eight years later. Salah, and his plight, sit at the center of an evolving legal-war architecture that would later constitute a central means through which the war on terror would be waged.

This chapter traces the evolution of this legal-war architecture, the centrality of Palestine to its development, and the geographically and temporally expansive logics that underpin it. Understanding the mechanics of the US material support ban is essential for understanding how the financial war on terror operates. It is this body of law that attaches to aid flows and financial transactions around the world, codifying into legal practice a preemptive model of punitive governance that authorizes state violence on bodies conscripted as threats-in-waiting. In so doing, the transnational operation of this law significantly expands the scope and reach of the prosecutorial web of the US security state. The material support ban thus constitutes an essential mechanism through which elastic imperiality operates. By extending the geographic scope of the US security state to cover the flow of money outside its territorial boundaries and by expanding its temporal reach to incorporate future-oriented, speculative action, this legal-war architecture stretches, transforms, and mutates the landscape and timescape of sovereignty. Accordingly, this chapter traces the historical development and evolution of this speculative and geographically expansive modality of warfare, a story that begins well before the official onset of the global war on terror. Thus, this chapter dwells largely in the 1990s as it is here where the legal foundation and tools for US preemptive war were established. Equally, even as this decade constituted a critical era wherein the legal and war-making powers of the global war on terror were established, the events traced herein (Muhammad Salah, the Oslo Accords, the Oklahoma City bombing) were powerful in shaping US discourse and policy on terrorism only insofar as they occurred on the heels of processes set in motion nearly two decades earlier in which the phenomenon of political violence was transformed into terrorism.[7]

PRELUDE TO THE GLOBAL WAR ON TERROR:
HOW VIOLENCE BECAME TERRORISM

The emergence of the discourse of terrorism must be understood within a broader set of racialized, transnational, and historical processes that date back at least to the 1970s.[8] Global events such as the 1972 Munich Olympics and the Iran hostage crisis—alongside two international conferences organized by the Jonathan Institute, an Israeli think tank—did much to consolidate what Deepa Kumar calls the "transnational production of terrorcraft," or a process of terrorist racialization with Palestinians and the Palestinian liberation movement at the center of that story.[9] The discourse of terrorism, as Lisa Stampnitzky suggests, emerged in large part in response to Palestinian resistance in the 1970s and was shaped in subsequent decades by transnational circuits between the United States and Israel.[10]

From the postwar period until the late 1960s, Palestinians had exhausted every possible tool at their disposal to attain their rights, freedom, and dignity. They had appealed to Arab states and to the international community including the United Nations to no avail, while their condition of statelessness, refugeehood, and denial of freedom persisted. By the 1967 War—wherein Israel would defeat surrounding Arab states and capture the West Bank, including East Jerusalem, Gaza Strip, Sinai Peninsula, and Golan Heights—Palestinians had become all too aware that the *nakba* was an ongoing condition. Strategies waged on the part of Palestinians to achieve dignity and freedom have never been a monolith; at different historical epochs, different strategies have taken shape. By the late 1960s and early 1970s, certain factions of the Palestinian national struggle turned to political violence, having exhausted all other avenues to achieve their return and freedom.[11]

While hijackings and other instances of political violence had occurred from 1968 to 1972, the attack at the 1972 Munich Olympics is often inscribed "as the spectacular event that inaugurated the era of modern terrorism."[12] Later that month, following Israeli air raids in Syria and Lebanon in the aftermath of Munich, the UN General Assembly would convene a series of debates on terrorism at the behest of Arab states. Israel opted not participate in the UN debates but did submit a defense to the secretary general of its decision to use force. It moreover argued that Egypt, Lebanon, Syria, and Libya had "initiated the establishment of terror organizations" and that it was the responsibility of Arab states to effectively disband them.[13] Meanwhile, the Soviet bloc and many non-aligned states argued that the struggle for self-determination was legitimate and accordingly put forth a forceful condemnation of colonial violence and foreign domination.

Despite objections from Western states, the Security Council passed UN Resolution 3034 three months later, which urged international cooperation to deal with the problem of terrorism, and equally affirmed the "inalienable right to self-determination and independence of all peoples under colonial and racist regimes and other forms of alien domination" and underscored the "legitimacy of their struggle." So too did it condemn "repressive and terrorist acts" by colonial and foreign powers in denying the right to self-determination. Two years later, the Palestine Liberation Organization (PLO) was conferred observer status in the UN. In 1977, the use of armed struggle in self-determination was inscribed as a protocol in the Geneva Convention.[14] Unsurprisingly, Israel's then UN Ambassador Benjamin Netanyahu was displeased with the UN approach to terrorism and would soon thereafter organize two international conferences on the subject along markedly different lines.

It was in the aftermath of Munich, Stampnitzky argues, that terrorism began "to take shape as a problem in the public sphere and as an object of expert knowledge,"[15] though there remained at the time, as Rumi Brulin has shown, no agreed-upon meaning of terrorism at the international level.[16] The UN debates on terrorism revealed a sharp divide between, broadly speaking, the Western and Eastern blocs, with many non-aligned states aligned with the latter on how to define and approach terrorism. Meanwhile, for many European states, including France and the UK in particular, as well as Israel and South Africa, "terrorism" was already part of political discourse given that these powers had directly interfaced with nationalist and anti-colonialist movements in their colonies and imperial holdings. However, in the United States, prior to the 1970s, the political discourse of terrorism was largely negligible.[17] "The terms *international terrorist* and *international terrorism*," Timothy Naftali argues, "did not yet appear in high-level documents or in the national consciousness."[18] Analysis of Nixon administration documents at the time, Naftali notes, "still referred to members of the PFLP [Popular Front for the Liberation of Palestine] as 'guerrillas' or the 'fedayeen.'"[19] Following Munich, the US State Department held its first conference on terrorism, and Congress passed resolutions proposing "all means be sought by which the civilized world may cut off from contact with civilized mankind any peoples or any nation giving sanctuary, support, sympathy, aid or comfort to acts of murder and barbarism such as those just witnessed at Munich."[20] Thus, even in the earliest days of enshrining terrorism within US political discourse, the seeds of the material support ban were being sowed.

The emergence of terrorism as an object of study in the 1970s, however, cannot be understood merely as a response to a "novel new problem" nor is it simply a creation of powerful states and elites in service of their self-interest. Instead, as Stampnitzky contends, "we must focus on the trifecta of the emergence of new sorts of events, new sorts of experts, and the means by which these came together: the application of specific forms of expertise to the problem."[21] Throughout the late 1960s and early 1970s, for instance, non-state actors utilized political violence in new ways, most notably, as demonstrated by the Black September Organization in 1972, through the use of hijacking as a political and theatrical tactic—as spectacle.[22] The transnational character of this political violence called forth new kinds of interventions and experts to manage it. And while terrorism did not become a primary focus of US foreign policy until the Reagan administration, Munich did impel the US government to foster the growth of terrorism expertise, funding research, conferences, and other institutional formations. By late 1972, the RAND Corporation became one of the primary centers for the development of terrorism expertise in the United States.[23]

The spectacular events of Munich and shortly thereafter the Iranian hostage crisis did much to mark the advent of "terrorism" as an object of knowledge and a thing to be governed. But it was quieter, less spectacular events that would do much to change the discourse around terrorism. The Jonathan Institute, an Israeli think tank founded in 1976 by Benjamin Netanyahu, which maintained close ties to the Israeli state, organized international conferences on terrorism in 1979 and 1984. These two conferences would play a decisive role in reframing the debate on terrorism. Bringing together Israeli state and military leaders, US governmental officials, and other foreign leaders—"experts" and journalists alike—the first conference in Jerusalem was explicitly framed as an "intervention to change the international discourse on terrorism" positing it as a direct assault on "civilization," "democracies," and "the West" and arguably fueled by the Soviet Union and Arab states, respectively.[24]

The opening speech would lay the conference aims bare. As Dr. Benzion Netanyahu, professor at Cornell University (also Benjamin Netanyahu's father), would proclaim, this is "the beginning of a new process—the process of rallying the democracies of the world to struggle against terrorism and the dangers it represents."[25] Conference speakers, who included a number of prominent Israeli military and governmental leaders, including then Prime Minister Menachem Begin, promulgated a discourse that explicitly linked modern terrorism to the conjoined forces of "communist totalitarianism" and "Islamic (and Arab) radicalism," as Benjamin Netanyahu would argue in his 1986 book, *Terrorism: How the West Can Win*. The speakers consequently called forth an alliance of the "democratic world" to defeat the "forces of terror."[26] There was, in other words, a concerted effort at this time to shift the politics of knowledge around political violence away from the UN General Assembly position, which enshrined the right of subjects under foreign domination to resist that subjugation, and instead to attribute political violence to irrational, fanatical actors whose main target was civilization itself.[27]

It is this sort of absolutist language, Tarek Ismail argues, that permeates the way "western audiences think about terrorism now and in fact how jurists do."[28] As a federal judge remarked in the 2012 trial of Tarek Mehanna, convicted of material support for translating documents from Arabic to English and putting them online, "Terrorism is the modern day equivalent of the bubonic plague"—it is constituted as an *essence*, an ontologically distinct category unmoored from history and context. Accordingly, in this framing, the naming of something as "terrorism" annihilates political space, conjuring the erratic, the fanatical, the irrational, the quintessentially queer. Stemming from a place of horror, it precludes any discussion of or engagement with politics.[29] With the production of this absolutist discourse, so too do we see the emergence of what Edward Said calls the "essential terrorist"—a figure "ontologically and gratuitously interested in wreaking havoc for its own sake"—or put differently, the discourse of the "essential terrorist" effectively eviscerates all the but the ontological *essence* of the "terrorist self."[30] The Jonathan Institute would play a decisive role in manufacturing not only a new discourse on terrorism, though one that would not fully take hold until roughly a decade later, but also in internationalizing the idea that terrorism was not just an Israeli problem but rather one that plagued the Western democratic world. Pleased with media coverage of the first conference, the Jonathan Institute's October 1979 *Bulletin* declared that the event "had a decisive impact on the Western perception of international terrorism and the central role of the PLO in it."[31] In this way, Israel's problem with the Palestinian liberation movement, as Kumar suggests, "became a problem for all democratic nations."[32]

But even as the phenomena of "terrorism" was introduced, in all its modern specificities, into international discourse in the 1970s, the US discourse on terrorism remained, until the 1990s, an "extraordinarily vague and imprecise concept."[33] The executive and legislative branches were locked in battle over which branch should have the power to designate entities to be included on the list; Congress, too, was unable to reach an internal consensus about what terrorism was or perhaps, more precisely, who the terrorists were. Saudi Arabia, for instance, was assisting the PLO, but it was not in the interest of the United States to designate Saudi Arabia as a terrorist state, nor was the Reagan administration particularly keen to include the Nicaraguan Contras. Meanwhile, the African National Congress, for the Republicans, was considered a terrorist group, while for Democrats, South Africa was a terrorist state.[34]

Even as a subcommittee on terrorism was created in 1981, ambiguity over the definition of terrorism and who constituted a terrorist persisted until the end of the Cold War. It was only then that a consensus emerged within the US government concerning terrorism. US foreign policy, as Remi Brulin argues, would now be filtered in large part through the prism of the Middle East—a region where "everyone can agree" (who the terrorists are)—a consensus shaped, in no small part, by US geopolitical interests in a region wherein Israel was seen as an indispensable ally.[35] Accordingly, the scope and parameters of the US–Israel relationship would inform US policies vis-à-vis Israel and the Palestinians in the post–Cold War era, manifesting perhaps most evidently, as Osamah Khalil suggests, in "America's wholesale adoption of Israeli definitions of the conflict and support of its negotiating position."[36] In this context, the figure of Palestinian-as-essential-terrorist would gain prominence in US domestic and foreign policy circles and become a key refracting point through which US terrorism law and policy would develop. And it is in this context that a famed historic agreement between Israel and the Palestinians would take place.

THE OSLO ACCORDS

While Salah was imprisoned in Israel, a much-celebrated handshake halfway around the world would take place. On September 13, 1993, Israeli Prime Minister Yitzhak Rabin and PLO Chairman Yasser Arafat signed the Declaration of Principles on Interim Self-Government on the White House lawn, inaugurating the beginning of the Oslo peace process.[37] Hailed by many as a historic move towards peace, more sober analyses, such as those of Edward Said, foresaw the agreement as "an instrument of Palestinian surrender, a Palestinian Versailles."[38] Arafat's Fatah movement, the dominant party in the newly formed Palestinian Authority, largely supported the accords. But Hamas, along with other Islamist and leftist Palestinian parties, opposed it, contending that the underlying two-state framework it promoted would concede fundamental Palestinian territorial and political rights, including the return of Palestinian refugees to homes from which they were displaced in 1948. The United States, meanwhile, remained committed to seeing the agreement through.

The Oslo Accords sit at the center of what would, roughly a decade later, become a centerpiece of the global war on terror. As part of a broader strategy to shore up a post–Cold War geopolitical arrangement amenable to US interests globally and in the Middle East specifically, on January 24, 1995, President Bill Clinton signed Executive Order 12947, which blocked assets in the United States of "terrorists who threaten to disrupt the Middle East peace process."[39] Invoking authority under the 1977 International Emergency Economic Powers Act (IEEPA), which authorizes the president to impose economic sanctions to deal with a declared threat to the "national security, foreign policy, or economy of the United States," and in so doing, folding Israel/

Palestine into the ambit of US national interest.[40] EO 12947 imposed US sanctions on the newly designated entities and prohibited transactional relations with them. Significantly, even as the regulatory powers of IEEPA had always necessarily been transnational in scope, Clinton's invocation of IEEPA with EO 12947 marks a definitive shift in its application.[41] Prior to 1995, US presidents had exercised their authority under IEEPA predominately against foreign governments, including Sudan, Burma, Libya, and Iran, and "against individuals and entities only if they were citizens of sanctioned foreign nations."[42] In 1995, Clinton extended its use beyond foreign countries to organizations and individuals suspected of having terrorist ties, and notably those linked to Palestine and the Palestinians, thus folding a conflict some 5,000 miles away intimately into the sphere of US national interest.[43]

Clinton's order identified twelve organizations it deemed to pose a threat to the Middle East peace process—including Hamas, Palestinian Islamic Jihad, and Hizballah, as well as eighteen individuals associated with them—as Specially Designated Terrorists (SDTs).[44] This marks the beginning of the shift to a "list-based" approach to criminalizing support for terrorism, wherein any support to or contact with the blacklisted entity is rendered criminal under US law. (The use of lists is explored more extensively in Chapter 3.) It moreover set into motion processes that ultimately culminated in passage of the US material support ban in 1996 with the Antiterrorism and Effective Death Penalty Act (AEDPA). A secret cable released one day after Clinton signed into force EO 12947 (1995) revealed:

> On January 24, President Clinton signed an executive order to block assets in the United States of twelve designated terrorist organizations that threaten to disrupt the Middle East peace process. The order also prohibits financial transactions with these groups. The White House also announced January 24 that the president will soon send to the Congress new, strengthened, anti-terrorist legislation. These initiatives, together, respond to a rising incidence of terrorism aimed at the peace process, the problem of funding of terrorist groups by donors in the US, and the continuing threat from international terrorism of all kinds, worldwide.[45]

The cable goes on to include a number of talking points to be used to urge foreign governments to broaden their counterterrorism laws, including the framing of terrorism as a distinct "threat to the Middle East Peace process" and the assertation that "international concern about terrorism is rising."

Notably the memo concludes with a reminder that Clinton would be undertaking two important initiatives: "First, to strengthen United States efforts to counter the danger of terrorism to the peace process, and second, to combat the global terrorist threat." Israel/Palestine was firmly at the center of evolving US terrorism law and policy. It is in this period that the US terrorism list was born.[46] Meanwhile, Salah, while incarcerated in Israel and without knowledge of the evidence against him, was designated a Specially Designated Terrorist by the US government.[47] He was the first US citizen to bear that designation.[48] Not long after Clinton signed EO 12947 into force, a pivotal event in the United States would consolidate support in the US Congress for legislative action around the problem of terrorism.

OKLAHOMA CITY

In 1995 two American citizens, Timothy McVeigh and Terry Nichols, bombed the Alfred P. Murrah Federal Building in Oklahoma City. While the first World Trade Center bombing just two years earlier resulted in the passing of 18 USC §2339A, which outlaws the provision of support for terrorism in service of a list of enumerated felonies,[49] it was Oklahoma City that fostered a political climate for the passage of an exceedingly broad material support ban that remains in effect to date. Building on the trend started by Clinton with EO 12947 to designate non-state entities as terrorist actors, Congress passed the Antiterrorism and Effective Death Penalty Act of 1996. Referred to by Barry Sabin, chief of the Department of Justice's Criminal Division Counterterrorism Section, as a "watershed legislative development of terrorist financing enforcement,"[50] AEDPA instituted an unprecedented broadening of federal counterterrorism laws by expanding the "definition of criminality in the context of terrorism."[51]

AEDPA established 18 USC §2339B, which imposes a blanket ban on material support to foreign terrorist organizations. The statute specifically prohibits persons subject to US criminal jurisdiction—a definition that has expanded considerably over the last four US administrations—from knowingly providing material support to a foreign terrorist organization irrespective of intent.[52] As Chapter 4 explores, the "US jurisdiction" clause has been interpreted broadly to encompass any institution, entity, or individual through which US financial flows are passed—it is this clause that compelled the Palestinian Authority to refuse all US security funding in 2019. With §2339B, Congress codified into federal law blacklisting practices that make not only tangible support but also interactions and relational exchanges with a designated foreign terrorist organization a federal crime.[53] Critical to the statute's promulgation was the "money-is-fungible theory" wherein FTOs, as it was argued in congressional legal proceedings, are so tainted by their terrorist inclinations that any support to them could be used to bolster their terrorist aims.[54] The terrorist status of a designated entity becomes all determining, and thus functionally any assistance to and interaction with a terrorist group is deemed ipso facto "material support."[55]

From the outset, the US material support ban has been predicated on a dual but interrelated set of presumptions: first that the threat faced is amorphous, flexible, and always potential, and two, that the threat is decidedly foreign and racialized.[56] Irrespective of the fact that the Oklahoma City bombing, for instance, was a domestic act of terrorism, congressional hearings in its wake focused almost exclusively on the threat of international terrorism, thereby weaving Oklahoma City into the geopolitical imaginary of threats abroad.[57] Ambassador Philip Wilcox Jr., one of the key drafters of the proposed act, made a direct link to an ominous "Islamic threat" seeking both to disrupt the Oslo Accords underway in Israel/Palestine and create "turmoil" around the world. As he warned,

> Islamic extremist groups are fighting a vicious rear guard action against the [Middle East] peace process and they are creating turmoil in countries like Algeria, Pakistan, and Egypt. Other extremist Islamic elements, like the group which attacked the World Trade Center and plotted attacks against US civil aviation in the Pacific in recent months, are also a menace.[58]

Similarly, the Anti-Defamation League scripted Oklahoma City within the context of overseas-related terrorism, citing numerous terrorist acts it sutured distinctly to foreign actors, such as the World Trade Center bombing of 1993, the death of an American student in a bombing in Gaza, and a plot to bomb American airliners in the Philippines, among others.[59] Put differently, we can see how this emergent, and invariably racialized, discourse around material support displaces "threat" from geographic proximity, fostering instead a geographic imaginary of connectivity and relationality across global space: the death of an American student in Gaza and a plot to bomb a plane in the Philippines are somehow related and, at least legally, proximate.

Passed into law in April 1996, AEDPA placed a heightened emphasis on international terrorism. Specifically, it amended the Immigration and Nationality Act to authorize the secretary of state to designate an organization as a foreign terrorist organization and established penalties for providing material support or resources to a designated FTO. It is here where the US terrorism list would be born. AEDPA brought into being a regime of listing foreign terrorist organizations and rendered any support administered to designees to be criminal activity punishable under US law.[60] The material support ban was thus, from the outset, a transnational legal architecture established to curb a perceived foreign, racialized threat.[61]

For Salah, these developments in Washington had implications of immense proportions. The "specially designated terrorist" classification that was applied to him while imprisoned in Israel imposed upon his body a relation of ban once released and returned to the United States in 1997. Pursuant to the SDT classification, Salah was placed under an internal embargo: his assets were blocked indefinitely, his bank accounts frozen, and he was prohibited from traveling, seeking services, and engaging in economic transactions absent approval from the Treasury Department Office of Foreign Assets Control (OFAC). Moreover, pursuant to EO 12947, it became illegal for anyone in the United States to engage Salah in any kind of economic transaction without OFAC approval.[62] Dick Marty, rapporteur to the Council of Europe, called the form of isolation that such blacklisting practices bring as *Zivile Totesstrafe* (a civilian death penalty).[63] The embargo would remain in place for seventeen years, removed only after extensive legal challenges on the part of Salah's lawyers. Despite the Treasury Department's classification, the Clinton administration ultimately refused to indict Salah, having found no evidence to be used against him, and his case was subsequently closed in 2000. The Department of Justice, however, would reopen Salah's case in the wake of September 11, 2001, enrolling it in the frontlines of the financial war on terror.

The two-year trial of Salah, which began in 2006, was precedent setting on a number of grounds. The overwhelming majority of the secret evidence used in the trial was extracted from Israeli classified documents, and Salah faced charges that neither he nor his lawyer could see. Among other things, Salah's case established that secret evidence and confessions obtained under torture, in this case by Israeli interrogators, could be used in trials conducted in US criminal court.[64] What resulted, as Salah's lawyers describe, amounted to a "military court sitting in the city of Chicago."[65] It was moreover Salah's forced confession that provided the intelligence for a series of FBI investigations and federal grand jury probes into Hamas financing in subsequent years.[66] As Michael Deutsch and Erica Thompson contend, the "tentacles of almost every known Hamas-related investigation or prosecution in the United States, including the case against the Holy Land Foundation (formerly the largest Muslim charity in the United States), lead back to Salah's coerced confession" at the hands of the Shin Bet.[67]

Salah specifically, and Israel/Palestine more broadly, sit at the center of an expanding legal-war architecture that would later become the centerpiece of the war on terror's preventive paradigm. Material support prosecutions and the financial war on terror more broadly have become, as Marieke de Goede suggests, "one of the war on terror's prime avenues for banal preemption" wherein the threat of potential violence in the future is deemed so potent and dangerous that the security state must take action against it in the present.[68] Differing from most other US criminal codes, the material support statute does not require that a crime be committed, nor that there be any direct link to violence. It relies instead on a rather elusive definition for offense that encompasses a broad swath of relations, associations, and activities, including speech, which, it can be argued, support or enhance the legitimacy of a US-designated "terrorist entity." This mode of policing and speculative security practice that underwrites the material support statute works though the "temporal and the uncertain"—it seeks to intercept threat before its materialization.[69]

The development of the material support regime in the 1990s and the broad criminalization it authorized for acts that *might* occur established the legal foundation on which the post–9/11 doctrine of preemption directly builds. In congressional testimony for the *9/11 Commission Report: Identify-*

ing and Preventing Terrorist Financing, for instance, Barry Sabin, chief of the Counterterrorism Section in the Department of Justice, pays direct homage to the legal regime Congress developed in the 1990s, which proved invaluable in the turn to preemption by the Bush administration. Sabin states:

> I must first stress our main priority since 9/11: preventing terrorist attacks *before* they occur. . . . A prosecutable crime occurs when [demonstrable] acts occur in combination with a requisite mental state. This presents a challenge where we seek to use the prosecutorial function to prevent terrorism, for we do not want to wait until the terrorists show their hand by taking a significant step towards a deadly attack in order to assure that we have enough evidence to convict.
>
> Thanks to Congress, we have a legal regime that allows us to avoid this thorny operational issue. The crimes of providing material support to terrorists and terrorist organizations—18 USC. § 2339A and 2339B—criminalize conduct several steps removed from actual terrorist attacks. These crimes are specifically designed to redress the problem of the terrorist financier, someone whose role in violent plots is not obviously lethal but involves the act of logistical and financial facilitation. . . . Quite simply, we seek to intercept the money that is being transferred to purchase the explosive components, rather than intercept the terrorist with the bomb on his way to the scene of the attack.
>
> Stemming from this legal regime, especially since September 11, we may glean some themes that illustrate important aspects of what Congress has provided us, how we have used those legislative tools, and what type of additional legislation may be in order.[70]

As Sabin underscores, the broad reach of US counterterrorism financing legislation, most notably §2339B, effectively circumvents prosecutorial challenges to criminalize terrorist acts *before* they occur. Likewise, as legal scholar Wadie Said argues, §2339b would prove to be "by the government's reckoning, the most important statute employed in terrorism prosecutions" and the centerpiece of the war on terror's preventive paradigm,[71] what Andrea Miller and I have described elsewhere as the preemptive orientation of the US security state.[72] Arguably a quintessential manifestation of the politics of preemption, the material support ban, by definition, is predicated on an associational logic that requires "policing wide" and policing into the future to intercept what might occur. There is, in other words, very little tangible *material* on which guilt is constructed. Rather guilt is constructed through a presumed intentionality; the alleged terrorist's imagination and desire, then, are sites for interception and capture.[73] The preemptive paradigm underwriting §2339b speaks more broadly to a speculative security model oriented around interventions in emergent, uncertain, and possible futures—a "politics of possibility."[74]

RACE AND THE SPECULATIVE

The speculative nature of contemporary security practice has been of increasing interest to legal scholars, political geographers, and critical security theorists, and certainly not least to Foucault, for whom technologies of security act on an uncertain future and in accordance with a series of probabilistic events.[75] Focusing on the speculative dimensions of terrorism financing, de Goede shows how the pursuit of potential threats is rooted in "preemptive decisions and speculative techniques" that involve "looking forwards," anticipating and acting upon imagined terrorist activity in preparation, and "looking sideways," "identifying, pursuing, and intervening in the associations of suspect individuals."[76] In a similar vein, Louise Amoore, taking insight from Foucault, coins this mode of governing oriented around emergent, uncertain, and possible futures the "politics of possibility."[77] Differing from discipline or law that prohibits, the politics of possibility seeks not to forestall the future but rather to embrace an uncertain one "by acting on its variations and circulations through a series of probabilistic interventions."[78] Or as Andrea Miller insightfully puts it, preemption "produces conditions of possibility, modulating emergent potential to delimit future actualizations."[79]

Meanwhile, Brian Massumi considers how the doctrine of preemption, which he contends denotes a new ecology of powers that comes to fruition in the post–9/11 era, operationalizes metaphysical problems, threats indeterminate yet always potential.[80] The future becomes an urgent matter of the present: the *what might be*, a potential eventuation must be precluded in the now. Massumi explores the operationalization of this logic in the leadup to the Iraq invasion of 2003.[81] The argument, so it went, was that Saddam Hussein *could* have weapons of mass destruction, and if he did, he would use them. Empirical proof of weapons became less important than the catastrophic future that could result *if* weapons did in fact exist. Second, the politics of a *could be* was extended to other sites of racialized threat. The Bush administration repeated the rhetorical trope that Iraq was linked to Al-Qaeda, and had the Iraqi regime possessed weapons of mass destruction, terrorists, the logic followed, would then be enabled to fulfill "their stated ambitions."[82] The politics of the *could be* here creates a vacuous space of the uncertain. However, that space is filled with the presumption that racialized threats are poised to enact violence. Curiously absent from much of the critical work on preemptive and speculative security forms and technologies emergent in contemporary war-making (with some notable exceptions) is attention to the racialized constructions of potentiality itself. All bodies and all states are not conscripted with the same potentiality of enacting violence in an undetermined future. Not all thought crimes are crimes. Not all populations are equally subject to preemptive policing and capture.

As feminist, critical race, postcolonial, and critical security scholars have long pointed out, race constitutes the unmentioned axis around which imperial policing and warfare turns; so too is preemption invariably predicated on constructions of racialized threats and anxiety that prefigure racialized subjects as poised to enact violence in an indeterminate future.[83] We can see the manifestation of this logic in "radicalization theory," adopted by US domestic policing forces, including the New York City Police Department (NYPD), which presumes the path from Muslim to terrorist is a predictable one; this policy has, in turn, has given rise to new laws, norms, and mechanisms. As Amna Akbar details, the FBI and NYPD have emphasized the need for proactive intelligence gathering and "forward-leaning" preventative terrorism prosecutions, which in turn have significantly expanded what is considered the legitimate scope of police work.[84] This preemptive logic manifests in interventions like stop-and-frisk programs, predictive policing software, and the NYPD's Mapping Muslims program, wherein the city, in collaboration with the FBI, carried out a sweeping and comprehensive "human mapping" and intelligence-gathering operation, implanting spies or rakers throughout Arab, South Asian, and Muslim communities to "keep tabs" and comb for threats.[85]

While not a new development—preemption has long animated the colonial relationship of the US settler state to its racialized others—it has become a central structuring logic and orientation of the US war state, both at home and abroad, in the two decades since the onset of the global war on terror. Such is the logic animating contemporary colonial war-making practices from drone warfare across Southwest Asia and the Horn of Africa to the use of material support for terrorism prosecutions to target individuals and organizations within the United States. As argued elsewhere, preemption is not simply a temporal orientation of the colonial state toward the future but also a distinctly racialized one, circumscribing capacities for life and intimacies while designating those who will be made subject to imperial violence.[86] We might think of preemption, as Miller suggests, "as the enactment of emergent infrastructures aimed to maximize and expand colonial capacity."[87]

EO 13224 AND PREEMPTIVE POLITICS

When President George W. Bush signed into force Executive Order 13224 on September 24, 2001, he described it as a major "strike on the financial foundation of the global terror network." The order significantly expanded the Treasury Department's power to target the "financial infrastructure of terrorism," setting into motion the doctrine of preemption that would underwrite the Bush administration's war on terror and US foreign policy more broadly in decades thereafter.[88] Predicated on an anticipatory logic (threats must be intercepted before they can come to fruition) and on an associational one (threats are invariably linked across a range of relations), EO 13224 conferred especially broad powers on the Treasury to disrupt the "support infrastructure" of terrorism, casting an ever-expansive net on who and what could be sanctioned under material support laws.

The executive order broadened the scope of those targeted from individuals directly belonging to Treasury-designated FTOs to those deemed "otherwise associated" with an FTO, and it nullified the humanitarian exemption in terrorism-related cases. It furthermore expanded the list of sanctioned entities from those specifically related to the Middle East peace process to a list of global entities and actors. EO 13224 created the Specially Designated Global Terrorist blacklist, consisting originally of twenty-seven organizations and individuals, which has since grown to thousands of entries. And finally, EO 13224 conferred powers on the Treasury to block US assets and deny access to US markets for foreign banks that refuse to freeze terrorist assets, which has had especially grave implications for global aid flows, as many transactions flow through US banks and are therefore subject to US federal law. Significantly, the range of those who could be caught in the prosecutorial net of the US security state expanded considerably to now include those "otherwise associated" with designated FTOs, as well as a range of humanitarian actors operating in zones deemed "high risk" and "terrorist inclined." In effect, EO 13224 significantly expanded the reach and capacities of the US security state to police and criminalize a range of activities and associations in sites well beyond US "formal" jurisdiction and ensnarled organizations deemed as part of "suspect publics" within the prosecutorial ambit of the US security state.[89] The case of the Holy Land Foundation lays bare the implications of these expanded state powers.

HLF AND CRIMES OF ASSOCIATION

Regarded as the government's "flagship terrorism-financing case," the Holy Land Foundation (HLF), a Texas-based Muslim charity with a mission of providing humanitarian aid in Palestine, was targeted and shut down by the US government shortly following the issuance of EO 13224 as part of the Bush administration's proclaimed "strike on the financial foundation of the global terror network."[90] In December 2001, HLF—at the time the largest Muslim charity in the country—was designated a Specially Designated Global Terrorist based on information obtained from Foreign Intelligence Surveillance Act (FISA) warrants that allegedly showed HLF's support for Hamas, which had been designated by the United States as an FTO in 1997.[91] Pursuant to the designation, all funds to the organization were frozen. HLF petitioned the Specially Designated Global Terrorist designation on the basis that the government's classification rested on "foreign-derived evidence"[92]—evidence obtained during Mohammad Salah's forced confession in Israel[93]—and on the basis that the government had misinterpreted the word "martyr." The contextually derived meaning of "martyr," as it is used in Palestine, refers to any Palestinian killed by Israel, not only those who have died in the commission of political violence. As Wadie Said recounts, HLF "petitioned for relief from the designation on the grounds that OFAC did not consider all available evidence and that it was prevented from submitting evidence in its own defense."[94] HLF's arguments were rejected by a trial court, and the designation was permitted to stand. Soon thereafter, HLF and seven of its staff were indicted and charged with conspiracy to provide material support to Hamas. The criminal prosecution of HLF would begin in 2004.

Relying on the "money-is-fungible" theory in §2339B, the government's argument rested on the associational logic enshrined in US material support law.[95] The prosecution charged that HLF had provided material support in the form of humanitarian donations to *zakat* committees (charities) in the West Bank, which, it was argued, were affiliated with Hamas. The *zakat* committees themselves, however, were not under sanction by the Treasury. The government argued that the *zakat* committees were "otherwise associated" with Hamas and that HLF's humanitarian donations *indirectly* supported Hamas by strengthening its image and presumably winning the group new recruits and community support, thereby constituting material support for a designated FTO.[96] Relatedly, the government did not allege that HLF had supported violent acts and admitted that the funds were used for schools, hospitals, and other charitable programs. The prosecution however contended that the jury should not be persuaded by this fact given that any support to Hamas was rendered illegal as per the fungibility argument in §2339B.

The case of HLF brings into view the selective nature of where the fungibility argument applies and where it does not: the US Agency for International Development, for instance, funded the same *zakat* committees but did not come under sanction by the US government. Indeed, what is considered to constitute "legitimacy" to an FTO, as Andrea Miller argues, is a "blurry and mutable border, one that shifts and stretches to encompass myriad speech acts by the racialized Muslim body."[97] Following two trials (the first trial ended in a mistrial in October 2007), HLF was found guilty not of directly supporting, funding, or abetting a terrorist act; rather its relations of association were criminalized.[98] In May 2009, five Arab Americans associated with Holy Land Foundation were administered sentences on charges ranging from supporting a terrorist organization to money laundering and tax fraud. Two of the five, Shukri Abu Baker and Ghassan Elashi, were each sentenced to sixty-five years in a federal prison; the other defendants received between fifteen and twenty years in prison.

Particularly notable in the HLF case is how constructions of racialized threat were mobilized by the prosecution and presented as evidence of HLF's guilt. As one juror recounted, "A lot of evidence that we saw was fear-based . . . [They showed us] bomb-belts, and they showed us explosions of buses. . . . Many times, at least a handful of times, they mentioned Osama bin Laden and 9/11."[99] HLF, in this case, is folded into the specter of a global jihadi threat. Much like the congressional hearing in the wake of Oklahoma City, a geographic imaginary of connectivity and relationality is fostered across disparate events and moments in time that somehow brings attacks in New York City and Washington, DC, into intimate relation with the second Palestinian *intifada* halfway around the world—moreover, somehow, this is all related to humanitarian donations channeled from Texas into the West Bank. The case of HLF, and that of Muhammad Salah before it, bring into view the racialized constructions of threat that underwrite material support prosecutions specifically and preemptive logics of racialization in the war on terror more broadly.

THE WAY OF WAR

The material support ban for terrorism, and the speculative security calculus on which it is predicated, has evolved into one of the primary means through which the global war on terror is waged. As pressure has mounted surrounding more controversial tactics of US warfare, notably torture and indefinite detention, US prosecutors have invoked the material statute more than any other in pursuit of the US global war on terror. The ensuing financial war on terror has come to dominate, in all its banal details, the preemptive focus of the war on terror.[100] Notably, since its onset after September 11th, an expansive legal-war regime, global in scope (see Chapters 3 and 4), has evolved to identify, manage, and regulate terrorist financing, from the proliferation of national and supranational sanctions and restrictive lists, to the emergence of global surveillance architectures, to ever-intensifying banking regulations and preemptive controls, among other regulatory techniques and technologies.

Even as greater attention is being cast on the less spectacular, banal, and largely concealed practices of contemporary warfare, relatively little attention has been afforded to the centrality of Palestine in constituting this central legal-war architecture. From the case of Muhammad Salah, the first US citizen to be branded with the SDT designation, a classification that would later grow to thousands of entries on the US OFAC list; to the role of the Oslo

Accords in expanding the US sanctions regime to encompass organizations and individuals, notably those linked to Palestine and the Palestinians; to the inclusion of Israeli intelligence in US courts as "evidence" for US material support prosecutions; to the evolution of terrorism law and policy through transnational circuits and "lessons and borrowings" between the United States and Israel from the 1970s on, Palestine has played a central role in the formation and evolution of a legal-war technology that today animates contemporary war-making and counterinsurgency—not just in the United States or Israel/Palestine but the world over. The following chapters examine the global circuits through which this law travels, foregrounding the racialized regimes of securitization and war-making to which they give rise.

Two

ELASTIC SOVEREIGNTY

THE PAPER

It was late July. I departed the bus from Ramallah and walked toward the city center. I had been to Nablus a handful of times prior—the first, years ago, during the second *intifada*. The city now looked different, busier, but the marks of that time were still worn on city walls: sketches of martyrs, plaques commemorating massacres, vacant spaces where houses once stood—scars on a city bustling, lively, moving on. The street faded into the suk, the pathways of which were lined with nuts, children's clothes, a soap factory, fresh knafi. I turned into a narrow alley; at the other end was signage for Yasmeen Hotel where I was due to meet Yousef.

Yousef and I had been introduced through a friend of a friend. I had just arrived in Palestine to begin my research on humanitarianism and protracted human displacement. I had hoped to speak with him about his work as a teacher at a nearby United Nations Relief and Works Agency (UNRWA) administered camp. I was curious about the relationship between temporality and crisis; I wanted to know what happens when an entire population is suspended some six decades under a regime of supposedly short-term humanitarian management. I prepared my questions accordingly.

Shortly into our conversation, I realized Yousef was speaking in the past tense. During a pause in the conversation, I asked him if he still worked at

UNRWA. "Not anymore," he said. "What do you do now?" I asked. "I over-see projects," he replied. What unfolded over the next hour was a detailed account of his work as part of an oversight team for a US Agency for International Development (USAID)–funded project in the West Bank. "It pays well," he said, "but we have to sign the paper." Embarrassed the reference had been lost on me, I inquired, "the paper?" "Yes," he repeated. "We all have to sign it. You know, to say that we aren't terrorists."

The paper (*watheekat monahadet al-erhab*), and passing comments to it, became a recurring theme across multiple interviews conducted over the next month. I tried to escape it; I tried to keep my questions focused on UNRWA. That is after all what I had come to research. After a month had gone by, I decided to look more decisively into "the paper" and why exactly it was so important to those with whom I was speaking in Palestine. Some rather cursory research on the subject took me straight back to Washington. The paper, or anti-terrorism certification (ATC), is connected to Executive Order (EO) 13224, the order signed into force just weeks after September 11, 2001, among a host of other statutes.[1] The ATC stipulates that recipients receiving US monies certify that they do not provide support for terrorist acts or to designated foreign terrorist organizations (FTOs) identified on the US Office of Foreign Assets Control (OFAC) list.

The OFAC database includes a number of Palestinian parties, groups, and individuals to whom US monies are prohibited from being channeled. Banned parties might also include those "otherwise associated" with designated entities. The ATC is one component of a more complex national security infrastructure that transposes regimes of surveillance, sanction, and punishment far beyond the sites and domains where the US claims jurisdiction. The paper offers insight into the topological relations at play in contemporary imperial formations, which rely, in large part, on mobile technologies, mediated arrangements of power, and indirect mechanisms of rule that link far-flung places in often intimate ways.

THE TIES THAT BIND

It had taken months to gain access, though finally it happened, largely by a fluke. I had my scribbled notes in hand and laptop bag in the other. I entered the multi-story building that overlooked the Mediterranean, a world away from Ramallah from where I had departed, a mere thirty-five miles southeast—a trip, nonetheless, that took five hours. The security guard at the entrance directed me to the appropriate floor.

Upon reaching the main office, my ID was taken, scanned, and I was directed to the room down the hall. The door was slightly ajar; I knocked anyway. The usual, but not entirely usual, customary performance began. I was welcomed in and invited to sit down. As I approached the table, I saw a dossier containing my picture on the front: "We do our homework," my interlocutor said. I sat down; I was glad to cut the performance.

I had waited months to get here—to the USAID West Bank/Gaza Mission headquarters in Tel Aviv. After my conversation in Nablus with the former UNRWA teacher turned USAID compliance overseer, where I had first learned about *watheekat monahadet al-erhab*, I knew I needed to know more what was behind the processes I had seen unfolding across the West Bank— the prohibitions, the fragmentation, the dizzying bureaucracy, the crippling oversight. I wanted to gain a clearer sense of the logics behind them, at least in an official capacity, from one of the key experts on the subject. As I sat in that room, one point was made abundantly clear: "We [USAID] have to negotiate within the parameters set by Congress," my interlocutor underscored, and those parameters are defined by US counterterrorism law. Mission policy here, he drove home, derives from a legal basis, which, as critical race and Indigenous scholars have long pointed out, cannot be cleaved from the political realm.

The curious thing about this interview, aside from my intelligence file sitting atop the desk throughout the duration of our conversation, was the largely untroubled yet invariably interesting political-legal geography at play. Here in Tel Aviv, as in Nablus just months prior, the US security state was intimately present, its security regime palpably felt. The contentious ATC and the broad gamut of terrorism legislation simply applied. This is not something we can negotiate, aid staff would often lament. US aid distributed in Palestine was topologically linked to US law, drawing the application of a national legal system into the global environment.

Aid flows; it flows globally. It flows in and through sites of war and colonial occupation and across landscapes of dispossession. It embeds into the lifeworlds of those on the receiving end of these flows. What, then, happens when a security regime is enfolded into the humanitarian infrastructures on which populations weathering wars, displacement, and dispossession are dependent? What kind of sovereignty arrangement takes shape? And more-over, how are the lives of those on the receiving ends of these securitized flows rearranged, constrained, and reconfigured? Of course, the bundling and dispersion of state security and legal regimes is not a new or novel ar-rangement. The borders of powerful states are embedded in all kinds of flows. European territorial borders, for instance, as Gabriel Popescu ob-serves, have "moved online through the digitization of personal records and massive database storage."[2] Or, as geographies of National Security Agency surveillance attest, the US security state operates through a "transnational web of security agencies, public authorities, and private corporations [that] do not sit nicely within a Euclidean territorial template."[3]

If we return, then, to the simple fact that aid flows are topologically linked to the US security state, an interesting spatiality of sovereignty emerges, one that does not cohere with a conventional, realist accounting of sovereignty as an ultimate law-making authority within defined territorial boundaries,[4] and external recognition of that authority,[5] the "sovereign-territorial ideal," as Alexander Murphy has coined it.[6] Instead we are presented with a spati-ality better defined topologically: one that bends and flexes unevenly across global space, what I call *elastic sovereignty*.

I foreground the analytic of sovereignty here as I am specifically trac-ing the articulation of US counterterrorism law (and its attendant regime of policing, surveillance, and punitive administration) as it manifests in Pales-tine. The architectures of the US counterterrorism regime, as explored sub-sequently, detach, bundle, embed, and traffic through mobile technologies, global circulations, and relationships that stitch far-flung sites—in this case Washington to Palestine—in intimate, though often obscure ways. By trac-ing the transnational operation of US terrorism law through the architec-tures of care and relief in Palestine, this chapter foregrounds geographies of de facto or effective sovereignty,[7] which foreground the concealed sites, per-formances, and gray spaces through which sovereign power takes hold, yet in such a way that does not necessarily eschew law (or the performance of law).[8]

The exploration of elastic sovereignty undertaken in this chapter follows in two parts. First, I trace how the US counterterrorism regime attaches and bundles to non-human objects (aid) and non-state enforcers. Here I home in on processes of securitization and displacement inherent in what I call the (inter)mediary sphere—that is the broad assemblage of aid actors that manage US aid flows around the world. This sphere, I argue, constitutes an agglomeration of what Bruno Latour calls intermediaries and mediators: like the former, these aid actors serve as conduits through which US security and legal regimes travel, and like the latter, they "modify the meaning or the elements they are supposed to carry."[9] I then turn to two snapshots or instances of elastic sovereignty at work. In line with Chris Harker's work on the topology of debt in Palestine, which he describes as a string that "becomes twisted in increasingly complex figurations,"[10] I track in particular the variant embeddings and enfoldings of the US security-legal regime in the daily infrastructures of Palestinian life, in a greenhouse in Gaza, across West Bank roads, and in municipal halls.

INTER(MEDIARIES)

When walking through Ramallah one is certain to encounter how aid and capital are making (and unmaking) Palestine. If you head northwest from the city center to Ramallah *tahta* (downtown), you will stumble upon an array of upscale cafés hosting a smattering of English-speaking patrons, illuminated Apple logos, and espresso prices comparable to those of London or New York. If you head southeast towards al-Masyoun, you'll come upon a number of high-end hotels and upscale restaurants, embassies, and PA ministries. En route you'll likely also pass Berlin or La Grotta: smoky, Ottoman-style pubs where on any given night the city's *ijanaab* (foreigners) can be found. If you head north, though a short drive, you'll perhaps come up upon Snobar tucked beneath trees and hosting an open-air pool, where a mixed crowd of foreigners, Ramallah's upper class, and resident families can be seen mingling, smoking argila, perhaps partaking in dinner and conversing in a variety of languages. Less visible to the eye are three refugee camps bordering the city, inflated rents, and the slow in-migration of workers from surrounding villages who now constitute the backbone of Ramallah's service sector. Palestine's de facto capital, Ramallah is home to the governing elite, foreign diplomats, international aid organizations, and foreign aid workers, what one interlocutor called the "coordinator class."[11]

It was March 2010, and I was sitting in one of those Ramallah-based international NGO headquarters. My interlocutor was the head of an international organization that was managing and implementing USAID-funded projects there.[12] "When it comes to the US government it's a law. What people don't recognize, it's a law *ya jama'a*. It's not something that you can negotiate. The legislators call the shots. . . . It all goes back to the legislation and the politics in the US."[13] I had come here to talk about aid. My interlocutor, in turn, recounted to me the workings of counterterrorism law.

"We have been living through a new era globally when it comes to anti-terrorism law," she explained. This period has played out unevenly across the globe with Palestine, like other sites where racialized populations are placed in the crosshairs of US war-making. "What happened in 2001 has nothing to do with here," she said, yet the US "targeted here [which] tells you when it comes to the Palestinian issue, there are other layers that you have to analyze that go beyond the anti-terrorism law." However, of primary concern to us, she added, are the "practicalities in terms of [the] implementation of this law and the policies" that flow from it.[14] "The bad side of [our situation]," she pointed out, "is when it comes to politics—the politics of the Palestinian issue, the internal Palestinian politics, the regional politics, and the global politics: somehow we are linked with all of them [and] now US government aid is definitely not outside this." She then joked, "I've worked with only one Norwegian aid [program]. I wish they had the millions."

USAID, like most bilateral agencies operating in Palestine, operates exclusively through (inter)mediary bodies—the broad array of international nongovernmental organizations and contractors that manage and distribute aid flows in the West Bank and Gaza Strip.[15] I employ the term "(inter)mediary" as a fusion of Latour's distinction between mediators and intermediaries.[16] An intermediary, Latour contends, "transports meaning or force without transformation" while mediators "transform, translate, distort, and modify the meaning or the elements they are supposed to carry."[17]

The institutions with which USAID contracts do both. These bodies constitute, on the one hand, a critical infrastructure or set of nodes through which US counterterrorism law and national security infrastructures are transmitted and projected onto landscapes and bodies afar. At the same time, they modify and transform US security architectures in often unpredictable and unforeseen ways, creating new kinds of synergies and contingencies that cannot entirely be calculated or accounted for—in some cases by magnifying and proliferating architectures of US securitization, and in other cases, by subverting and/or playing with the security state in creative and often humorous ways. In the snapshots that follow, I home in on the variant processes that take shape within this sphere—a sphere that while neither monolithic nor stable nonetheless constitutes a crucial web of relations through which US power takes hold.

In line with broader global trends towards contracting, especially since the 1980s, responsibility for ensuring compliance with US terrorism law and security mandates has shifted onto the many international NGOs and private firms that receive American, and specifically USAID, monies around the world, what one interlocutor referred to as USAID's "many arms."[18] These agents are conscripted as enforcement bodies, tasked with ensuring that US terrorism law, and the prohibitions that flow from it, are upheld across the many sites where US aid is distributed. The contractual relationship to which these bodies are enlisted is best distilled in a document integrated into the USAID West Bank/Gaza (WB/G) Mission in 2003—Mission Order 21.

As laid out in Chapter 1, Executive Order 13224 constituted a key legal infrastructure of Bush's global war on terror. An emergency declaration that created a Specially Designated Global Terrorists list and barred transactions with them, EO 13224 also nullified the humanitarian exception in the 1977 International Emergency Economic Powers Act (IEEPA), thus barring the provision of humanitarian aid where listed groups operate.[19] The nullification of the humanitarian exception in the US sanctions regime posed a distinct challenge to US-funded aid-administering organizations around the world, which now had to ensure that US assistance was not channeled to entities and individuals designated on the US Treasury's OFAC list, including those "otherwise associated" with designated entities. The issuance of EO 13224 posed an acute challenge to USAID missions operating in zones scripted as particularly prone to terrorist influence.[20] The answer, USAID officials concluded, was to offset responsibility for ensuring compliance onto the civilian agents that receive US grants and contracts. This practice of risk diversion has resulted, in turn, in the diffusion of surveillance and policing tactics through those civilian bodies that handle US monies. Put differently, bordering work—or the work of both producing and policing the boundary between aid recipient and terrorist, with the former always potentially slipping into the latter—was effectively offset and re-embedded within the civilian agencies through which US funds are channeled. Mission Order 21, in effect, conscripted a host of civilian aid agents into undertaking the work of the security state.

As part of a growing transnational legal-security architecture that expanded to new domains during the early years of the global war on terror, Mission Order 21 was integrated into the USAID West Bank/Gaza Mission as a compliance measure for Bush's EO 13224, Clinton's 1990s laws, the PATRIOT Act, and other terrorism statutes. Specifically, the order mandates a set of compliance measures with which all prime awardees (international NGOs and contractors) must adhere to ensure that US assistance "does not inadvertently provide support to entities or individuals associated with terrorism."[21] As per the US material support ban, alongside other associated terrorism laws criminalizing the provision of material support to OFAC-designated terrorists (a classification applied to a number of Palestinian political groups and individuals of the Palestinian resistance movement[22]), the (inter)mediary body (the prime contractor or grantee) is required to collect the personal information of key individuals and organizations receiving US funds under an award, to be screened or vetted against US intelligence and counterterrorism databases for "derogatory" information.[23] The agency then channels the information to USAID's Program Support Unit, and from there it is transferred to USAID's Office of Security in Washington. In DC, the information is screened through US intelligence databases, including the FBI Terrorist Screening Center, which houses the US Terrorist Watchlist.[24] In select cases, another round of vetting is undertaken by the US Consulate General in Jerusalem.

The model of "extreme vetting" established in the USAID WB/G Mission has served as a template for other USAID missions around the world. In 2012, USAID implemented its Partner Vetting System (PVS), a pilot program modeled on the USAID WB/G program, to five countries: Guatemala, Kenya, Lebanon, the Philippines, and Ukraine. PVS required humanitarian organizations to "collect and report identifying information on their partners to US government officials who then ran the information against secret government intelligence databases."[25] In short, Mission Order 21 set into motion hyper-securitized aid practices and surveillance technologies that policed far and wide and that would be replicated globally in years to come. Palestine, in more ways than one, served and continues to serve as a testing ground or laboratory for evolving tactics and instruments of global counter-insurgency and imperial pacification.[26]

In addition to requiring extreme vetting of US monies flowing into Palestine, Mission Order 21 also mandates that the prime awardee obtain antiterrorist financing certification ("the paper") from both US and non-US NGOs. The paper is a deeply divisive and fragmentary technology in Palestine, effectively sowing division among those who agree to endorse a US definition of terrorism (though many in this camp would argue that this endorsement is merely instrumental) and those who unequivocally refuse it. It has accordingly served as an object around which a politics of refusal has emerged, the focus of Chapter 3. Lastly, the order stipulates that all contracts, grants, and cooperative agreements include a clause barring facility names that recognize or honor those who commit or who have committed acts of terrorism.[27]

Mission Order 21 functions, in essence, as a technology of risk transference: responsibility for upholding the US counterterrorism regime across global space is offloaded onto the international bodies that handle American aid monies, resulting in a diffusion of securitized managerial power. Accordingly, the outsourcing of responsibility for adherence to US law onto aid intermediaries has meant, as one intermediary concluded, "We could be held up in court, you know, as internationals. It's a way of USAID protecting themselves; all of the emphasis is placed on the people procuring these contracts. This means they can't be affected, but we could."[28]

The implications of this transference of risk have been profound, most especially for racialized aid workers, some of whom have been sentenced to extensive prison terms (see the Holy Land Foundation case discussed in Chapter 1). Concerns over potential violation of US terrorism law, itself a body of law that dwells in gray space, has meant that many agencies receiving any kind of US funding have built expansive surveillance and policing mechanisms into their aid programming, such as screenings, certificates, and restrictive contractual terms, and in some cases have cleaved off entire regions and spaces, such as the Gaza Strip or municipalities coded as "derog" (a term often used by contractors, short for "derogatory") from aid flows to protect themselves against legal violation and corresponding punitive measures. The director of one international NGO handling US funds noted that "money does not go to anything that is considered risky by [US] law."[29] The director of another organization running a youth democracy program noted, "Entire municipalities were simply eliminated."[30]

Routinely, contractors talked about how they had incorporated expansive policing mechanisms and preemptive strategies to ensure they were viewed as low-risk bodies by those administering US aid contracts, in turn lending a power to the security state that it might not otherwise have. As another NGO worker noted, "Our home office in Washington has 'warned us to be very careful.' "[31] In the case of this NGO in particular, which had an established presence in Gaza, the organization's activities, in toto, were cast in an ambit of suspicion. The NGO's Gaza program director, Samir, revealed that they had to be excessively cautious about initiating contact with any individual or organizational body "outlawed by the US government."[32] This is why, he stated, a colleague in their Jerusalem office spends the majority of his time "checking the names we send to him on OFAC." As Samir detailed,

> We send the full names of the people on the board with organizations they are considering working with which he checks on the OFAC site. [They screen] not only organizations, but also the contractors, suppliers, partners, whoever will be benefiting from projects; whoever receives money from us has to be OFAC checked. All the board members of any organization we work with have to be cleared.

The embedding of the OFAC list into aid flows, translated from vague law and policy into concrete practices, has material results, effectively casting certain bodies, infrastructures, and geographical spaces under sanction. This NGO in particular had been awarded a multi-million-dollar grant for the rehabilitation of water and sanitation infrastructure in the Gaza Strip. However, given that the governing authority of the territory was also an OFAC designated FTO, the NGO was prohibited from coordinating or having any contact with any government-linked body, including municipalities, village councils, and ministries in Gaza. As Samir explained, "Traditionally in Gaza, and in Palestine in general, water sanitation usually is owned, run, and maintained by the municipalities. If we have to implement a major water and sanitation project, we usually start by contacting the municipality [and] the technical people in the water department in particular."[33] However, as per conditionalities mandated by the US counterterrorism regime, the agency was prohibited from initiating any contact with municipal bodies responsible for water management, which ultimately hampered the full development of the water sanitation project: the folding in of the US regime of prohibition in Gaza resulted in the casting out and severing of residential units from life-sustaining systems and infrastructures.[34]

Equally, the adoption of the "precautionary principle"[35] by (inter)mediary bodies to minimize the risk of legal violation has, in turn, breathed new life into the US counterterrorism regime circumscribing, in some cases, how agencies operate even in the absence of US funds, constituting a kind of agential absence. In the case of the aforementioned NGO operating in Gaza, the US sanctions regime was applied to all of its projects—US funded or not—as one employee recounted. "It's not only USAID money," Samir stated: "This policy is being applied by [the NGO] even for money that comes from different sources, not necessarily USAID."[36] Fear of potential violation of US law, in short, circumscribed how and with whom the organization could interact across all sectors and all spaces in Palestine, as exemplified in its milk-for-preschoolers program.

The milk-for-preschoolers program supplied milk and biscuits to roughly 20,000 children daily in 120 partnering preschools across the Gaza Strip. The program, which ran for multiple years, contained no US funding. Each of the roughly 120 participating preschools was affiliated with a local NGO (coined the "mother organization") that oversaw and coordinated milk and biscuit distribution in each of the participating preschools. As per warnings from the home office, the US NGO routinely screened the partnering mother organizations overseeing the milk programs in the respective schools to ensure they were free of links or associations to any US banned entity. Biannually, Samir explained, they had to screen each partnering NGO to ensure it had "no affiliation, whatsoever, to Hamas, Jihad, or PFLP, or whatever. . . . We cannot continue to serve a preschool as part of our program if it's not OFAC cleared," he underscored. Samir went on to recount how concerns arose with regards to mother organizations operating in some thirty-two preschools. "The only thing we can do," he lamented, "is to exclude the schools" in their entirety, which eventually they did. In this instance, the mere potentiality of violation of US counterterrorism mandates meant that the NGO effectively applied the sanctions regime across all of its aid programming. "This is [now] our general policy," he noted. "In recent years, we changed our partners; we excluded many local partners with whom we used to work for years just because we have some information that some of the board members are Hamas or have some contacts or affiliation with Hamas." Processes of securitization are centrifugal, in this case proliferating well beyond US funding streams to embed and move expansively throughout Gaza's social webs and relations.

The broad assemblage of aid agencies that handle US funds, while neither monolithic nor mere instruments of empire (indeed many of these bodies are themselves private agencies interested foremost in accumulation) nevertheless constitute a critical, and highly mobile, infrastructure through which the security state is cast across multiple domains and on far-flung subjects. Equally, these bodies amplify the work of the state through heterogeneous mechanisms and means, which obscure the work of the state while unmooring it from any single source of power or domination. In this respect, these bodies are, on the one hand, merely conduits through which the US security apparatus is transmitted, but equally, it is here, too, where securitized technologies and practices proliferate, magnify, evolve, and transform. It is within this sphere wherein the "stuff" of imperial statecraft is performed and made into something anew. The vignettes that follow explore these heterogeneous processes in turn.

THE US SECURITY STATE WALKS INTO A GREENHOUSE

The whole thing, it's all about Mission Order 21.
That's really where it starts and ends.[37]

In December 2008, the Gaza Strip was bombed, again. Israel's 22-day military assault killed some 1,400 Palestinians and injured 5,000 more. Approximately 20,000 Palestinians were made homeless, many made refugees again. Damage to civilian and urban infrastructure—including electricity networks, water pipes, sewage systems, and residential building—was widespread.[38] Operation Cast Lead, as it was coined by Israel, compounded conditions of crisis created by Israel's blockade imposed on Gaza in 2007, which regulated life-sustaining flows into the territory often to a minimum with the intended effect of managing the Palestinian population on the "red line."[39] When Cast Lead began in December 2008, the Gaza Strip was already in a humanitarian crisis.[40]

The blockade combined with devastation wrought from the 2008 incursion exacerbated an already dire situation of food insecurity for Gaza's nearly 1.6 million inhabitants, over three-quarters of whom were already dependent on food aid.[41] The military assault wrought significant destruction to Gaza's agricultural areas and cultivated lands, especially in the northern and eastern parts of the territory. The UN Food and Agriculture Organization (FAO) estimated that between 35 and 60 percent of the agricultural sector had been destroyed, and nearly a third of the Gaza's arable land—producing crops such as wheat, barley, beans, citrus trees, olives, almonds, and various vegetables—had been confiscated by Israel for a buffer zone.[42] The United Nations Office for the Coordination of Humanitarian Affairs estimated losses to the agricultural sector at $268 million.[43] Much of Gaza's most productive land, as Amnesty International concluded, had been turned into "condemned wastelands."[44] The conjoined violences of military assault and sanctions compounded a crisis of food insecurity in the Gaza Strip, making the area a priority for aid from international donors.

It was October 2010; Gaza, still under blockade, was struggling to rebuild from the destruction of Cast Lead. I had just made it to Jerusalem to speak with a US contractor who, like many aid actors, had honed their efforts on Gaza. This contracting firm had recently expanded its work in Palestine in agriculture and agribusiness: "70 to 75 percent of the population in Gaza is food insecure," my interlocutor, a senior-ranking employee of this particular firm, relayed to me.[45] The aim of this project, he explained, was to address food insecurity in Gaza. The project, funded by USAID, supplied greenhouses and drip irrigation systems, as well as inputs (seeds) and training to grow fresh vegetables to Palestinians identified as in need. As part of an effort to meet pressing humanitarian need, these US-supplied greenhouses, he explained further, would help families produce food for their own consumption, as well as food to sell on the local market.

This particular contracting firm had worked on USAID projects elsewhere in the world. It cut its teeth in Latin America in the 1980s, where it concentrated for most of the decade. In the 1990s, it expanded its operations into the former Soviet Union and Eastern Europe, and then in the early aughts, developed further into parts of Africa, Asia, and the Middle East. While the firm serviced a number of government, private business, and international development clients, the US Agency for International Development was among its core clients.

This greenhouse project entailed the distribution and installation of greenhouses and drip irrigation systems throughout Gaza. "By the end of this week," the contractor told me, "we will have installed ninety-eight greenhouses from the trial phase and ninety-nine drip irrigation systems, most of which have been installed in the north." They had also ordered another 300 greenhouses to be manufactured. That greenhouses could be a plausible fix to the problem of food insecurity in Gaza seemed straightforward enough, as my interlocutor framed it. But as he began to recount the assemblage of actors that stitched the project together, a more complex picture emerged. The greenhouse project involved a network of contractors and subcontractors, experts and engineers, including an Israeli manufacturer of greenhouses; a Gaza-based contractor for the installation of the greenhouses; a Palestinian firm with offices in both Gaza and the West Bank responsible for assembling the drip irrigation systems; an Israeli transportation and logistics firm that coordinated the greenhouse and drip irrigation loading transport through the Karem Shalom checkpoint along Gaza's southernmost border; and a Gaza-based NGO responsible for overseeing regulation and compliance, coordinating between different subcontracting bodies and undertaking routine reporting. The Gaza-based NGO, believed to have especially privileged knowledge of beneficiaries, including their political affiliations and economic conditions, was responsible for the original collection of the identifying information, which was then submitted to the prime contractor.

Listening to my interlocutor recount the web of actors and steps involved was dizzying. I asked him to walk me through the process. As he explained:

> We do not install anything until a beneficiary has been identified through an application process, passed both technical and social criteria, is vetted by USAID, approved by a local committee, which includes a representative from USAID, approved by COGAT [the Israeli Coordination of Government Activities in the West Bank and Gaza] and the grant agreement is signed and the area prepared for installation.

I asked if he could elaborate on the process a bit more. He continued:

[The Gaza-based NGO] starts the process. [The beneficiary] applies through an application process. There are two different criteria. There's the technical criteria: You know, does she own a plot of land that can hold a greenhouse structure? Is she a farmer? Is she part of the civil authority? Does she have an official position? If they pass these technical criteria, then there's a set of social criteria. Is this a woman-run household? Does she have a certain number of children? . . . Once they pass that, that's just the first step. Then [the Gaza-based NGO] brings it to us and they say, "This person has passed our technical and social criteria." Now it's our turn to take it over from them, and we send them to USAID for vetting. Once USAID vets them, they just let us know that this person has been vetted and they are eligible to receive some kind of assistance. That's the second step. The third step in the process is that a local committee in Gaza which [has a] USAID representative [does] a second verification.

Once that person is deemed eligible then they say this person is still ok then we actually have to send that person's information to COGAT, well USAID does it for us, and so USAID sends a list to COGAT with this person's ID number and the longitude and latitude of where we are going to put their greenhouse and COGAT basically gives us silent approval. If they don't say, "No you can't use that person," then it's basically silence is concurrence as far as we are concerned. And we give them like a two-week window. Once they've been concurred by COGAT then we go out and prepare their land. And that's again where [the Gaza-based NGO] gets back into it. They do the preparation. [The Gaza-based NGO] is involved in collecting information on every step of the way and so are we.

This passage is instructive on a number of fronts. First, it lays bare the politics swimming beneath and within the galvanized steel frames, gutters, and nylon sheeting for the greenhouse structure, certainly not least with regards to the structural entanglements of Palestinian life with Israel's settler–colonial regime. Here, greenhouses deemed "humanitarian aid," necessitated because of conditions created by the dual violences of military incursions and blockade, must be sanctioned by COGAT, a unit within the Israeli Ministry of Defense, which coordinates directly with the Israel Defense Forces (IDF). Second, and the more sustained focus of my inquiry here, is how this dizzying array of actors and logistical transactions is entwined with the US material support ban. When I commented on the extensive layers of compliance and oversight entailed in just this project alone, the contractor confirmed as much and then laid bare the simplicity of it all: "The whole thing, it's all about Mission Order 21. That's really where it starts and ends."

What, then, does Mission Order 21 mean for this greenhouse, its beneficiaries, and for an accounting of global counterterrorism formations more broadly? This vignette points to the political work that the US sanctions regime, as configured through transnational aid networks, does on the ground in Gaza. As the interlocutor describes, potential beneficiaries for a greenhouse plot must successfully pass a set of preliminary criteria divided into *social* and *technical* sets. The technical criterion for this project includes things such as: "Does she own a plot of land that can hold a greenhouse structure? Is she a farmer? Is she part of the civil authority?" This last point, while subsumed under the technical category, is anything but. Since June 2007, Gaza has been governed by Hamas, an OFAC-designated FTO. Accordingly, the beneficiary who is gifted a greenhouse in Gaza "from the American people"[46] cannot be associated with the civil authority, nor have links to any group, appearing on the OFAC list. Conversely, this means that the beneficiary of the greenhouse is, at least overtly, unaligned with the aforementioned groups. This greenhouse, thus, is a political marker, both in terms of its material components (poles, seeds, soil, and the like) and in terms of the particular subjects to whom these infrastructures are distributed. Notably, in the West Bank arm of the greenhouse project, it was the local cooperation that had to be vetted and OFAC-cleared, not necessarily the farmers themselves. One consultant who worked on the West Bank greenhouse program revealed that the local farmer had to be "vouched for" by the local cooperation—risk, in this case, was deferred onto the local cooperating entity.

The greenhouse structures, across these divided territories, index the presence of multiple contingencies (the greenhouse recipient, or recipient's sponsor, for instance, did not contain a duplicate name to someone on "the list") and heterogeneous forces bound up and embedded in galvanized steel frames, nylon sheeting, strawberry seeds, peppers, molokhia, and eggplant. These infrastructures and the objects that populate them are not merely political but rather "politics in matter," as per Eyal Weizman—a product of heterogenous forces and linkages folded into matter, including, not least, the US counterterrorism regime.[47] The matter, its geographical coordinates, and the technical language used to designate beneficiaries obscure the work of the US security state therein. Indeed, part of the work that elastic sovereignty (or sovereignties, in this case) does, to return to Weizman, is to obfuscate "facts of domination" in this case repacked and delivered as humanitarian "offerings," critical infrastructures, and foodstuffs.[48] The productiveness of what is visible here (i.e., the greenhouse) and invisible (the US counterterrorism regime) is the trick of the elastic security state. Equally, we must remain attuned to another iteration of US power in Palestine, including the billions administered to Israel each year in the form of military aid and weapons contracting. Israel's routine bombing and razing of the Gaza landscape has resulted in, among other things, the widescale destruction of farmland and greenhouses, thereby necessitating more aid to address the problem of chronic food insecurity, and the cycle repeats.[49]

ELASTIC SOVEREIGNTY AND ITS (LOCAL) SUBJECTS

You are always in conflict with yourself.[50]

Just as proxy forces have long been crucial to the implementation and "success" of colonial and imperial exploits,[51] so too do "local" staff working within these aid (inter)mediaries constitute a critical infrastructure for the transnational enforcement of the US counterterrorism regime.[52] It is particularly notable that many of those enlisted with performing the work of the US security state are themselves Palestinian. It is most often Palestinian staff who are sent to collect the personal information of potential recipients for vetting, are tasked with the procurement of anti-terrorism certification, and are placed on local committees, as in the case of the greenhouse project, to ensure recipient bodies are clear of suspect links. Equally, Palestinian subjects working in these agencies also come under suspicion both by the United States and by local governing bodies that are themselves targeted by the US security regime, as in the case of the Gaza Strip. Samir revealed the challenges inherent in this delicate dance:

> They [Hamas] would often stop us in the streets and ask, "Why you avoiding us? Why you working against us? You cannot keep avoiding us forever.... The balance is very difficult: you need to abide by US and USAID

policy but you [also] need to continue working in Gaza without being exposed to any kind of danger by Hamas.... This is how the situation is.[53]

The balance of which he speaks is instructive—it captures the heterogeneous forces at work. In this instance, the interlocutor, both Palestinian and inadvertently an enforcer of US counterterrorism infrastructures, must navigate between varying and often countervailing forces: the dictates of the US security state, on the one hand, and the governing authority of Gaza, also a direct target of the US security state, on the other. The paradoxical positioning of Palestinian staffers working within these (inter)mediary agencies as enforcers of US mandates situates them in awkward, often contradictory ways—essentially having to police the communities and beneficiaries with whom they work while also purportedly being their partners. As one staffer working for one of the most lucrative US contractors in the West Bank and Gaza Strip explained,

> It's hard for us because a lot of us are Palestinian so when we pick up the phone and say, "Hello my name is ____ and you know you are participating in our training but for us to get you through USAID requires a special approval," that's what I call it. "Can you please send me a copy of your ID, sorry." I start sounding like a whiny little girl, "*Ma'lesh* I know it's hard, but it's just a requirement." Basically I accuse USAID of being bureaucratic and stupid while I am in the process.[54]

She went on to describe how collection of personal data was highly insulting to recipients and vendors alike. "We ask them to sign the anti-terrorism clauses [which] they find offensive. To them, its accusatory, insulting language. They don't want to sign," she added. Palestinian staff implementing these projects, as she described it, are constantly negotiating contradictory positions: "We are constantly apologizing for having to do work on behalf of USAID."[55]

In another case, one Palestinian worker had to check the names of the schools the contractor would potentially fund to ensure that they didn't contain the word "martyr."[56] The director of a Palestinian mental health organization remarked that a human rights organizations could not defend a client if said client had a family member on the list. "They are making us police our beneficiaries," she said. "We are monitoring our people."[57] In another instance, a Palestinian staffer, formerly employed by a US contractor but who had since left the aid industry, remarked that Palestinian staffers were at times more strict than officials in the mission itself: Palestinian employees, my interlocutor noted, were in constant fear of losing their jobs or worse.[58] "They become more Catholic than the Pope," she added.

This fear is not unwarranted. Mohammad El Halabi, the manager of operations for World Vision in Gaza, as but one example, was arrested at the Erez checkpoint in August 2016 by the Israeli military. After fifty days in Israeli detention and allegations of torture, Halabi was charged with funneling millions of dollars of the charity's humanitarian funds to Hamas. Halabi's secret military trial in Israel has proceeded for over four years, and Israel continues to hold Halabi to date. Following Halabi's arrest, World Vision suspended its work in Gaza, including canceling the contracts of some 120 Palestinian employees, and commissioned an "externally-conducted forensic audit [which] found no evidence of diversion of funds and no material evidence that Halabi was part of or working for Hamas."[59] The Australian government too found the claims baseless in a separate investigation. Halabi's story was often referenced by Palestinian aid workers across the West Bank and Gaza, and while Halabi's case is exceptional in terms of the severity and stakes involved, Palestinians know all too well that their bodies are marked as already-always suspicious, and can, at any time, be cast in the crosshairs of the US security state on the one hand, and Israel on the other. In the many exchanges I had with Palestinian employees in the (inter)mediary sphere, self-policing was a recurring theme.

Yet, the benefits afforded to those who are absorbed into foreign aid circuits are, as many underscored, substantive. Many middle-class Palestinians have charted opportunities for physical and class mobility through employment in foreign aid institutions. Not only are the salaries, especially for USAID contracts, exponentially higher than most other professional jobs, including those in the private sector, but integration into foreign aid circuits grants Palestinians a set of rights and privileges otherwise denied to them as subjects under Israeli military rule. Israel maintains a strict im/mobility regime throughout the West Bank and over Palestinian borders, which severely curtails Palestinian internal and external mobility. However, Palestinians who procure employment in foreign aid agencies, such as with the UN or USAID, are granted special permission to move and travel. As one Palestinian worker put it, "People who work with USAID have a life. They have permits to go into the Israeli areas. They have these cards that allow them to pass any checkpoint. Even the drivers get that. . . . You are treated like a human with it." However, signaling a limit, she added, "You do it until you get tired, just like I did."[60] Her story is not unlike that of many middle-class Palestinians for whom employment in international and specifically US organizations affords opportunities for social and physical mobility.

Likewise, for Palestinians living abroad, employment with international aid agencies provides an opportunity to return home—a possibility otherwise denied to them under Israel's restrictive permitting system. Employment in foreign aid agencies is one of the few ways Palestinians are granted permission to visit and work in Palestine, as aid organizations, and especially US-funded agencies, are often able to procure the necessary permits from Israel. As Ahmed, a Palestinian with UK citizenship formerly living in London, recounted when discussing his decision to accept a USAID-funded job in the West Bank, "This was my ticket back."[61] Towards this end, he noted, "I realized that USAID was my main party on my side" to enable him to return. Ahmed secured employment in Palestine for nearly half a decade, jumping from aid contract to aid contract. He spoke of the perks of having cleared vetting, which signaled to other organizations that he was a "safe" hire, as well as the complicated dance he would have to do while working on USAID contracts. When writing reports, "You can't talk about the occupation," he recounted. "You can't mention the wall or checkpoints." He described how he was instructed to use language that described the built environment and its impact but that he couldn't talk about the objects themselves. He spoke too of the disciplinary work that terrorist regulations do. "Their [the contractor's] biggest fear," he recounted, was "to break the rules which would preclude them from receiving future contracts. . . . They would only work with safe organizations." He continued working from project to project for roughly six years until a persistent but gnawing internal conflict surrounding his role to "police other Palestinians" propelled him to leave. "You realize what you are doing," he stated, "but you are bound to it at the same time." The enfolding in of bodies denied rights, and then dually affording rights-turned-privileges in exchange for performing the work of the state, is itself an age-old tale of imperial governance. Equally it is a testament to their very elasticity and how easily these bodies can be cast out.

THE OFAC DANCE

Yet, even as the security state invariably shapes social and material relations across the sites where aid flows, producing new kinds of linkages and disconnections, it is not all-determining. (Inter)mediary bodies handling US monies, while conscripted into carrying out the work of the state, also navigate this security field in creative, often comical ways. As one aid worker enlisted in the West Bank greenhouse project noted, "We had to be creative without being in violation."[62] Likewise, the aforementioned NGO operating in Gaza devised a host of strategies to enable it to continue operating in the region while not technically violating US counterterrorism mandates.

As one among a host of challenges it encountered, the organization had to coordinate the entry of shipments into the blockaded territory. This required, on the one hand, that the agency remain in close communication with Israel. On the other, it required contact with Hamas as the governing authority of the territory. This presented them with, as Samir explained, a "sticky situation." Hamas required that communication be initiated in the form of written correspondence containing all necessary information about incoming shipments. "But we cannot initiate an official letter on our letterhead to them," he underscored. "So we tried to be creative." The NGO received a "green light" from its home office in Washington that contact could be made between the "lowest level possible of Hamas government and the lowest level possible at [said organization]."

What transpired was a rather comical situation wherein all correspondence involving the facilitation of US shipments containing medical supplies and pharmaceuticals inbound to the Gaza Strip occurred between a warehouse manager working in a Hamas ministry and the NGO's office manager. As Samir explained, laughing intermittently,

> Our contact person is the warehouse manager. He's very low level. He's a nice person [but] he doesn't have any authority. Whenever our man talks to him, he smiles and says, "I don't know anything but I accept it." He's a

very nice person. . . . He says, "Where should I sign? Here? Okay, I'll sign. Show me where should I sign." And he would sign.

In other instances, low-level NGO staff were at times stopped by Hamas authorities on the street as they were delivering correspondence to the various ministries. The messenger, equipped with letters needed to obtain necessary shipments, carried a recorder containing dictation of exactly what should be said if questioned by Hamas authorities. The written correspondence carried by the messenger moreover could not contain the NGO's letterhead or logo. "Funny isn't it? Yeah it's funny," Samir said between a laugh and sigh.

Other (inter)mediaries adopted similar strategies when operating in the Gaza Strip. As the chief of party of a different US contractor disclosed, their administrative assistant was tasked with delivering all correspondence to Hamas in the Gaza Strip. "Whenever we have to send a letter or do anything, we have to go to our lowest admin employee to go and deliver and talk and do these things. She has to take these letters to the deputy ministers. We cannot address these letters to their name [or] to anyone in particular." They simply read, "To whom it may concern," he stated. "They then grill her."[63] Hamas had allowed them to continuing operating in Gaza: "It's a bit of a don't ask don't tell situation," he explained, "but we've got it down now." In another case, a French humanitarian organization operating on funds from a US contractor described the rather humorous performance that took place whenever they had to purchase anything in Gaza. One of the organizational staff described the process of obtaining the ATC ("the paper") from Gaza vendors:

> We have these forms. They are actually quite funny. I probably shouldn't say it's funny, but they must know it's funny. It's this two-page thing that basically says, "I swear that I'm not a terrorist and I don't support any of these groups and I would never have anything to do with terrorism." . . . It's in English; it's not translated. And we have to get this signed every time we want to buy anything. If we are buying coffee, we have to get it signed by the shop owner. . . . Can you imagine? So obviously we just take it and when we get the coffee and receipt we just say, "Can you sign here please?" And everyone just signs it. No one knows what they are

signing. . . . Any shekel you spend you have to have one of these papers to go with it. Our staff have a printed stack in the car. If they need to buy something, they just take in the document and have them sign there.[64]

There is indeed a dance at play here—part comedy, part finesse, but one nevertheless that can come to an abrupt end if and when the security apparatus determines one has exceeded the bounds of permissible action. The stakes of violation are not even, of course. US aid contractors might lose future contracts if proven to be too risky and potentially lose direct funding. Palestinian, Muslim, and other racialized subjects can and have been prosecuted under US material support statutes. Where that line is, however, is ever shifting. It is within this inchoate space that the security state wields its power. It is through the fear of enforcement rather than enforcement per se that that the security state governs.

The following vignettes track a slightly different articulation of elastic sovereignty: that of the work of the US security state at the scale of the municipality in Palestine. Municipal space has been largely neglected in accounts of Israel's settler colonialism on the one hand, and on the other, in terms of US warfare and imperial exploits on the other. The following vignettes examine a more obscure mode of warfare that makes itself manifest in Palestine's roadscapes, municipal halls, and water infrastructure.

ROADSCAPES, WATERWORKS, AND MUNICIPAL HALLS

The space of the municipality has long been a paradoxical one, serving dually as an arena for local political expression and a site of intervention for colonial and foreign powers. A central dilemma facing Israel's control over the territories it occupied in 1967 was how to cultivate a pliant, proxy class through which to rule.[65] In 1976, local elections were held across the West Bank, the results of which presented a dilemma for the realization of this strategy. Israeli authorities had permitted the elections that year, believing the outcome would yield local leaders hostile or at least unconnected to the Palestine Liberation Organization (PLO). The result proved the opposite as a number of PLO supporters won mayoral and council seats throughout many West Bank cities.[66]

Israel soon changed course. The Likud government disbanded indirect rule and adopted a more interventionist strategy aimed at weakening PLO infrastructure through the promotion of an alternative Palestinian leadership.[67] The Palestinian rural sector served as a key target of intervention. In 1980, inspired in part by Menahem Milson, who became the head of the Civil Administration in 1981, Israel utilized the Movement of Palestinian Leagues (Harakat al-Rawabet al-Filistiniyya), or the Village Leagues, to foster an alternative Palestinian leadership to the elected PLO-affiliated leadership.[68] Drawing in part on an earlier strategy executed by the Jewish Agency in 1924, which sought to strengthen rural opposition to the anti-Zionist al-Husseini family through Hizb al-Zurra' (the Farmers Party), this strategy aimed to mobilize rural sectors in the West Bank against the urban-based nationalist elite as a means of weakening the PLO and undermining the "social base for Palestinian nationalism."[69]

The Village Leagues figured as key instruments in a broader counterinsurgency strategy. Accordingly, Israel sought to intervene in the daily life of Palestinians by cultivating "village potentates whose ability to provide services and patronages rested directly in power delegated by the Civil Administration."[70] The authority of the Village Leagues derived, in essence, from Israel's military government. League heads (often appointed *mukhtars*) who collaborated with the Military Administration were "invested with sufficient intercessionary power to provide services most desired by villagers" including, as Salim Tamari outlines:

> family reunion permits for relatives residing abroad; travel permits for crossing the bridge to Jordan; appointments (and transfers) in the civil service; building permits and the cancellation of orders to demolish buildings illegally constructed; intercession on behalf of detained family members, and the reduction of prison terms for prisoners; and permits to acquire driving licenses.[71]

Meanwhile noncooperating villages and recalcitrant *mukhtars* were denied such rewards, had local funds blocked, were stripped of their powers, and were forced to resign. Others were arrested, imprisoned, and deported.[72] Cooperating Leagues, on the other hand, were allocated village electrification schemes, piped potable waterworks, and internal road networks.[73] "Development" was understood by architects of this strategy as a key instrument in the broader counterinsurgency objective of eroding the PLO power base and fostering an alternative local leadership, more amenable to Israeli rule.

This counterinsurgency strategy proved largely ineffective as the Village Leagues did not enjoy legitimacy among their constituencies, nor among the urban-based nationalist elite.[74] Israel was largely successful in undermining the power of municipalities, annulling the appointment of certain mayors and municipal council members, and in damaging national institutions, including three major Palestinian universities.[75] However, with the start of the first *intifada*, Palestinians sought to reclaim municipal spaces, and in 1987, the Palestinian National Unified Command called on mayors and municipal council members appointed by the Israelis to resign from their posts.

The role of municipalities and local government shifted slightly again following the establishment of the Palestinian National Authority (PNA or PA) in 1994. Prior to that, Palestinian municipalities and village councils were responsible for providing public services to Palestinians in occupied Palestinian territory.[76] The Palestinian National Authority, however, sought to promote local government as part of its broader state-building-cum-development strategy.[77] Accordingly, the PA promoted a policy of "decentralization" or "municipalization" wherein it supported the rehabilitation of local governing capacities and infrastructures to ensure districts had the means to partake in the state-building project.[78] Donors too have regarded municipalities as key sites of intervention, particularly over the last decade.[79] Municipalities have thus long constituted a kind of paradoxical political space in Palestine, serving as a critical arena of local administration and as a strategic site of intervention for Israeli counterinsurgency and donor interventions, precisely because of their critical role with respect to the former.[80] It is against this backdrop that the case of Bethlehem and the workings of the US security state therein is refracted.

In 2005, Palestinian municipal elections were held across the West Bank and Gaza Strip.[81] These were the first local elections to be held since 1976 and the first to take place under Palestinian Authority administration. Carrying echoes of 1976, the election yielded pockets of local leadership disagreeable to Israel, thus presenting a distinct dilemma for US aid flows inbound to the Palestinians.[82] Fatah (the dominant party of the Palestinian Authority) secured a majority of mayoral and municipal council seats in the West Bank.

Meanwhile in the Gaza Strip, Hamas procured a majority. Equally, Hamas and the Popular Front for the Liberation of Palestine (PFLP), both appearing on the US Treasury OFAC list, also won a number of municipal seats across the West Bank.[83] The 2004–2005 election would mobilize the full weight of the US sanctions regime. It would also spur the United States, just a few years later, to target the municipal scale as a key site of aid intervention.

While much has been written about the fracturing of Palestinian national politics in the wake of the 2006 parliamentary election, caused in no small measure by interventions undertaken on the part of states and supranational bodies to purge the PA of Hamas ministers from its ranks, less attention has been afforded to the more subtle, political work sanctions regimes do, how they rearrange, consolidate, and fragment, at the scale of the municipality. Over my decade of fieldwork, including multiple trips to Bethlehem and surrounding municipalities and interviews conducted with mayors and municipal workers, I grew to understand the political work of Washington's terrorism designation within and around the space of a banned municipality, and in particular the violences enacted in the space of void or withdrawal.[84] Bethlehem proves an especially generative case through which to refract broader questions about the quiet, often undetected work of empire regimes in the absence of spectacular warfare or a globally indexed event—in this case, a local election.

BETHLEHEM AND THE BAN

I had allocated roughly two hours for the trip from Ramallah to Bethlehem. The direct route between these the two points (about eighteen miles) is through Jerusalem. By car it takes roughly thirty minutes. Restrictions on Palestinian travel into Jerusalem forced our vehicle, a shared taxi (*serveece*), onto a lengthier alternate route, covering some thirty-four miles. We cut along the eastern side of the separation wall and along an elliptical path deep into the West Bank, around Greater Jerusalem and south through the mountainous area of Wadi al-Nar. This more circuitous route has become the main passageway for all Palestinian commercial and residential traffic between the northern and southern parts of the West Bank. The trip between Ramallah and Bethlehem on this route takes one-and-a-half to two hours. Space, like time, is pulled, stretched, and distorted. Connectivity between points is reworked by sprawling colonial settlements and accompanying infrastructures, prohibited military zones, and permanent and makeshift checkpoints. Geographies of settler colonialism, as per Weizman, "shrink and expand the territory at will."[85]

Our taxi traveled southeast from Ramallah past the Qalandiya checkpoint, rounded the northern tip of East Jerusalem settlements, and then transited to a smaller road snaking us through a string of Palestinian villages. At the fork of the juncture there was a watermelon stand and makeshift car garage; in front, scrap metal, old tires, and a sign in Hebrew, Arabic, and English warning passers-by of their entry into Area A. Dodging potholes and speed bumps, we made our way through the narrow streets and to the foothills of Wadi al-Nar, or Hell Valley. Previously a dirt road connecting the villages of Sawahreh and Ubediyyeh, this path was rarely used aside from local villagers. However, with progressive restrictions imposed by Israel on Palestinian mobility, including the prohibition of Palestinian traffic into Jerusalem, this road has become the main link for Palestinians between north and south.

The driver downshifted, and we began the treacherous climb. Trying to consume my thoughts with anything but the steep drop below us and the truck in front, which I was convinced would tip at any moment, I jotted notes for my interview in between the bumpy parts. The woman next to me, having grown tired during the thirty-minute trip thus far, had fallen asleep, her head bobbing as we hit stones and ditches. My nervousness marked me as a foreigner.

Nearing the top we came onto the Palestinian village of Sawahreh, which is surrounded by the settlements Ma'ale Adumim from the northeast and Kidar from the east and by the separation wall to the west. Its southern entrance is blocked by the Wadi al-Nar checkpoint, or "the container," the main crossing between north and south. Passing through the morning rhythms of Sawahreh, we neared the checkpoint and shuffled through bags and pockets for our identity documents. Two soldiers approached, looking more bored than usual, and opened the door. While delays up to an hour are not uncommon, this time the soldiers decided we were not worth holding, and after randomly checking the ID cards of four Palestinian passengers, they walked away, permitting us to pass. As we pulled through to the other side, the mood lightened, and we started shuffling for the required fare of thirty shekels. No one pays before the container.

Once on the other side, we began the descent through the windy down-hill. Just a couple of years later, Wadi al-Nar would be enlarged, paved, and equipped with guardrails around the more treacherous bits. Wadi al-Nar's rehabilitation would be part of a donor-funded alternative roads project that would, in effect, consolidate a segregated Palestinian road network through-out the West Bank. The plan, first introduced by Israel in 2004, though originally rejected, and later funded in large part by USAID, rehabilitated a number of secondary, rural, and unpaved roads deemed vital to Palestinian "fabric of life."[86] The "fabric of life" roads were widely understood to be key in-struments in the normalization of colonial infrastructure packaged, accord-ing to signs bearing the USAID emblem, as a "gift from the American People to the Palestinian People."[87] The USAID signs poised along the main artery connecting north to south indexed a particular kind of American presence. Bethlehem would index another.

I had arrived at the Bethlehem Municipality (*baladiyya*) for my meeting with Dr. Victor Batarseh with just a few minutes to spare. Dr. Batarseh had

FIGURE 1. USAID sign along Wadi al-Nar Road.

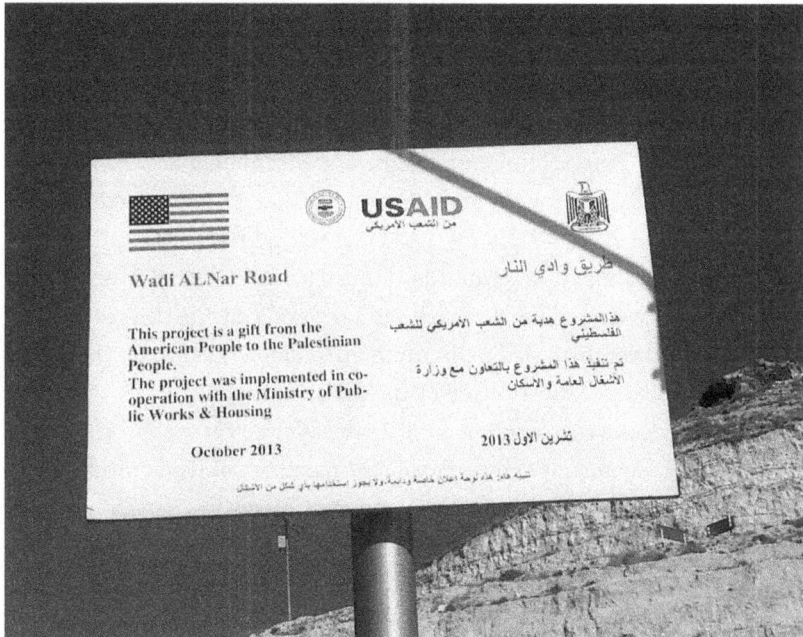

Photo by author, 2015.

been elected mayor of Bethlehem in 2005, a time during which the political composition of Bethlehem's municipal council had shifted.[88] The denominational quota of the council was upheld in the 2005 elections, with eight seats going to Christians and seven to Muslims. However, the Fatah movement secured only four seats (a minority), while the remaining seats went to groups listed on the US OFAC list, including Hamas (five seats), PFLP (three seats), and Islamic Jihad (one seat). Also included, though he ran as an independent, was Batarseh, arguably affiliated with PFLP. Batarseh is also a US citizen.[89] In the wake of the elections, the United States imposed sanctions on Bethlehem. In practice, this meant that Bethlehem became a no-contact zone for American money: all ties to the city and to joint bodies of which Bethlehem was a part were severed. The logic of fungibility written into US material support law prevailed here: any assistance to Bethlehem could defray the cost to a listed entity, and therefore no relations, financial or otherwise, were permitted. I would later speak to a US contractor who disclosed the classifications used. Municipalities, he told me, are either "derogatory or non-derogatory. [It] depends on who sits on the councils." This particular contractor was working in the Bethlehem area but "Bethlehem Municipal Council," he told me, "is 'derog.' "[90] Washington's list was intimately here.[91] I wanted to understand more fully the work that it was doing here and across the landscape of Bethlehem.

"Anything with Bethlehem Municipality they [agencies with US funds] run away from," Baterseh told me.[92] Most of their funding now comes from the *sudlooq baladiyat* (the PA municipal fund), "but it's not enough," he underscored. Bethlehem, he told me, had been struggling to maintain municipal services and repair deteriorating infrastructure, some of it worn from time, much of it destroyed by Israeli military raids during the second *intifada*. The repair of roads, old piping, and dilapidated wastewater treatment systems had been greatly arrested by the deficit of funds.

Meanwhile, the surrounding municipalities of Beit Jala and Beit Sahour had, in 2005, elected city councils void of members of listed groups (predominately Fatah and independents), and accordingly had seen a relatively healthy inflow of US funds for municipal services, infrastructure, recreational spaces, and city services.[93] USAID packages, both mayors underscored, were among the largest of any donor. Beit Jala, just to the north of

FIGURE 2. Bethlehem Governorate including Bethlehem, Beit Jala, and Beit Sahour municipalities.

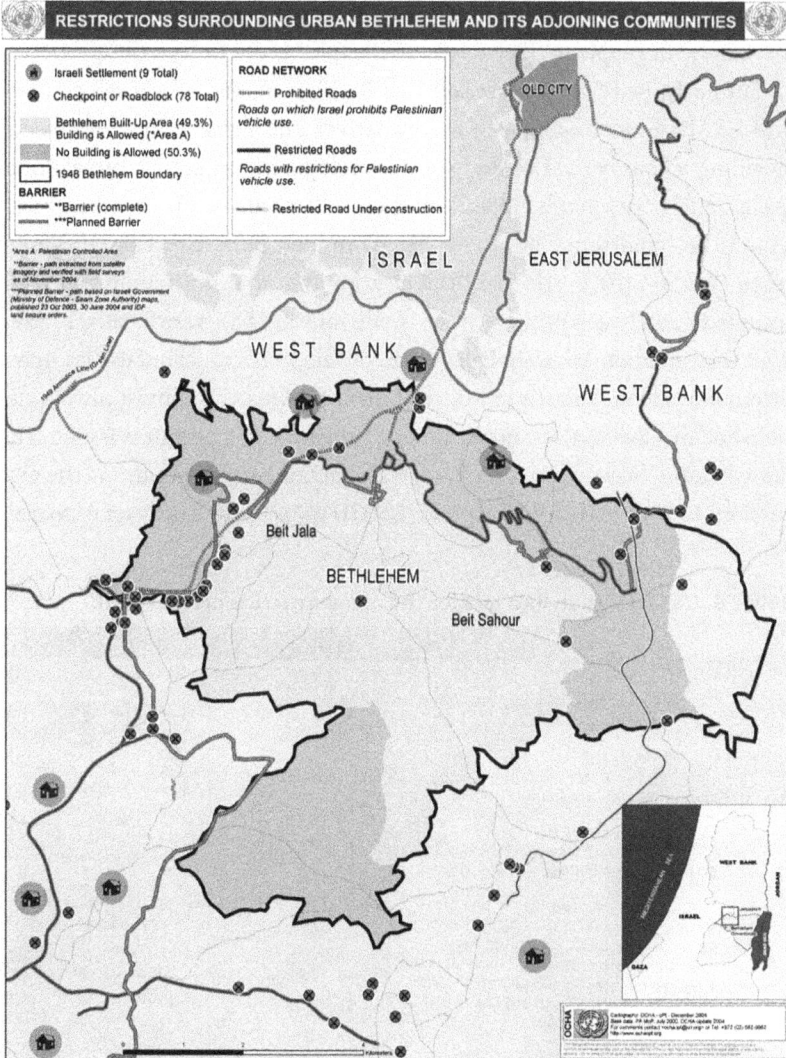

RESTRICTIONS SURROUNDING URBAN BETHLEHEM AND ITS ADJOINING COMMUNITIES

Bethlehem, at this same time had seen the rehabilitation of Beit Jala Government Hospital, the upgrading of health services, road rehabilitation projects (including the St. George Road, a main artery that links the Arab Society Hospital to surrounding villages), a sewage pipeline, and other new infrastructure projects including a new library bearing the slogan, "A Gift from the American People to the Palestinian People."

Similarly, Beit Sahour, just south of Bethlehem, had also received plentiful USAID-funded quality-of-life initiatives and infrastructural projects, including a commercial center, youth development programs, recreational spaces, and new schools. When I met with Beit Sahour's mayor, he underscored the importance of a new USAID-funded park, Ush Ghurab Public Peace Park, on the outskirts of the city, an area that until 2006 had been occupied by an Israeli military base. Israeli military bases are located in Area C, an Oslo creation, wherein Palestinian development and land use is almost strictly forbidden. Palestinian development in Area C is almost always demolished by Israel unless, under rare circumstances, a permit is issued. The United States, he went on to explain, was instrumental in obtaining the permissions to zone and build the park. "USAID gives us the safety for us to con-

FIGURE 3. USAID sign in Beit Jala for the reconstruction of a hospital.

USAID
من الشعب الأمريكي

Rehabilitation of Beit Jala Government
Hospital / Bethlehem Governorate

Funded by the
People of the United States of America for
the Benefit of the Palestinian People

Implemented by
American Near East Refugee Aid (ANERA)
for the United States Agency for
International Development (USAID) Under
the Emergency Water and Sanitation and
Other Infrastructure Program (EWASII)
November 2009

ANERA
AMERICAN NEAR EAST REFUGEE AID

مشروع اعادة تأهيل مستشفى بيت جالا
الحكومي / محافظة بيت لحم

يتم تمويل هذا المشروع بدعم من الشعب
الأمريكي لإفادة الشعب الفلسطيني

تقوم مؤسسة أنيرا بتنفيذ المشروع
بدعم من الوكالة الأمريكية للتنمية الدولية
ضمن برنامج
المياه والصرف الصحي و البنية التحتية
الطارئ
تشرين ثاني ٢٠٠٩

Photo by author, 2010.

FIGURE 4. Sign hanging in the entranceway of Beit Jala library.

Photo by author, 2010.

FIGURE 5. View of Beit Jala Public Library.

Photo by author, 2010.

tinue working there because it is Area C," he said. The Israelis put a military tower near the park, he said, but we were able to build most of it. "USAID negotiated with them [Israelis]," he underscored. "The Israelis announced that they will not demolish this place." I inquired as to whether other donors such as the EU, French, or Germans have the same ability to negotiate with Israel. "No," he said. "Who can negotiate with Israel? Only the Americans."

While it would be facile to draw a direct line between motivations for residents electing leaders based on the material rewards they might accrue (or not), the case of Ush Ghurab is a stark, very material reminder of the rewards that will follow if behavior conforms in a particular way. Beit Jala and Beit Sahour had both been aptly rewarded. Even as the two municipalities were also receiving other sources of funding, principally from European donors and the PA, it was repeatedly underscored that USAID packages were virtually unmatched. "It gives the most money," as Beit Sahour's mayor said.[94] Fatah-controlled municipalities, he underscored, have a better quality of life.

Yet, equally, there was a glaring void—a definitive limit to awards amassed by a "safe" city council: Beit Jala and Beit Sahour were invariably, too, caught up in the punitive web of the US material support ban and US Department of State "no contact" policy. Given the close proximity between Beit Jala, Bethlehem, and Beit Sahour, which together comprise the Bethlehem Governorate, these three municipalities collectively share seats on the joint water and sewage council. The presence of a blacklisted entity on the council resulted in the United States blacklisting any projects running through the council or that might benefit the Bethlehem Municipality.

"One of [our] first projects" Beit Sahour's mayor told me, "was in water and sewage [and] the construction of water lines." However, when Bethlehem was placed on the banned list, these projects were terminated. When I inquired about the status of these sectors now, some five years after the boycott had gone into effect, he told me, "No one is funding it now. [We haven't] develop[ed] this sector since the last five years. Fayyad [the PA] funds some pumps and some wells but it's not enough." At the time of this interview, Beit Sahour was awaiting funding from the European Union and the French to upgrade dilapidated water pipes and the sewer network throughout the city. "We've had these pipes since the 1950s," he said. "We have changed not more than 20 percent of this network," which had resulted in up to 45 percent water loss in some cases. Many houses, the mayor told me, do not have connections with the main sewage line, resulting in sewage leaks upwards of 20 percent. Similarly, Beit Jala's mayor lamented that the situation had presented significant challenges for them. "Bethlehem, Beit Jala, and Beit Sahour are the owners of the water department, together," he said. "Now to get something we must go only as Beit Jala or only as Beit Sahour."[95] It's all very embarrassing. . . . I hope they will fix it by the next elections."

Bethlehem did. In 2012, with the election of a new mayor and municipal council (Hamas and PFLP boycotted the election), US sanctions would be removed. The next election held in 2017 also yielded a cabinet of nondesignated groups. That year I would return to Bethlehem to meet with the new mayor, Anton Salman. As I walked through the crowded streets to Manger Square, USAID signs indicating rehabilitation projects underway, including that of the civic center, could be seen along the main road that cut through the market. When I reached the municipality, I saw, adorned on the building itself, a sign reading, "This project is a gift from the American people to the Palestinian people"—USAID was funding Bethlehem's municipal center. Accordingly, facing the entrance were a handful of computers with stickers of the USAID logo.

FIGURE 6. Plaque at the entrance to the Bethlehem Municipality.

Photo by author, 2017.

FIGURE 7. A printer inside the Bethlehem
Municipality.

Photo by author, 2017.

The following year, some six years into the new post-sanctions era, I
would return to Bethlehem to meet a municipal staffer, also an engineer,
at a restaurant near Manger Square. The mood felt lighter than during previous trips—perhaps it was the moment at the outset when we realized we
had first met years ago, when I was just beginning my doctoral fieldwork,
and he was a new staffer at the municipality. US money was now flowing,
he told me. At that time, a US contractor, Tetra Tech, had tried to design a
strategic plan for the municipality. We declined, he told me, "we can do our
own plan."[96] We would also speak about the dilapidated water infrastructure
that Mayor Batarseh had spoken about those many years ago. With French
aid (administered through the Agence Française de Développement), rehabilitation of the water network had just been completed—a project for which
Batarseh had struggled to procure sufficient funds almost a decade prior.
He noted that another US contractor, AECOM, an infrastructure firm, was
rehabilitating five major roads, one of which would run from the Bethlehem
checkpoint to the city center, where we were sitting.

Bethlehem's story indexes a different kind of presence—a present absence, a withdrawal but not a void. It is absence that is itself active; it shapes space and acts on bodies and landscapes; it fractures and consolidates; it rearranges. This absence presents itself in Bethlehem's dilapidated water pipes and aging roads, in the fragmented spaces between broken sewers and new libraries, in the yawning gap to rehabilitate a water grid and lush "peace parks," though pressed against a military base. The US sanctions regime does a certain kind of work.

STRINGS AND EMBEDDINGS

Palestine, as any other place, is made and undone, remade and reworked by heterogenous forces, dynamics, and actors. Here I have not necessarily attempted to chart the complex amalgam of powers, historical contingencies, engineered colonial designs and their slippages that have made and continue to remake Palestine. Rather, I have told a different kind of story: one of interconnectivity and presence, one of the weaving and embedding of a securitized counterterrorism regime into the landscape, material infrastructures, and bodies of Palestinians themselves. This is not the whole story in Palestine, of course. Washington is not all-determining, but it is, nonetheless, intimately present, a force, though in ways often obscured. The topological workings of the US counterterrorism regime as it bends and flexes across extraterritorial domains, de-linking legal and territorial borders and recasting the US security state through aid flows, folds in far-away (non-citizen) bodies as objects of security to be hyper-surveilled, policed, and punished while excluding them from the space of politics. They are objects of empire, but in ways, often unknown. In one sense, then, the story I have sought to tell here is one of silent wars, of regimes of domination obfuscated by humanitarian claims and how these become reworked in the most insidious of ways. Yet it also, I hope, holds open the promise and possibility of how the "ties that bind" can, and often do, come undone. Such is the subject of the following chapter.

Three

WORK OF THE LIST

Empires are controlled from a distance, using [the] simplest of
technologies. . . . The material culture of bureaucracy and empire is not
found in pomp and circumstance, nor even in the first instance at the point
of a gun, but rather at the point of a list.

—*Geoffrey Bowker and Susan Star,* Sorting Things Out

LISTS, SEEMINGLY MUNDANE TECHNOLOGIES OF ENUMERATION AND classification, do "discrete but hard work."[1] From no-fly, kill, and sanctions lists, to border preclearance programs and "whitelists,"[2] lists filter and sort bodies, marking some for premature death, others for the "good life," some to be fixed in place, and others for unfettered mobility; they enact new kinds of legal orders, jurisdictions, and targeting. Lists, too, morph and play with time. The organizing logic of the security list, as but one example, is that of preemption that brings into being "novel modes of targeting" predicated on predictions and projections that enable security interventions in absentia of any crime committed and outside the scope of judicial protections.[3]

Lists act on the world, splitting, connecting, and rearranging, bringing disparate elements into abstract relation—they are topological technologies. The UN sanctions list, for instance, creates what John Law calls a "collateral reality,"[4] bringing into abstract relation "diverse entries associated with lo-calized political violence and historically embedded (Islamist) movements" spanning from Somalia to Indonesia.[5] In this vein, Palestinians would often differentiate themselves from other groups and entities included on any one of these lists. As one Palestinian interlocutor remarked,

> We are not Al-Qaeda or ISIS. We are not Al-Nusra. We are not part of these terrorist groups that are fighting in Lebanon, in Syria, or in Libya, or in other areas in Yemen. We are people who have the right to struggle for our own liberation, and that is what our people [are] doing.[6]

Differentiating the Palestinian liberation movement from other, predomi-nately Islamist, movements operating around the world, he pushes against the homogenizing work the terror list does, effectively constituting diverse political actors operating across the world into a single classificatory scheme that then subjects them to sanction, punishment, and violence.

Lists, put differently, do not merely represent pre-existing phenomena; rather they actively produce new kinds of epistemological orders and re-lationalities. As Urs Stäheli contends, the list is too often conceived as an "instrument or tool for political processes exterior to the list" rather than un-derstood as constituting the very entities and categories included therein.[7] "List-making," Stäheli explains, is "not only a problem of selection, but it is necessarily a transformative and performative practice."[8] Lists are "inscrip-tion devices that are heterogeneous, unpredictable, and *productive* in un-foreseen ways."[9] Lists have a "liveliness" that demand our attention.[10] Such is the focus of this chapter.

Security lists in particular have proliferated in the post–9/11 era. The US government, for one, has developed an expansive watch-listing system, cloaked in secrecy, opaque in its construction, for monitoring and tracking individuals suspected of being national security threats.[11] The US Terrorist Screening Database (TSDB) contains hundreds of thousands of listed sub-jects, some US citizens, who have been blacklisted absent due processes on secret "derogatory information" (also the term used by NGO workers con-ducting security checks of aid beneficiaries in Palestine).[12] Notably, criteria for inclusion in the US terrorism database requires only reasonable *suspi-cion*, not proof of any wrongdoing or crime committed.[13]

Information stored on this list is used to construct other lists, including the no-fly list and the selectee list (designated by an "SSSS" on a plane ticket, for instance), which subjects individuals to enhanced security at border crossings, airports, and in encounters with local law enforcement. By 2017, the TSDB included roughly 1.2 million people, among them about 4,600 US citizens or permanent residents.[14] The US list has gone global: TSDB data are shared with some sixty foreign governments with which the United States has entered into "foreign partner arrangements," along with a sprawling network of private partners.[15] Once a subject is listed in the TSDB, even if later removed, she always runs the risk of capture, detention, and disappearance by other foreign sovereigns in the network. The list tethers to marked bodies, bringing them into intimate relation with a global terrorism infrastructure that renders individual terrorism suspects effectively prisoners without any political or legal redress.[16]

Meanwhile the US National Counterterrorism Center Terrorist Identities Datamart Environment database contained over 1.6 million people as of February 2017, and Thomson Reuters World-Check, a private sector database (thus having looser listing standards than states), marketed to financial institutions and charitable organizations, contained an estimated 2.7 million entries of "individuals and entities deemed worthy of enhanced scrutiny" as of 2016.[17] "The list" has emerged as central, though subtle, war technology in the long arc of the global war on terror: it is through the list that the more spectacular modes and modalities of US warfare—from "targeted killings" to rendition and torture—are built, filtering bodies into a space governed by sovereign violence alone.

While the politics of lists and the epistemologies, technological arrangements, material-semiotic relations, and juridical regimes they bring into being have garnered greater attention across legal, critical security, and geographical scholarship,[18] there remains scant ethnographic engagement with the *work* that lists—and terrorism lists in particular—perform on targeted subjects and spaces. We know, for instance, that contemporary security listings affect ever-increasing numbers of individuals and that lists generate new knowledge practices and modes of ordering. Predicated on the elastic concept of "reasonable suspicion"—wherein subjects are deemed "listable" by virtue of their associations, connections, and relationalities, or by belonging to designated population categories—these lists sweep ever-greater numbers of racially coded "suspect" subjects into their dragnets.[19]

But what of the listed subjects? In most accounts, the listed remain largely statistics, aggregate sums, stored databases if they appear at all. What kinds of work does the "point of the list" do on targeted bodies and populations? What kinds of exclusions are produced from list inclusion? Put differently, what is the topological work of the list as it moves across global space, enfolding certain subjects into punitive regimes of rule while exempting them from rights and protections? This chapter reorients the view of the terrorism list from the sites where these lists are often generated (Washington, New York, London, Brussels, and so on) to the work these lists do on targeted bodies and populations, while equally remaining attuned to how the targeted push back on these lists, refusing the epistemologies and the logics they impose and demand. Accordingly, the chapter theorizes war waged through the list not from the geohistorical location of the Global North, as so often the privileged optic, but instead from the nodes, landscapes, and bodies on which the technology of the list intimately presents itself, on which it operates, rearranges, and is indeed refused. Here I theorize the list broadly, less as a material artifact, or database, per se, and instead as a topological technology that is itself "lively"—that does particular kinds of work—enfolding and isolating, fragmenting and consolidating, disassembling and reorganizing sociopolitical formations and relationalities.[20]

LISTS AND THEIR FRAGMENTS

Terrorism lists infuse aid space in Palestine.[21] "All donors and UN agencies now have them," one aid worker relayed.[22] Donor agencies operating across the West Bank and Gaza Strip, including USAID, the Canadian International Development Agency, Australian Aid (AusAid), the UK Department for International Development, to name a few, each host their respective national lists, such as the Proscribed Terrorist Organizations list in the UK or the Office of Foreign Assets Control (OFAC) list in the United States. The UN Security Council maintains a global sanctions list (the Consolidated List), which first targeted the Taliban pursuant to UN Resolution 1267 (1999) and then later incorporated Al-Qaeda and the Islamic State in Iraq and the Levant (ISIL) and associated entities. The Consolidated List, as Gavin Sullivan argues, has been "radically repurposed into a preemptive legal weapon for disrupting global terrorist networks and their perceived supporters worldwide."[23] Alongside the growing expanse of national and supranational lists, a burgeoning industry of private firms, such as Thomson Reuters World-Check, consolidate sanctions, counterterrorism watchlists, regulatory and law enforcement lists, public sources, and media sites, often cobbling together identities featured in online content that are used by financial institutions and charitable organizations alike. Likewise, lists of high- and low-risk clients, "Know Your Customer" guidelines, and "other 'filtering devices'" are used "by banks in ambiguous and unpredictable ways."[24]

These lists touch down in Palestine in different ways, proliferating through aid flows and financial transactions, in governing technologies, and throughout political institutions. Everything depends on the list, aid workers constantly remarked. NGOs and contractors often spoke about how project timelines were delayed as they waited for clearance from Washington. Other times, aid projects were aborted midway through implementation, as happened in 2007 following the Hamas victory in the parliamentary election.[25] Implementing partners commonly remarked on the extensive security checks mandated for even small-scale activities such as trainings and workshops—though some aid bodies found a workaround to this. As one Palestinian employee of a US-funded health program noted, "You have to choose your language carefully."[26] He went to explain that they always have to vet for "trainings" (which are defined as anything that has a "learning outcome"), as well as workshops over four days.[27] However, if a workshop runs under this allocated time and does not involve any learning outcomes, he remarked, they could bypass participant vetting.

Some NGOs and contractors were able to dance creatively around the list and the mandates it enforced; however, the power of the list and the punitive measures it could potentially wield if a group or individual was targeted always lurked in the background. Meanwhile the discursive work of the list posed a more complicated set of issues for Palestinian aid recipients. Palestinians were continually forced to make difficult decisions regarding whether or not to denounce as terrorists, and accordingly sever relations with, Palestinian factions that had long been part and parcel of the Palestinian national movement. As one Palestinian NGO employee involved in debates in the early 2000s surrounding US terrorism certification noted, "You want me to denounce half of my people?"[28] In another instance, the director of a Palestinian mental health organization noted that the key question Palestinians were debating during this period was "whether we as civil society should consent or not consent?"[29] The work of the list, and the politics of fracture it has produced between groups cleared by the security apparatuses of foreign capitals, has caused significant fissures within and across Palestinian civil society actors.

The list too permeates the institutional structures and fabric of daily life, such as in banking. One high-level manager of the Arab Bank in Ramallah described how employees were required to screen customers through security databases for many financial transactions, including new accounts, loans, banks transfers, and other kinds of transactions.[30] "We enter all of their information into a database," he explained, where it is screened through other databases. If the person comes up as being on the blacklist, then they are denied an account. "We can't tell them why," he lamented. At times a blacklisted subject might appear on a list due merely to a subject's associational and/or familial relations or as the result of a duplicate name appearing on any number of the screened lists. He discussed incidences when entire families of listed subjects were blacklisted: risk here is calculated relationally. The list in Palestine is everywhere.

Amid the interlinked and deeply entangled set of lists at work in Palestine, I focus here on one in particular, the US OFAC list, though its impacts reverberate globally through the host of other terrorism lists with which it interfaces including those managed by Israel, Canada, Australia, and European states, as well as the United Nations. I start the story with the United States because moves undertaken during the early years of the global war on terror, and in particular the infusion of the terrorism list into aid packages bound for Palestine, set in motion the trend for intensified aid securitization, which has today nearly entirely impaired Palestinian organizations and formations reliant on foreign assistance (see Chapter 4). A disproportionate number of Palestinian parties and political figures are featured on the OFAC list.

REFUSING THE LIST

It was 2003 and the United States Agency for International Development had just introduced a host of compliance mechanisms in accordance with President George W. Bush's recently declared war on the "financial foundation of the global terror network." Palestinian NGOs were just beginning to grapple with the implications of these new conditionalities. My interlocutor, who was central to these conversations, shared with me internal debates circulating within a prominent coalition of some hundred Palestinians NGOs—the Palestinian Non-Governmental Organizations Network (PNGO)—as it strategized a response to Washington's new counterterrorism stipulations.

Formed during the early Oslo period in 1993, PNGO began as an initiative undertaken by a number of NGO leaders, political independents, and left factions, including members belonging to the Palestinian Communist Party (PCP) and the Popular Front for the Liberation of Palestine (PFLP). A central function of the network during these early years was to advocate on behalf of NGO interests in light of Palestinian Authority (PA) attempts to enforce greater regulatory controls over NGO activities and funding.[31] It was also intended to function "as a bulwark and guarantee for both national sovereignty and democracy."[32] In the first instance, PNGO was to serve as a counterweight to the PA; nearly a decade later, it would assume a central role in countering the trend towards aid securitization. The interlocutor with whom I was meeting, Samira, was centrally involved in debates surrounding the growing trend towards aid securitization.

Samira, who was active in internal PNGO debates in the early 2000s, described the mood at the time:

> At the time the USAID anti-terrorist document was being disputed, there was a lot of discussion worldwide about the terms in that document— whether we as civil society should consent or not consent—here and in Egypt and other places. Now unfortunately that kind of regional discussion and global discussion did not go very far because it was obvious at that point that we as Palestinians were the most targeted because the number of the number of people and organizations included. There was a US presidential decree—it had a number [13224]. My colleague and I researched it. . . . In the annex many Palestinian organizations [were listed] so our discussion was [based on the question]: how can we accept a document that is basically asking us to refuse to acknowledge people

who we actually consider nationalists and announce them to be terrorists because of financial requirements?

[B]asically what we were saying [is]: first off, all political conditional
funding is not acceptable in principle; second, that it is targeting us, Palestinians; [and] third, [who] they are considering as terrorists are actually national figures for us. The list included, among others, the PFLP . . .
there was even the al-Aqsa Brigades and also [George] Habash and names
that are very much national figures [for us]—and of course Hamas and
Hizballah. So we were saying that in principle, first of all, the whole anti-
terror war that the US is waging is very much a distorted war and that the
US has intentions by waging this war and that is to put the whole world in
a state of defense . . . and all these are instruments of that war.[33]

PNGO's internal debates weave together a number of threads calling, in
the first instance, for an adherence to Palestinian Law (specifically Chapter
Seven, Article 32), which stipulates that Palestinian NGOs are not permitted
to receive conditional assistance. Second, PNGO conceives of the ATC as an explicit instrument of US warfare, a technology of counterinsurgency that would
invariably fragment Palestinian political formations and networks, criminalize acts of non-submission, and ultimately enroll Palestinians into practices
of self-policing and surveillance. It was on this basis that PNGO announced a
boycott of USAID on July 12, 2003: "Some donor agencies," its statement reads,
"are setting unacceptable conditions for providing financial support to Palestinian NGOs. Such conditions include a pledge titled 'Certification Regarding
Terrorist Financing' that must be signed by Palestinian NGOs prior to entering
into funding agreements."[34] Accordingly, PNGO expressed concern that Palestinian NGOs were being required to sign a document stipulating that they
would sever relations with individuals and groups the United States had designated "terrorist entities."[35] To sign the ATC was seen as a direct sanctioning
of the conjoined Washington–Tel Aviv position that criminalizes in toto all
but Palestinian complacency under conditions of ongoing dispossession. The
ATC, put differently, was clearly understood as a technology of proxy warfare,
one embedded and expressed through the "point of a list."[36]

PNGO's concerns regarding the fragmentary and disciplinary work the
list would enact on the ground in Palestine were not unwarranted. As Samira
recounts above, "If I want to provide you with services I have to check your
background, your security record [and check to see] if you are affiliated

[with any group on the list]."[37] The most dangerous thing about the ATC," another PNGO interlocutor stated, is that it "splits and fragments." "We cannot work together," she added.[38] Moreover, the vetting, she asserted "is also very dangerous. . . . The most important thing is not the proposal and your intervention. The most important thing is to have clearance." In one instance, it was revealed that a Palestinian human rights organization could not defend clients if they appeared on the list.[39] In another, a PNGO member remarked that Palestinians who had been imprisoned by Israel would not pass US security screenings to receive aid.[40] "It's not our job to police our people," one NGO director underscored.[41]

For those who did accept US money, and accordingly its associated conditionalities, self-policing was a recurring theme. "We simply don't work with every municipality," the director of one US NGO admitted. "Some are restricted."[42] She then proceeded to list a range of municipalities in the West Bank including Nablus, Jenin, and Ramallah with which they were prohibited from having relations, at the time given that their respective municipal councils contained members belonging to groups on the US foreign terrorist organizations (FTO) list. A considerable number of beneficiaries, she lamented, were preemptively eliminated. The director of another international NGO remarked, "It's humiliating; you cannot work with anyone on the list."[43]

Even well before the political work of the list had been made abundantly clear, PNGO foresaw its implications. The decision to call for a boycott, as the interlocutor underscores above, was a refusal to be put in a "state of defense."[44] And while USAID was made a central target of the boycott, the issues PNGO sought to address with the call were broader than this institution alone. As one member on the steering committee stated, "It was not just USAID, but USAID was the most striking issue in conditional funding."[45] The issuance of USAID's anti-terrorism certificate (ATC) in 2003 brought to the fore, and underscored with a certain urgency, a number of debates ongoing among Palestinians for decades surrounding the thorny problem of how to contend with the political projects into which they were being integrated, through the channels of aid upon which they were dependent. The problem, PNGO made clear in its boycott call, is not Palestinians themselves, nor their NGOs; the problem is the settler–colonial regime that creates a need for aid in the first place. PNGO issued the following statement:

While NGOs are against any form of terrorism, including state terror practiced by the Israeli army against Palestinians, it is imperative to note that Palestinian NGOs have affirmed their opposition, on several occasions, to any and all acts of violence against civilians whether Israelis, Palestinians or internationals.

It is not clear on what basis and upon which criteria the definition of "terror acts" [by the United States] has been set, especially in light of Israeli attempts to portray the struggle of the Palestinian people for freedom and independence as "violent and terror acts." . . .

The root problem in the West Bank and Gaza remains the continued illegal Israeli military occupation of Palestinian lands, and not the work of Palestinian NGOs and their constituencies. . . .

Palestinian NGOs believe that any conditionality in funding beyond the accepted international norms and standards constitutes a violation to the legality of funding, as the Palestinian NGO law prohibits accepting such conditions in pertaining funding from any international body.

We believe the conditions stated in the annex entitled "Certification Regarding Terrorist Financing" and in the contract presented by American PVOs should be considered invalid and be annulled.[46]

PNGO's reconstitution of the frame lays bare the politics of the terrorism list. First, it calls into question the construction of the very definition of terrorism itself in the ATC, underscoring the clear omission of political violence waged on the part of Israel. Second, it foregrounds Israel's historical flattening of the Palestinian anti-colonial struggle into the ambit of "terrorism," emptying it of meaning and reinscribing it with irrational, terroristic intent—a discourse endorsed and promulgated by the United States as well. The decision to accept USAID funding and the conditionalities attached to it means acquiescing to a discourse that prefigures almost any activity, behavior, or speech that challenges Palestinians' subjugated position within the current political order as a security threat. As the interviewee above notes, "How can we accept a document that is basically asking us to refuse to acknowledge people who we actually consider nationalists and announce them to be terrorists because of financial requirements?"[47] As another Palestinian NGO worker in the West Bank noted, "No group actually wants to use the funds to support terrorism. Rather, this is a battle over principle. Who has the power to define?"[48] PNGO's boycott of USAID was a declaration of limits: it refused the discourse that prefigures Palestinians as, per Edward Said, ontologically and gratuitously interested in waging political violence for its own sake.[49]

PNGO's position would delineate one set of Palestinian responses to US securitization, though it is crucial to underscore that its politics of refusal drew inspiration from developments underway in less high-profile networks, including the refusal of Jenin's residents to accept American aid after Israel's massacre at Jenin Camp carried out with US military aid and weapons in 2002. As one activist noted, PNGO's boycott "was not only because of PNGO. Even people in Jenin refused to accept USAID in their most dire situation."[50] The politics of refusal deployed by Jenin's residents in the aftermath of Israel's 2002 siege and cited and reproduced in PNGO's boycott of USAID are part and parcel of a longer tradition of Indigenous refusal to participate in eliminatory efforts wrought upon it by settler states.[51] The call to boycott refuses a colonial rationality that normalizes the discourse that Palestinians are the problem to be managed and effaces the problem of the regime of dispossession in which they are enmeshed. Demonstrating a commitment to that colonial rationality, PNGO's boycott politics would soon meet a more creative security state.

RISE OF THE *DAKAKEEN*

The introduction of the list and its attendant policing and surveillance mechanisms in Palestine, and the politics of refusal with which it was met on the part of PNGO and other Palestinian institutions, meant too that a new host of strategies would be deployed by the United States to override the resistance it encountered.[52] While the boycott of USAID instituted by PNGO and other sectors of Palestinian civil society had been applied with the intended goal of consolidating a united Palestinian position against the imposition of the US security state through the mechanisms of aid, it, at the same time, effected a host of other transformations that yielded an opposite result. PNGO cautioned against capitulation to EO 13224, understanding that it could easily serve as a mechanism to enhance the monitoring of Palestinians by Palestinians. What had not been foreseen is the way in which the boycott could serve as a pretext to marginalize and isolate the network and diminish its influence. Not long after the boycott call, a new wave of NGOs began to set foot in Palestine, as recounted by one PNGO member:

Then there were all these kinds of ways to go around [the boycott]. Now at that time, we didn't have a long-term vision. We did know that part of it was to get us to monitor and police our people. But what we didn't understand [then] but what we understood later, was that it was also a way to justify the presence of an American organization contracted by USAID to come here directly and to completely exclude us from the whole setting . . . because we refused to sign. . . . So contractors, private contractors, from the US were given government money and they came and opened offices. There was the mushrooming of all of these organizations. This was the pretext: all these Palestinian organizations do not want to sign but we want to spend the money. OK we open the field to all these private, especially private organizations. . . . It took us ages until we reacted. . . . Now later it is not only the Americans that require us to sign—the Australian and the Canadian have decrees or these ATCs that were no better than the American one.[53]

This passage brings into view the creative refashioning of the US security state in response to the resistance it encountered to the imposition of its executive power in Palestine. Not long after the boycott of USAID was put into effect, a new wave of *dakakeen* (shops), or small-scale organizations created to absorb aid money, began to emerge in Palestine. USAID, as one Palestinian staffer with the Palestinian Popular Art Center noted, started to assume "different masks and [took on] a number of forms. It's not always clear-cut where it is operating," she added.[54]

Dakakeen were first introduced during the early years of Oslo as donors had earmarked funds in support of the peace process. This was followed by a relative decline of such entities during the early years of the second *intifada,* and then a resurgence again in the early to mid-2000s when resistance to the new USAID counterterrorism conditionalities grew. In 2004, as recounted by one NGO staffer, "the Americans started working with organizations [established] to implement their programs."[55] Usually focusing on key sectors such as youth, community development, and education, these organizations were created specifically to absorb US monies. The *dakakeen,* as many Palestinian recounted, enjoyed little to no grassroots support, and the entities soon dissipated once the USAID boycott waned in popularity and efficacy.

The gradual weakening of PNGO's boycott however was due only in part to the *dakakeen* themselves. Over the course of the decade, more and more

Palestinian institutions began accepting conditional funds due to a confluence of factors. First, the funding pool shrank as funds were gradually consolidated within fewer donors, with more aid flows channeled through multilateral agencies, such as the UN. Second, other donors (including Canadians, Australians, and Europeans, among others), increasingly integrated similar "anti-terror" clauses that are, as the interlocutor above suggests, "no better than the American one."[56] As one NGO director put it, "The circle for the 'good' organizations who accept all [of] these conditions now is expanding; the other one is shrinking. It's one space—that space is donor space. . . . You had several organizations that refused [the conditionalities] so their space shrunk and others came to replace them."[57]

Even as the 2003 boycott is still technically in effect, there has been a gradual weakening of opposition to the agency.[58] So too has the governing technology of the terrorism list, and the broader counterterrorism paradigm to which it is connected, become increasingly normalized across donor practice in Palestine. The intensified trend towards aid securitization is due in part to post–9/11 developments in national contexts, as many states passed draconian emergency legislation that expanded their executive powers exponentially and engaged in preemptive security actions under pressure from the United States. But it is also on account of new legal developments at the global level within the United Nations Security Council.[59] As Gavin Sullivan observes, changes within the Security Council, including the adoption of new binding resolutions on terrorism, required states "to change their laws to criminalize terrorism and terrorist financing."[60] As a result, the council, Sullivan argues,

> was transformed from an executive policing body into a new global legislator, "imposing general and permanent obligations on states . . . not tied to any particular conflict." . . . . [T]he UN1267 list was radically repurposed into a preemptive legal weapon for disrupting global terrorist networks and their perceived supporters worldwide, with unprecedented powers (temporally and spatially unlimited in scope).[61]

These developments had dire consequences for Palestinians: their aid world would increasingly be governed by the list.

Today almost every major bilateral and multilateral donor operating in

Palestine has integrated enhanced security technologies, terrorism clauses, restrictive programming, and expansive surveillance mechanisms into their aid programming. The United States has been at the helm of this trend. As the director of an NGO in the West Bank remarked in August 2018, while counterterrorism laws and terrorist databases predate September 11th, heavily securitized aid practices did not become common practice until recent decades. The global war on terror has given rise to enhanced security infrastructures and surveillance practices that are fundamental to the way aid works in Palestine today. "This is now normalized," he stated, and "the US paved the way for this trend."[62]

The counterterrorism model aggressively promoted by the United States in the early years of the war on terror would become a de facto norm of aid governance over the course of the next decade. This framework would also be taken up by Israel's Ministry of Strategic Affairs and used to steadily undermine the Palestinian non-governmental sector (see Chapter 4). Terrorism lists, and their accompanying security infrastructures, have proliferated across heterogeneous spaces of Palestinian everyday life. At the same time the *work* of the terrorism list is not all encompassing or absolute. PNGO's refusal to confer the US terrorism list authoritative power over how and with whom Palestinians can enact politics under a regime of occupation demarcated one strategy for how to negotiate the US security state. Other sectors of Palestinian society have deployed different tactics, including opting to work within, though not entirely capitulating to, the punitive logics and dictates of the list.

MEDIATING THE LIST

In September 2011, the Sharek Youth Forum held its second annual Youth Summit in the central hall of the al-Bireh Municipality. The event included some 500 youth who had gathered to discuss strategies for garnering greater youth participation in local politics. Khaled Qawasmeh, the PA Minister of Local Government, and Hasan Abu-Libdeh, the Minister of National Economy, had also been invited to participate. Meanwhile, outside of the municipality, a group of university-aged Palestinian activists had congregated to call for an end to US funding of the organization. According to one of the protest's organizers, an activist with the youth movement Herak Shababi, the protestors had gathered to oppose not only the aid system as a whole but more specifically "USAID's desire to influence the political dialogue of young people," which as the youth organizer underscored, is "particularly provocative in the context of the Palestinian struggle for justice."[63] Protestors highlighted various dimensions of US interference in the region. One sign read, "Arab Spring: Youth Set the Agenda, Sharek Youth Summit: U$A Set the Agenda." Another protestor highlighted the circuitous, reinforcing nature of US intervention in the region: "The USA is feeding and killing us," he stated.[64] Virtually all participants objected to USAID's "terrorism clause."[65]

Sharek had not always received funding from USAID. In 2010 the organization reversed its long-held position of refusing US funds. Sharek's trajectory is not dissimilar to that of many Palestinian institutions over the last two decades. Increasing political conditionality on the part of most large-scale foreign donors coupled with a relative decline in foreign funds in the post-Oslo period led many Palestinian organizations that had previously refused US funds to modify their stance. As more and more donors began to integrate counterterrorism apparatuses into their West Bank and Gaza programming, there was a general shift in the kinds of conditions Palestinians had to accept if they were to continue accepting foreign aid.[66]

Sharek's trajectory from a position of refusal to acceptance of US funds is but one example of the steady shift towards a more complex politics of negotiation and mediation, what many referred to as a politics of pragmatism that would increasingly dominate the post-Oslo period. While I use USAID as a focal point here, the processes discussed and the predicaments Sharek encounters speak to a broader set of trends in Palestine: as aid securitization intensified over the course of the global war on terror, Palestinians would be faced with the predicament of how to navigate an aid landscape increasingly shaped by the counterinsurgency aims of foreign states, including Israel, alongside their political realities as subjects under an ever-intensifying project of settler–colonial rule. As the mayor of Birzeit would remark in 2010, "We've been given marginal space to make marginal decisions."[67] Many Palestinian organizations found themselves renegotiating the "red line" demarcated in 2003 by PNGO, as the war on terror waged on.

Sharek began as a youth initiative of the United Nations Development Program (UNDP) in 1999 and evolved over the years to become an independent organization in 2004.[68] For the first six years of its existence as an independent body, Sharek refused to accept money from the United States despite multiple invitations from international NGOs with USAID money. A number of interviews conducted with staff and directors of the organization demonstrated that, from 2006 to 2010, it was relatively easy for Sharek to turn down USAID money despite multiple attempts to recruit these circuits.[69] Other times, US-funded organizations preemptively excluded Sharek from projects knowing full well their position on the ATC and USAID more broadly.

While Sharek had entertained the idea of taking US funds in 2006 for a project pertaining to the Palestinian elections, this decision was soon revoked following the US response to the Hamas electoral victory wherein the United States cut aid to the Palestinians and imposed sanctions on Hamas and the Palestinian Authority. As one of Sharek's staff recounted:

> Then the election happened and everything stopped. We were really annoyed by the reaction of USAID after the election so we took another decision and said, no thank you, we're not going to work again with USAID.

Sharek's position changed however in 2010 when, as recounted by one of the core staff at the time, "[W]e opened the newspaper and we found a quote from CHF [the Cooperative Housing Foundation] that there is a call for NGOs to implement the youth shadow local councils project. The youth shadow local councils project had been the dream of Sharek's for ages."[70] Following deliberation among the organizational leadership and a vote of approval, Sharek submitted an application to be the local implementing partner. It won the bid.

The intermediary implementing the US-funded project, CHF International (which later became Global Communities), indicated that it had long been interested in partnering with Sharek for the youth shadow councils; however, knowing Sharek's position with respect to the ATC and USAID more broadly, they had refrained from suggesting a partnership.[71] Sharek revealed that it was willing to revise its former position for this particular project given that it aligned, in lockstep, with its vision and goals. In the words of one of the organization's core staff,

This doesn't mean that we will take any money and funds from USAID. [But] we never found a project that goes with our philosophy. This project it really fits one hundred percent with our strategy, and we believe that we can take and leave whatever we want.[72]

She acknowledged the limitations this decision entailed. "We know there are regulations on US side. We're not doing it with any Hamas municipalities, and Gaza is excluded." The vision behind the shadow council project was to build local bases of power through the establishment of formal mechanisms for youth participation across the West Bank and Gaza. They would establish youth shadow municipal councils that would emulate the local municipal council or local governing unit in that community in select municipalities across the West Bank.

Part of the impetus to target the local/municipal scale, as revealed by one employee, was that the national scale was viewed as deeply compromised due to international and Israeli conditions imposed on Palestinian national and political spheres, as well as PA complicity in upholding the occupation.[73] The local scale, it would turn out, was also a target of foreign interventionary power. Sharek still believed that it could maintain its principles, ethics, and vision despite the conditionalities attached to US funding and the restrictive parameters imposed upon it by the US terrorism list.

Soon after winning the bid, which required among other things, Sharek signing US anti-terrorism certification and the vetting of staff,[74] Sharek began the process of selecting municipalities in which to establish ten youth shadow councils across the West Bank. Just as with the US boycott of the Bethlehem Municipality, US terrorism mandates stipulated that Sharek could not work with any municipality that contained, on its city council, members of groups classified as FTOs on the US terrorism list. Banned municipalities included, among others, Jenin, Hebron, and Nablus, along with Gaza in its entirety. Indeed the irony of upholding a foreign prohibition on the inclusion of political parties in a democracy project for Palestinian youth was not lost on the included and excluded municipalities and beneficiaries alike.[75] Many of the excluded municipalities, as one of Sharek's high-level staff disclosed, "called us and asked, 'Why are you not doing this with us?' We said it's within our plans." She continued,

We didn't make it clear the reason was because of USAID. Some of them they understand, like Nablus, they understand. And Gaza . . . everybody knows about Gaza and USAID, so it was clear to other municipalities too. The good thing is that Sharek has a presence on the ground. [The excluded] municipalities understood this is the piloting phase for us and there might be something in the future. . . . It was really embarrassing because we never linked our activities to donors. We crossed that but it's ok. For the current phase, it's ok.[76]

The decision to cross the formerly held "red line" in relation to US funding was anchored in a temporal strategy, one predicated on the short-term abeyance of a political approach to aid, yet one viewed as neither wholesale capitulation nor surrender. As one Sharek staffer remarked, "We will think of how to replicate [this project] with other municipalities that are not included in this phase" at a later date, presumably with different donor money. While there was an admission on the part of Sharek that a certain line had been crossed in affording the United States the power to demarcate the field intervention, the transgression was deemed acceptable in light of larger aims, or more precisely, in order to achieve these larger aims. While this particular phase of the project was circumscribed by dictates of the US security state, it did not necessarily mean, according to Sharek's leadership, that these dictates functioned as an iron cast that predetermined everything; rather they were seen as an elastic set of criteria that could be modified and circumvented over time. Equally, staff overseeing the shadow councils deployed a number of creative strategies to work around the imposed restrictions. One Sharek employee who had worked on an earlier pilot phase of the project indicated that they would refrain from holding meetings in village councils or municipalities that contained Hamas members.[77] "Material support," in this instance, was translated quite literally into the physical infrastructure of a building.

At the same time, the geographies of fragmentation and exclusion that the US terrorism list produced within the youth shadow project could not be ignored. The stipulation of US terrorism mandates produced a tangible geography of exclusion across the West Bank and Gaza in full. Nearly all the major cities were excluded from the USAID–CHF funded phase of the project, including Nablus, Jenin, and Hebron, with which Sharek had previously signed memoranda of understanding. "Because of stipulations from USAID," a staffer remarked, "we are forced to work in predominately very small municipalities," which invariably will "have a very different experience with such a program than a larger municipality would. It's going to be very different doing this in Beit Fajar—a tiny, tiny town—than in Nablus, Hebron, Jenin, Ramallah." The adoption of a pragmatic approach to aid, as Sharek staff called it, would be increasingly adopted by Palestinian NGOs.

Sharek's story is reflective of larger trends across the West Bank and Gaza as donor funds were increasingly compromised by political conditionalities throughout the second decade of the global war on terror. Increasing numbers of Palestinian NGOs would abandon a politics of refusal, opting instead for a more pragmatic approach wherein conditional aid would be accepted in light of more narrowly defined institutional aims: in the case of Sharek, building a youth base in line with its vision for increasing youth democratic participation in Palestine even if the scope of that project would be delimited by US counterterrorism mandates, resulting in the exclusion of almost all municipalities and local governing units not governed exclusively by Fatah.

In 2018 I would return to Palestine to meet again with one of Sharek's core staff at the time when USAID funds were first being considered. Sharek, he noted, had opted for a pragmatic approach to aid, especially as there was a general "drying up of the sources of income." He further explained,

> Some NGOs found themselves desperate to actually bend their principles a little bit but not to the level that they can, you know, be vetting people. So it was a convenient project, let's put it this way. So it's not an issue of principle—they were more pragmatic about it unlike other organizations that took a principled position to boycott USAID. These organizations [that boycott] are to be respected for that decision. I, myself, as pragmatic as I was, think maybe it would have been better to stick to principles and to see the bigger picture with USAID.[78]

He later added, "We tried taking American money. We since altered course. . . . This is a process of attrition," he further underscored. "Eventually things break." Or as another Palestinian NGO worker noted, "The circle [of available funds] for the 'good' organizations who accept all [of] these conditions" has expanded.[79]

A shift among Palestinian NGOs from a politics of refusal, as represented by PNGO, to a more flexible, arguably more politically compromised, approach of mediating US terrorism mandates took place over the course of the first two decades of the war on terror. Many West Bank municipalities also followed this course, as was the case for Birzeit. Birzeit Municipality would accept US funding shortly after the 2005 municipal election for infrastructural development and again in 2009 as part of the USAID-funded, CHF-administered Local Democratic Reform (LDR) program.[80] The LDR program, which purportedly sought to enhance the democratic local governance system, was launched in 2005, the same year as the Palestinian municipal elections. Birzeit was one of the forty municipalities with whom CHF had partnered for the LDR program. I would speak at length with Birzeit's mayor, Yousef Nasser, roughly two years into the program.[81]

The Birzeit municipal council in place at the time of this interview was the first elected council since 1976. The Israelis, he explained, did not allow any more elections after 1976 due to the high number of PLO candidates that had successfully secured seats in local government (discussed in Chapter 2). From the late 1970s to the Oslo period, the capacity of municipalities had been systematically undermined. In 1994, when the Palestinian Authority was established, municipalities were more or less marginalized due to the PA focus, and donor-inflected trend, on developing a central government, resulting in general neglect of the local scale. The 2005 local election yielded a new municipal council that encountered, in the words of Birzeit's mayor, a "dire situation" in terms of the institutional capacity of the municipality. "It wasn't really an institution; it was more like a fiefdom," he stated. "Everything the mayor was said was law." Notably, the existing law at the time (Jordanian municipal law), was based on the 1924 British Mandate law, which did not delegate authority and control to local powers. To date, Nasser asserted, municipalities are limited in terms of their ability to develop policy in key sectors like education and health.

Birzeit, like Bethlehem (as discussed in Chapter 2), required significant rehabilitation of the water network. From 1967, when Israel seized control over the West Bank, to 1995 (the Oslo Accords), Israel did not permit the expansion of the Birzeit municipal boundaries. The city was limited to 2,000 dunams (about 500 acres) within which it had authority over licensing, building, and infrastructural projects. Beyond the 2,000 dunams, any development required a license from the Israeli military governor. Moreover, over half the population lived beyond the Birzeit municipal zone and thus, under the Absentee Property Law, were considered absentee landowners. Accordingly, the Israeli military governor exercised jurisdiction over their lands, thwarting any kind of centralized or systematized planning. From 1967 to 1995, the water network was expanded haphazardly resulting in, at some points, "thirty to forty households or buildings connected to a two-inch pipe by a half-an-inch or one-inch pipe."[82] Moreover, dilapidated pipes meant considerable water leakage. "We were losing 50 percent of what we paid for," Nasser asserted. "If we had water coming in twenty-four hours a day, seven days a week, it would take a week for that neighborhood to fill up with water."[83]

The economic crisis from 2006 to 2007—when Israel, the United States, and many Western states placed sanctions on Hamas and the PA—meant that many Birzeit residents could not pay their bills. When the new council was elected in 2005, it made the overhaul and revamping of the water network a municipal priority. It hired new engineers, mostly new graduates, and developed project proposals to pitch to donors. The city needed $1 million to revamp and rehabilitate the entire system. USAID had made infrastructure a priority in its West Bank/Gaza aid portfolio. As Nasser disclosed, "I heard that USAID had $1 million USD for basic infrastructure work." "We approached CHF," Nasser disclosed. "We went knocking on their door.... We've become expert beggars."

CHF and another US NGO would spearhead the reconstruction of Birzeit's water infrastructure. Birzeit, much like Beit Sahour and Beit Jala discussed in Chapter 2, did not feel as though they had conceded too much: they all had material needs that needed to be fulfilled, and money, albeit from the United States, was made available to them. "Our process," Nasser noted, "is that we identify what we need and then we fundraise for it. That's how we deal with CHF." The water sector was identified as a primary need. "We needed aerial photos in order to do proper town planning and infrastructure development and the water sector. That was very important at the time."

CHF indicated that Birzeit would have to be vetted prior to moving forward. "We said vet us. I have no problem with vetting. We were vetted. We

got approved. We started a relationship. We started building our capacity."
The minutiae of who had been elected to the city council in 2005 was at best
a backstory if it made an appearance at all. Despite politics being a precon-
dition of their having received funding for rehabilitation of their water network, it was not believed that their political position had necessarily been
compromised. At the same time the political implications of Birzeit's decision to accept US funding were not entirely discounted: they simply were
not given the force one might assume.[84] The central question, for Nasser, re-
volved around how to maneuver within the marginal space Palestinians had
been allocated within the contours of colonial rule:

> People realize that if you don't get this money it is going to be gone. Right
> now this money is not influencing our political position in terms of re-
> sistance, in terms of going after our freedom. And it's building the water
> network; it's building the road; it's building a school room. And so we
> take it and we can fight the struggle later because right now the struggle
> is—we don't have a consensus on how to struggle, once we do we can go
> back to the struggle again. It hasn't divided us into pro-liberation, anti-
> liberation groups, the difference is in the approach [we take in regards
> for] how to deal with it. At the same time, even people that have signed
> the ATC would say that we can never have true development unless we
> have freedom, as long as the occupation exists within certain parameters
> you can improve your life, you can have improvement but you cannot
> have development because as long as we don't control our borders, to
> import and export, Israel can close the door at any second and decide.
> Even now when it's open it's not completely open; it's conditional. . . . I
> consider what's happening now to be slow motion, slow process ethnic
> cleansing, and despite this we are still trying to build institutions. . . .
> Right now liberation has been put on hold.

In the meantime, Nasser would conclude, "we need institutions, flexible
ones." Nasser's position, like that of Sharek, reflects a tactical approach to
navigating the long arc of settler colonial time. And right now what is required, Nasser argues, are the material infrastructures required to live,
to survive, and to build for a future not yet arrived. The present is already
compromised, and aid is always necessarily conditional. As one Palestinian active in the first *intifada* now turned NGO director remarked, "Nobody

came and said, I am here to support the Palestinian resistance and the plight of the Palestinians and their right for self-determination and for an end to the occupation. No one. No one."[85] In the meantime, money is here, as Nasser underscores. And so is the occupation. At a time when the horizon of Palestinian politics was deeply uncertain, those who could increasingly accepted conditional aid as a means to subsist in the present. In the cases of Sharek and Birzeit, autonomy was believed achievable and compromise temporary. If indeed history is any indication of the future, the alliances forged and the divisions wrought by US and other foreign assistance have inscribed an indelible mark into the social and political field.

THE LIST AS COUNTERINSURGENCY

The terrorism list is but one instrument among an ever-evolving amalgam of counterinsurgency forces that work on and through Palestinians to fragment, pacify, and render them more easily governable in the long arc of dispossession. The work of the list does discrete but hard work, fracturing and disaggregating, disassembling and reassembling. It cleaves off entire spaces and zones for controlled abandonment; it inaugurates expansive regimes of policing, surveillance, and punishment upheld and maintained often across seas and vast geographies; it marks bodies for violence from blockades and enforced immobility to indefinite detention and death. The work of the list is not the stuff of spectacular warfare that has featured so centrally in the dominant canon of work on war, militarism, and empire. Though it is no less the work of empire. For the designated, the "point of the list" eviscerates entire lifeworlds.

For Palestinians, the tethering of terrorism lists into the flows of aid on which they are reliant has, in turn, imported an expansive regime of punitive regulation into the intimate lived spaces of daily life, fracturing the political field, aborting or allowing the development of critical infrastructure, and enrolling Palestinians into practices of self-policing and surveillance. At the same time, some Palestinians, as displayed by PNGO's ongoing boycott of USAID, act against the list and the punitive regulatory regimes it enforces. They refuse to be conscripted into and defined by the logics of a database that disallows them to be fully political subjects—that is, they refuse the false binary the list constructs as either irrational actors ontologically interested in waging violence or as agentless humanitarian objects. Others, such as Sharek and Birzeit have found ways to work in the interstices of the list—finding ways to build "flexible institutions," as Nasser suggests, amidst the counterinsurgency forces to which they are subject.

Regardless of the diverging approaches Palestinians have adopted with respect to the proliferation of terrorism infrastructures in their aid flows, the insidious effects of the terrorism list on their social, political, and material world cannot be understated. So too have the punitive logics and infrastructures of the terrorism list expanded to new domains. As the following chapter explores, the governing logic of the terrorism list, wherein a regime of prohibition is emplaced on any subject and entity branded with the terrorist classification—an ever-expansive category that has grown to include the boycott, divestment, and sanctions movement (BDS)—has proliferated beyond any single actor or donor to now constitute a new aid-governing norm. Indeed, this security architecture and its governing logic has grown so widespread that, as the next chapter tracks, it persists beyond the termination of US aid. The following chapter tends to the afterlives of US aid, asking what kinds of violence lives on in absence, in the repeal of US soft power.

Four

AFTERLIVES AND REVERBERATIONS

USAID is the architect of the security regime in development. Other donors have followed suit.

—Palestinian NGO director, Ramallah, July 2019

THE 2016 ELECTION OF DONALD J. TRUMP INTO THE HIGHEST SEAT OF US power ushered in a number of significant changes domestically and on the world stage. Across both fronts, the Trump administration continued the militarized expansion of the US security state while directly facilitating and affording cover for authoritarian forces at home and abroad. So too did the Trump era mark a departure from a decades-long US policy aimed at creating an integrated postwar world order under US leadership, including shedding any pretense of a commitment to liberal precepts of multiculturalism, human rights, and humanitarianism. The gradual eclipse of US soft power had direct and violent implications for those caught in the crosshairs of US wars, militaristic foreign policy, and imperial interventionism. The case of Palestine was no exception.

US policy vis-à-vis Israel and the Palestinians has, since the postwar period and especially since 1967, skewed sharply in favor of the former; yet so too has the United States been at the forefront of efforts that paradoxically attempt to buffer the impacts of Israeli settler colonialism on the Palestinians while directly enabling it to continue. Today, Washington stands as Israel's primary patron, providing it with roughly $3.8 billion in military aid per year, and since 1967, US military aid to Israel has totaled over $120 billion. The United States has also been the largest contributor to the United Nations Relief and Works Agency (UNRWA), established in 1949 to administer relief to Palestinian refugees, and is among the top six donors of aid to the Palestinians since the Oslo Accords, committing over $5 billion in bilateral assistance since 1994.[1] Since the 1970s, Washington has also sought to retain stewardship over the peace process and assert its dominance in the Middle East by promoting a resolution to the Israeli–Palestinian conflict. From Camp David in 1978 to the 1993 Oslo Accords to the Annapolis Conference of 2007, Washington has safeguarded Israel's political objectives while promising to deliver a compromise between Israel and the Palestinians.[2] US intervention in Palestine has long been defined by a mix of hard and soft power that has ultimately shored up Israel's settler–colonial project while attempting to manage its most deleterious impacts on the Palestinian population through civilian aid.

The Trump administration ended this veneer. Shedding any pretense of concern for the Palestinian population, Washington waged a series of unprecedented pressure policies on the Palestinians while directly facilitating Israel's most maximalist claims. This hardline approach to the Palestinians was made apparent in a number of broken diplomatic norms, including US recognition of Jerusalem as Israel's capital in May 2018 and the expulsion of the Palestine Liberation Organization (PLO) office from the US capital that September. Taken together, these moves returned Washington–Palestinian relations to the pre–Madrid Conference (1991) era wherein the US refused recognition of the PLO. In substance, US–Palestinian diplomatic relations all but disappeared.[3] Meanwhile, Washington passed two new terrorism laws that built on but also expanded to new dimensions the terrorism-financing legal-war architecture started under George W. Bush's tenure, which directly targeted the Palestinian Authority (PA) as part of a larger effort, as some have surmised, to "shut down the PA."[4] Such maneuvers by the Trump administration represent a moment when the US security state trips over itself in its zeal to criminalize the Palestinians. Under the pre-Trump system, US (and European) funds had been disbursed to the PA in exchange for compliance with a status quo—Palestinian self-policing—that serves Israel.[5] An aggressive lawfare campaign waged by a coterie of US lawmakers and lobby groups effectively undermined this security ecology.

In March 2018, Trump signed into law the Taylor Force Act, first introduced by Senator Lindsey Graham (R-S.C.) in 2016, as part of an omnibus spending bill. Charging the PA with incentivizing terrorism, the law terminates financial aid to the Palestinian Authority until it ceases payments to political prisoners and to the families of those killed by Israel, a practice that dates back, with the PLO, to the 1960s. The act effectively suspended all money from the Economic Support Fund that "directly benefits" the PA (with certain exceptions for wastewater projects, vaccination programs, and the East Jerusalem Hospital Network) so long as the PA continued to compensate prisoners and the families of martyrs. The Taylor Force Act similarly set the stage for Israel to punish the Palestinians in February 2019 by withholding taxes that Israel collects on behalf of the PA.

Combined, these cuts sparked an expanding budget crisis that compelled the PA to slash Palestinian civil servants' salaries, including those of some of its security forces. One high-level PA official interviewed in July 2018 asserted that ultimately Washington's hard-line approach threatened to undermine the PA's role upholding Israel's security designs, thus working contra to US foreign policy interests. The significant shrinking of the PA budget, as UNRWA was being rapidly defunded by the cessation of US funds, this official warned, carried the potential of stripping the PA to nothing more than a naked policing body. He warned that the PA could not survive this contraction given its already existing legitimacy crisis among Palestinians. With a bankrupt PA and devoid a political process, he argued, "the entire thing collapses"—the "thing" here being the fraught project of Palestinian pacification by a non-sovereign, quasi-governmental Palestinian body that operates in service of Israel's interests.[6]

A second blow to US–PA relations took place in October 2018 with passage of the Anti-Terrorism Clarification Act (ATCA). As one among a larger array of lawfare tactics deployed against the PA and the Palestinians, the purported intent of ATCA was to enable victims of international and specifically Palestinian terrorism to secure monetary damages from those alleged to have aided and abetted terrorist attacks through US courts.[7] Passed unanimously in both the House and Senate, ATCA effectively wielded US sovereignty extraterritorially through aid flows, stipulating that any entity that receives US assistance has deemed to have consented to personal jurisdiction in US courts.

ATCA was motivated in part by perceived failures of previous lawsuits, such as *Waldman v. PLO*, wherein US courts ruled that they lacked personal jurisdiction over the PLO and the PA.[8] To remedy the jurisdiction problem, ATCA stipulated that one consents to personal jurisdiction if she accepts US assistance, including economic support funds and international narcotics control and law enforcement (INCLE) aid. Accordingly, in the 2018 version of ATCA, any individual or entity that accepts US money consents to personal jurisdiction in the United States for lawsuits related to international terrorism, as well as past acts of terrorism—a definition that, under existing US material support law, is "treacherously ambiguous."[9] In effect, the 2018 version of ATCA rendered any recipient of American aid vulnerable to multimillion-dollar lawsuits in the United States.[10] Recognizing the potential of ATCA to bankrupt the Palestinian Authority through litigation, the PA announced that as of February 2019, when ATCA went into effect, it would no longer accept US funding. As Palestinian Prime Minister Rami Hamdallah informed US Secretary of State Mike Pompeo, "ATCA purports to alter the rules of jurisdiction over the Government of Palestine in US legal proceedings if it continues to accept such aid."[11] PA refusal here could be interpreted as an accurate read of the inherent dangers of elastic sovereignty at work.

Cognizant that ATCA posed a distinct threat to the security arrangement that ensures Israel's dominance via proxy, senior US officials scrambled to find a fix that would enable security aid to continue flowing to the PA. US lawyers drafted up an amendment—endorsed by the American Israel Public Affairs Committee as a "legislative priority"—that would eliminate "personal jurisdiction" from strategic funding streams.[12] A partial fix to ATCA would be enacted with amended language included in the 2020 federal spending bill. The amended version eliminated foreign assistance triggers for US jurisdiction, meaning that mere acceptance of security, economic, or law enforcement funding would not mean the party is consenting to the jurisdiction of US courts.[13] However, the "fix" continues to subject to US jurisdiction "anyone making a payment to a convicted terrorist or their family member."[14] In effect, ATCA left open ample space for US citizens to sue the PLO in US courts, a space that would be exploited by a growing network of lobby groups, lawyers, and organizations working across international lines to, as Lara Friedman suggests, "sue the PLO (and PA) out of existence."[15]

Even more, ATCA had implications beyond Palestine. Through ATCA, the US effectively exercised sovereignty over aid funds worldwide, presenting any NGO or aid-receiving organization that handles US monies, even if they maintain no footprint in the United States, with the potentiality of being sued in US courts.[16] The strategy of lawfare implemented under Trump would leave behind traces not so easily erased. Even as US aid flows would later resume under the Biden administration, they would remain subject to the legal legacy left behind by the Trump era. Layers of aid securitization only compound. "US terrorism law," as Lara Friedman aptly points out, "is like zombie legislation. It lives forever." "The best one can ever hope for," she suggests, "are little tweaks or temporary fixes like waivers [referring to the 1987 PLO Mission waiver]. What sits there always are these multiple Swords of Damocles hanging over the Palestinians"[17]—a latent, always lurking threat that can be wielded at any time.

Washington's iron-fisted approach to the Palestinians and corresponding unreserved support for Israeli political claims resulted not only in the abrogation of diplomatic norms and intensified criminalization of Palestinian national aspirations, but also in the termination of US aid to the Palestinians, thereby dispensing of any pretense of measured liberalism from US interventionism in the region. Starting in 2017, Washington scaled back and roughly a year later ended all US civilian aid to the Palestinians. In August 2018, the United States withdrew its contributions to the UNRWA, which totaled $360 million in 2017 and constituted over a quarter of the agency's annual budget, forcing the agency to curtail critical refugee programs and services in camps under its jurisdiction.[18] Washington's aggressive posturing went even further in January 2019, when it announced that the USAID West Bank/Gaza Mission would cease its operations in Palestine, only to be reopened under the Biden administration with ratcheted up terrorism financing laws. In the months following, the USAID West Bank/Gaza Mission shuttered the mission, abandoning half-finished infrastructure projects including water, road, and sewage systems and leaving underfunded local municipalities to pick up the pieces.[19]

Trump's hard-line approach to the Palestinians, some would speculate, was part of a larger goal to unilaterally remove key issues (such as refugees and Jerusalem) from the negotiating table in time for the grand reveal of Trump's "Deal of the Century."[20] More sinisterly, however, Washington's defunding of UNRWA could also be read as an attempt to dissolve the category of refugee altogether. As one Palestinian Authority official remarked, "UNRWA is a preamble to the refugee issue."[21] The velocity of the maneuvers Washington enacted amounted to, as Ilana Feldman aptly summarizes, a "full spectrum assault on Palestinian politics."[22]

AFTERLIVES AND PROLIFERATIONS

Even as US assistance to the Palestinians was officially terminated during the Trump administration, the afterlives of US aid intervention proved especially insidious.[23] The question of afterlives animates this chapter. Centrally, I ask what remains despite the official (if temporary) termination of US aid to the Palestinians? What continues after a declared end? Here I think alongside Avery Gordon, who speaks of "endings that are not over"—the "after" retains a vitality that breathes into the present.[24] This chapter tends to the afterlives of intervention, enduring presences that persist in absence and in withdrawal, to consider how social worlds are indelibly transformed long after aid has stopped flowing, after colonial infrastructure has been built and the last bomb has dropped. Indeed the legacies of intervention, what Ann Stoler might call "imperial debris," breathe on in torn flesh from landmines, in dilapidated medical infrastructures, and in the cancerous cells of bodies.[25] Ruination, Stoler reminds us, is an ongoing process rather than a static event.[26] It seems that the right question is, as Oliver Belcher asks, how do wars live on?[27]

Afterlives are necessarily a corollary to war. We might turn here to the enduring presence of US warfare in Iraq, as Kali Rubaii has done[28]—wherein the US dropped some 800 cruise missiles at the onset of invasion, expended 6 billion bullets containing shells of lead and mercury between 2002 to 2005, and dumped military toxins across the landscape—to see how war is never a temporally bound or isolated event but instead lives on in the tumors and cleft palates of children born in lifeworlds made and undone by war, their bodies testimonies to the "enduring life of toxic war materials."[29] Likewise, Lisa Hajjar, deploying Gordon's analytic of haunting, explores how the now-terminated CIA torture program—with its reliance on executive power, state secrets, and reinterpretations of law to rationalize practices that deviate from international norms—has enduring power in shaping US politics and warfare.[30] The Obama administration, Hajjar points out, utilized and refined the unitary executive thesis on which the torture program relied to justify its boundless extrajudicial killing program. Drone warfare and other forms of extrajudicial execution, which now constitute the norm of US warfare, put differently, were built on and through the afterlives of CIA torture and detention.[31] Afterlives constitute the present; the seemingly over-and-done-with invariably comes alive.[32]

Here I track the afterlives of US imperial power during the aid cuts of the Trump administration. Despite the official "end" to US civilian aid brought about by the bellicose actions of the Trump era, the securitized practices, technologies, and norms the United States had long promoted and normalized into its aid interventions in Palestine have lived on, metastasized, and perhaps most significantly, established new aid-governing norms that shape virtually all Western-aligned donor interventions in Palestine. Here I consider what remains living and breathing in absence—what kind of violence is embedded in a world that cannot be returned.

————

The terrorism regulations and policies developed
following September 11th are now the norm.
—*Director of a Palestinian prisoner rights organization, Ramallah, July 2019*

In December 2019, the European Union announced the integration of a new anti-terror clause into its aid contracts to the Palestinians and that it would henceforth also require that Palestinian organizations vet staff, contractors, and beneficiaries, including workshop participants, to ensure detection of any financial support to parties appearing in the lists of EU restrictive measures.[33] Palestinians were quick to point out that the list of EU targets included a greater swath of targets than those overtly or even moderately involved in the Palestinian resistance movement. Palestinians arrested by

Israel, as well as those engaged in civil society organizing and activism, could also be classified as terrorists and therefore disqualified from receiving funding. The terrorism designation effectively collapsed into its fold an exceedingly broad range of Palestinian subjects, laying bare ever-expanding architectures of securitized control exercised over and through Palestinian life. The clause would be applied not only to direct EU funding, but also all European country funding streams within the EU fold.

The EU contended that the enhanced counterterrorism measures were consistent with EU policy since 2001. But even as individual European states had followed the US lead in the early aughts in adopting a more aggressive counterterrorism approach, the clause had not been imposed on Palestinian civil society as a condition until July 2019, as per Annex II of the EU General Conditions. The Palestinian National Campaign to Reject Conditional Funding (PNCRCF), a coalition of some 300 Palestinian organizations born in response to intensifying political conditionality imposed on the Palestinians by the EU and its member states, was quick to point out that the EU move further constrained the ability of Palestinians to expose and challenge violations of their rights and criminalized the Palestinian national struggle at a time when Israel's settler–colonial project was accelerating to new heights.[34] As PNCRCF contended, the EU move is,

> [H]appening amid a growing institutionalized campaign of repression and attacks against us, designed to leave Palestinian civil society without funds, delegitimize our work and silence our voices. It is happening when we need that funding the most in order to challenge the more urgent issues such as Trump's "Peace to Prosperity"/so-called Deal of the Century plan for Palestine and the looming official Israeli annexation of strategic areas of the West Bank.[35]

Similarly, as Palestinian scholar Tariq Dana argues, the EU decision to formalize terrorism-financing regulations was not fortuitous. It came at a time of escalated attacks waged against the Palestinians:

> The EU move comes at a very difficult time for the Palestinians: Israel is preparing to annex most of Area C and the Jordan Valley; the Palestinians are weak, fragmented, and divided; the PA has become a de facto

enforcer of Israeli security. . . . The EU restrictions add to these factors by criminalizing many Palestinian organizations that embark on moderate forms of resistance through international law and advocacy and support the survival of communities. These restrictions will therefore not only contribute to further marginalization of the Palestinian cause but will also facilitate the institutionalization of Israeli colonial expansion because many organizations will not be able to sustain their operations in monitoring and reporting Israeli crimes if they fail to find alternatives to the EU funds.[36]

The EU conditions added yet another layer of control into the securitized aid regime that quells Palestinian political life under conditions of continued dispossession. It was not by happenchance that the EU counterterrorism stipulations could and did result in the termination of funds, in some cases, to Palestinian organizations and institutions engaged in documenting abuses of human rights and violations of international law.

BADIL was among the first Palestinian organizations to be defunded by the European Union when it refused to sign the "anti-terrorism" clause, resulting in a net loss of $1.9 million for a project that aimed to enhance the resilience of Palestinians and highlight Israeli human rights abuses and crimes in Jerusalem, underscoring the financial drain on Palestinian organizations that refused to comply with the EU condition. Its rationale for refusing to sign resonated with those put forward by Palestinian NGOs upon the introduction of the US clause over a decade earlier (see Chapter 3). The EU move, as Dana argues, must be situated in the context of "the ability of [Israel's] colonial enterprise to invent new mechanisms of control."[37] While the EU move did represent an intensification of processes of criminalization of Palestinians and their political struggle, the EU model was one well-worn and well-trod in Palestine. The United States had long been at the fore of the push to hyper-securitization to which the EU followed suit nearly two decades later. Even as US aid had been terminated during the Trump era, the hyper-securitized aid paradigm adopted and promoted by the US security state from the early years of the global war on terror lived on.

By the time the Trump administration officially ended US aid to the Palestinians, nearly every Western donor stream had integrated terrorist clauses, restrictive programming, and expansive surveillance and enforcement technologies into their Palestinian aid programming. "The US approach has become the model," the NGO director of a Palestinian human rights organization remarked. "Almost all donors are integrating similar mechanisms and aid conditionalities. This is happening not just in Palestine," he continued, "[it] is becoming a thing the world over."[38] European funders for his particular organization had just approached them to sign the newly introduced EU anti-terrorism clause. "We rejected conditional aid before because we have a right to self-determination, to live without occupation," he asserted, "but now," he lamented, "we have to accept some 'administrative' issues otherwise we will lose our funding." There is "shrinking space," as the term was often used, for aid that is not entirely conditioned by the political directives of war and foreign policy, he asserted.

The reverberations of the securitization regime have been profound, constituting new kinds of securitized norms and surveillance practices that are fundamental to the way aid operates in Palestine today. Reflecting on the spiraling circuits of aid securitization in Palestine, and the role of the United States within them, two employees of a Palestinian development NGO based in Ramallah had this to say:

> Interlocutor 1: The ATC emerged in 2003, and we boycotted this. It's not our role to do vetting; it's not our role to replace the police. [However] it didn't stop with USAID. It spread [to] UN agencies. They [other donors] started adding some articles in their contracts. Then it went to other organizations like the Scandinavian countries, and they started adding a BDS [boycott, divestment and sanctions] condition.
>
> LB: So it started to mushroom out?
>
> Interlocutor 1: Yes.
>
> LB: Was the US the first to do this?
>
> Interlocutor 1: Yes, the US was the first. [Then] some [donors] added the list of terrorist groups—and here you'll find the majority of our political parties: Hamas, Islamic Jihad, PFLP, DFLP, some individuals and also the Military Brigades, *Kitaab il-asulteen al-Qassam* and all of these. The majority of our people [are on the list and] you know you should not work with them. In addition, they started adding other things like vetting. This is done by everybody from the EU to all other

countries. They vet the board members, vet the key staff and the staff of the project.

LB: That's a lot more than it used to be.

Interlocutor 1: Yes, they expanded this. And now [they] do vetting for the staff of the project in addition to the board members and key staff. And they have a database.

Interlocutor 2: There are different databases and every government [has one].

Interlocutor 1: It didn't stop with the ATC. It mushroomed to other things. Also, recently over the last two and a half years, we have what they call due diligence.

Interlocutor 2: They do a spot check [every six months].

Interlocutor 1: A list of thirty-three questions.

Interlocutor 2: Forty-two.

Interlocutor 1: Forty-two questions and you have to provide them with all the documents needed. . . . You feel like you're doing something wrong. You always feel accused until you prove not. . . .

Interlocutor 1: You feel that you are accused until . . . you prove to be innocent. This is how they deal with Palestinian NGOs.[39]

The expanding circuits of securitization set in motion following Bush's "war on the financial foundation of terror" in the early aughts primed the stage for the deepening integration of war technologies into aid flows. As one NGO director contended, the counterterrorism paradigm started

to take shape in 2003 and spread. Now all the agencies do it. Just recently, last month, there was a new development that some of the Scandinavian countries adopted a new "anti-terrorism policy." And you have to do vetting and also there are [antiterrorism] clauses. . . . In the last four or five years, it spread rapidly.[40]

This new "aid norm," as often described by countless interlocutors, constituted a securitized normal that will live on whether American aid to the Palestinians ebbs and flows or is again entirely disrupted.

One of the most disconcerting developments, the aforementioned interlocutor asserted, is that Palestinian NGOs were being conscripted into the spiraling circuits of aid securitization. "They are now are asking the [Palestinian] NGOs to be responsible. . . . We should not be transferred into security apparatuses, you know, to run behind people and [ask them] about their affiliations. That contradicts with the [Palestinian] Basic Law [and] human rights." It is on this basis that many Palestinian organization refused to sign the EU terrorism clause. He further noted that Palestinian NGOs must also vet potential beneficiaries to ensure that a potential beneficiary's family member has not been accused of being a part of a terrorist organization.[41]

These circuits of spiraling securitization have morphed into related but new domains. In 2019, Israel's Ministry of Strategic Affairs (MSA) and Israeli-affiliated lobby and lawfare groups released a new report outlining evolving tactics deployed against Palestinians and their political struggle at an international scale.[42] The report renders synonymous the Boycott, Divestment, and Sanctions (BDS) movement with terrorism and calls for the defunding of organizations that advocate for or support the call to civil disobedience against Israel. It is only a matter of time, as the director of Palestine's oldest human rights organization lamented, before "BDS becomes the next 'untouchable' for funders."[43]

In February 2019, the Ministry of Strategic Affairs released a new report alleging links between the BDS movement and evolving strategies deployed by terrorists, with NGOs playing a central role in the grand design. Leaving little to the imagination, the report titled "Terrorists in Suits: The Ties Between NGOs Promoting BDS and Terrorist Organizations"—and featuring a split-image cover containing half a clean-shaven, suit-wearing NGO worker and half a keffiyeh-wrapped, gun-flaunting terrorist, a hybrid terrorist-executive—purports to have uncovered previously unexposed links between terror groups and NGOs promoting BDS.[44] The report leaves little speculation as to the ministry's aims. As part of a broader series of efforts on the part of Israel in collaboration with lawyers and Zionist organizations to undermine Palestinian civil society formations, the report casts Palestinian NGOs as key vehicles in a broader movement to delegitimize, defame, and destroy Israel.[45]

Centrally MSA alleges that terrorists view NGOs as a useful and strategic institutional infrastructure through which to advance "their ideological goal: the elimination of the State of Israel."[46] This approach, it is alleged, con-

FIGURE 8. Cover of MSA report "Terrorists in Suits."

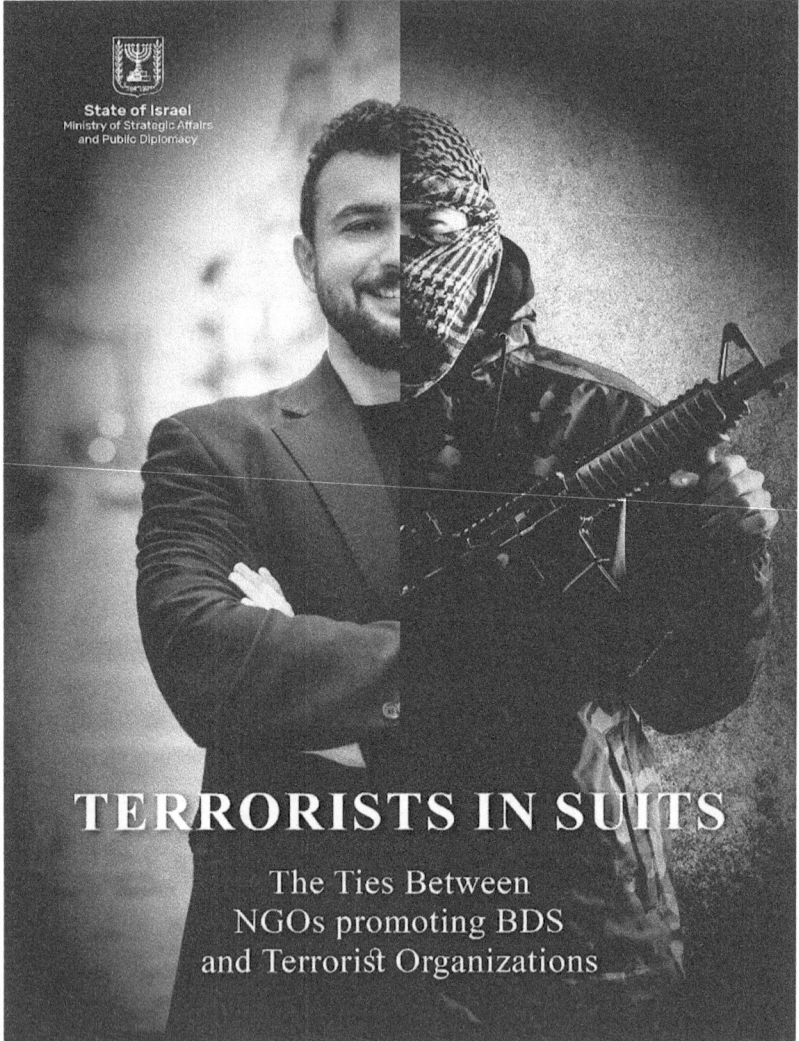

stitutes "an evolutionary development in the tactics of the terror organizations against the State of Israel."[47] The report claims to have uncovered over 100 links between terror groups and Palestinian organizations supporting BDS, including thirty alleged terrorists who occupy senior positions in thirteen of the identified BDS organizations. The MSA report was one among an evolving array of tactics and strategies levied by Israel to delegitimize and defund Palestinian institutions effective in leveraging the Palestinian struggle into the international arena.

European donors came under increasing pressure by Israel and affiliated organizations to terminate their funding to Palestinian organizations supporting or advocating for BDS. In a list of its accomplishments for 2017, the NGO Monitor, which maintains close ties to Israeli and Zionist governmental and lobby groups, described how Denmark ended its funding to Palestinian NGOs (through the Human Rights and International Humanitarian Law Secretariat).[48] This decision, it boasted, was made after the NGO Monitor traveled to Denmark to meet with government officials where it presented its research "exposing funding to NGOs with links to terror groups that support BDS."[49]

In the summer of 2019, I met a senior policy advisor of a Palestinian think tank who informed me of the recent publication of the MSA report. "Open it and look at the list of organizations mentioned," she suggested. "Just go down the list and you have a sense of who will be hit next."[50] I spent that summer meeting with organizations featured in the MSA report. The trend was clear: Palestinian NGOs had what was commonly referred to as "shrinking space" to undertake development and humanitarian work that was not dictated and shaped by the security and counterinsurgency aims of Israel and foreign states. The story of Ma'an Development Center is but one example of this trend. In the summer of 2018, Ma'an was placed under a terrorism financing investigation by one of its foreign funders. I would speak to Ma'an's staff over the course of multiple visits spanning two years.

THE TARGETED

The story first ran in Sydney's *Daily Telegraph*. In the summer of 2018, the Australian outlet began a series of articles charging that Australian aid administered through the Australian bilateral aid agency, AusAid, had been used to finance terrorism. The charge, so it went, was that AusAid provided funds to Union Aid Abroad—APHEDA (Australian People for Health, Education and Development Abroad) through the Australia Middle East NGO cooperation agreement. APHEDA had in turn had partnered with Ma'an, a Ramallah-based Palestinian NGO, as part of the implementation of the Australian Middle East NGO Cooperation Agreement (AMENCA): a multiyear, three-stage, Australian-funded development program for Palestinian agriculture.[51] The APHEDA-managed portion of the program came under intense scrutiny after a series of articles appearing in the *Daily Telegraph* alleged that a former contractor of Ma'an had links to the Popular Front for the Liberation of Palestine (PFLP). The PFLP appeared on US, EU, and Canadian terror lists and on the Australian "Consolidated" list.

"We had been working with the Australians for so many years," Ma'an director's Sami Khader, stated in his Ramallah-based office in the summer of 2018.[52] Ma'an had just been placed under a terrorism investigation by the Australian government. The terrorism allegations began, as Sami explained, when an Australian journalist published an exclusive on the front page of the *Daily Telegraph*. "The article is full of allegations against Ma'an and against our partner, which is APHEDA," he explained.

> Mainly what they are talking about is that the money that comes from the Australian government to APHEDA and from APHEDA to Ma'an and from Ma'an to terrorists and from the terrorists to PFLP and then to the funeral of this guy, who happened to be one of our employees, who was shot by a sniper in Gaza recently.

The employee to whom Sami is referring is Ahmed Abdullah al-Adine.

Al-Adine, formerly one of Ma'an's thirty-six Gaza-based staff, had been participating in weekly protests as part of the Great March of Return in the Gaza Strip, a series of protests held each Friday from March 2018 to December 2019 to protest of the ongoing blockade of territory, denial of the Palestinian right of return, and US recognition of Jerusalem as the capital of Israel. Of the approximately 1.9 million Palestinians in Gaza, 1.4 million are refugees. The demands of the protestors were simple: dignity and return. The weekly demonstrations were met with live ammunition, rubber bullets, and lethal force by the Israeli army. Over 200 Palestinians were killed over the course of the demonstrations, and 36,000 more were injured.[53] March 14, 2018, was a particularly harrowing day. As described in the account of one of the participants, thousands of Palestinians began "walking unarmed to the fence to demand their right to return."[54] Israeli soldiers were given instructions to "shoot any civilian trying to 'trespass.' And so the shooting began as early as nine o'clock that morning. . . . By the end of the day," he laments, "we lost 60 people, and more than 2,700 were injured." Al-Adine was among those killed. He was fatally shot in the stomach by an Israeli sniper meters away as he stood among other protestors.[55] Al-Adine's funeral, held shortly thereafter, would be attended by many, including members of the PFLP.

Pictures of the funeral showing the members of PFLP present were soon picked up by Australian media, as was a PFLP martyr poster of al-Adine. On June 28, 2018, the *Daily Telegraph* ran an exclusive describing the funeral as "guarded by more than a dozen armed men wearing balaclavas with the PFLP logo on bandannas, and his [al-Adine's] funeral image also had the PFLP logo on it."[56] *Telegraph* reporter Sharri Markson further asserted that the PFLP hailed al-Adine as a 'martyr' " (all Palestinians killed by Israel are referred to as "martyrs"). The PFLP, she revealed, gave al-Adine "a grand funeral . . . attended by at least a dozen PFLP terrorists."[57] Additional evidence wielded by Markson included Facebook posts (written in Arabic) along with the PFLP martyr poster, which were used to buttress the claim that al-Adine was a PFLP commander.

Just a week later, the story was picked up by Naomi Levin of the *Australian Jewish News*, who not only echoed Markson's narrative that Australian taxpayer money was being used to finance terror vis-à-vis the APHEDA–Ma'an–al-Adine/PFLP link, but cast greater suspicion on Australian aid to the Palestinians more broadly.[58] The web of relations that sutured AusAid to APHEDA to Ma'an to al-Adine in Gaza, it was argued in both the *Daily Telegraph* and *Australian Jewish News*, constituted material support for terrorism and warranted an immediate suspension of Australian aid to the Palestinian organization along with other entities of the APHEDA-funded consortium.[59] It mattered little that the allegation of terrorism financing had not yet been investigated or corroborated—the mere accusation was enough to warrant the freezing of a $1.2 million aid program for Palestinian agriculture.

Here we see the fungibility thesis at play, which has animated material support cases specifically and shaped processes of racialization of Muslims within the global war on terror more broadly (see Chapter 1). The key question is not whether one "can prove that money donated actually goes toward the deployment of violent or terrorist acts," as Marieke de Goede suggests.[60] Rather it is assumed that any act undertaken to benefit a designated group necessarily enhances its capacity to carry out terrorist acts. Once an entity is designated with the terrorist classification, any and all activity it undertakes is necessarily terrorist. All else is abolished; it exists as a singular identity and with a unilateral aim.

The allegations set in motion a series of punitive measures. The Minister of Foreign Affairs and Trade in Australia suspended the Australian aid program to Ma'an, and a team of investigators soon dispatched by Australia's Department of Foreign Affairs and Trade began a terrorism investigation of the organization and its alleged links to terrorism that would last approximately two years.[61] During this period, Ma'an's assets were frozen, and the agricultural work it had undertaken in the Gaza Strip and West Bank was suspended, resulting in significant net loss both for the organization and its beneficiaries. I conducted a series of visits and interviews with Ma'an throughout the course of the terrorism investigation.[62] The following vignette presents some insight into the processes that take shape when a charge of terrorism financing is levied. Ma'an director Sami Khader had this to say in July 2018:

> SK: Nobody consulted us and suddenly the Minister of Foreign Affairs decided to suspend our whole program. . . . They are doing a full audit for the program for the last three years. We don't mind having them to come and audit but we have one condition, to publish the results and not to be cowards because we have nothing to hide. . . . Everything was put aside and just because [the accusation was] terrorism, terrorist groups, etc. So everybody starts shaking about this.
>
> LB: So this trumps everything?
>
> SK: Yes.
>
> LB: So no one fact checked the accusations?
>
> SK: Of course not. And nobody is. . . . Because the damage happened you know—just to link you as an individual or as an organization with a

terrorist group, according to their definition of terrorism, you know. That's enough.

LB: So what happens at the moment when you get branded? What happens to your work? What happens to your alliances?

SK: Everything is suspended.[63]

The mere allegation that Ma'an was funding terrorism created an executive override; it effectively ceased the organization's work and abrogated its alliances with other institutions, thereby isolating the organization until it was cleared of terrorism allegations.[64] "Everything stopped," Sami stated: "We lost the [agricultural] season." Another Ma'an employee contended that the Australian ministry cared little about Ma'an's successes thus far with the AMENCA program:

> We managed to export 1,400 tons of vegetables to support the farmers. We have done around eight and a half kilometers of agricultural roads. We have done thirty-one water pumps for farmers to export their harvesting. We have done maintenance for artesian wells in Gaza.[65]

"It's irrelevant to them," he added. "We have done so many activities; we ranked number one in achieving all of these among the three main consortiums. [Then] everything was put aside just because this was terrorism and terrorist groups. Everybody started shaking about this."[66] The very speech act of branding a Palestinian organization as linked to terrorism is effectively equivalent to a conviction barring evidence.

Following the allegations, other Palestinian organizations with whom they worked were afraid to maintain associations for fear they would also be swept in the net of suspicion. Ma'an effectively became, in the words of Lara Friedman, "radioactive."[67] Ma'an staff also noted that they were faulted in the investigatory report issued by the Australians for failing to vet the gas station at which they fueled their vehicles. When I visited the organization again in the summer of 2019, Ma'an had just been cleared of the allegations following extensive auditing, investigatory, and vetting procedures, including the screening of all their partners, contractors, and staff. Some of those vetted, they noted, came back with matches to those in terrorist databases due to duplicate names, misspellings, and other errors. One positive match, they noted, was their procurement officer, who was sitting in the office when the Australians came to do the audit. The database indicated that he was a member of Hizballah and was currently incarcerated. "The margin of error," one employee remarked, "is huge. This has happened a number of times."[68] Another Palestinian human rights organization also targeted around the same time with terrorism-financing allegations similarly lamented that the mere accusation of terrorism itself does damaging work: it freezes your work and places you in a state of defense, he remarked. "It's like a war," he stated.[69] These *wars* have far-reaching implications—and tentacles—as the following case attests.

I had been given a number to call by Sami Khader. "Our story is not unique," he told me, "especially right now." An increasing number of Palestinian development organizations working in agriculture and food sovereignty, especially in Area C, were being targeted.[70] This organization, formerly the largest agricultural development institution in Palestine, had also recently been targeted by Israeli and settler groups for alleged links to terrorism. Founded by a group of agronomists in 1986, the Union of Agricultural Work Committees (UAWC) had grown into one the largest agricultural unions in Palestine. It was among the few Palestinian non-profits that specifically supported agricultural projects and assisted Palestinian farmers to cultivate land in Area C, an area spanning over 70 percent of the West Bank, the space demarcated for Israeli settlement development and where Palestinians are especially vulnerable to settler encroachment.

We received a letter in 2019, a high-level UAWC staffer noted. The letter came from UK Lawyers for Israel (UKLFI) informing the organization that it was suspected of having links to a terror organization, specifically PFLP, just as with Ma'an. The letter proceeded to cite the designation of the PFLP as a terrorist organization across multiple lists, including the US, EU, and Canadian terror lists. It also included a cataloguing of hijackings, suicide bombings, and assassinations undertaken by the PFLP dating back to 1969 and detailed connections it alleged linked UAWC to PFLP, including, in one instance, identifying a former president of UAWC's board of trustees "convicted of terrorist offences in 1969 and jailed for 15 years," and in another, highlighted that UAWC's secretary "spoke on a platform alongside Leila Khaled."[71] "Everyone gets the same letter," he remarked. "Sometimes they'll revise a sentence [but] it's the same information. They do it to everyone be-cause they know that it will put us in a position where we have to defend ourselves. They do it to disturb."[72] This is about disruption and attrition, he underscored.

UAWC had been targeted for years by an array of Israeli lawfare, settler, and advocacy groups with moderate success. In 2012 a sustained campaign waged by Shurat HaDin, an Israeli legal center, prompted Australia to tem-porarily freeze UAWC's funding subject to an investigation, relying again on the tenuous charges of PFLP affiliations. Following the allegation, my in-terlocutor noted, UAWC's funding was immediately cut, and no recourse to challenge the allegation was offered. Ultimately the Australian government resumed its aid flows to UAWC, arguing, contra to Shurat HaDin, that UAWC had not been designated a terrorist or banned organization by Israel at the time.[73]

The political landscape shifted for UAWC in the fall of 2019, however, when two of UAWC's employees, Samer Arbeed and Abdel Razaq Farraj, said to be connected to the PFLP, were arrested by Israel for allegedly overseeing a bombing that killed an Israeli, Rina Shnerb, near a West Bank settlement. In the wake of their arrests, UKLFI and NGO Monitor, two Israeli groups lead-ing the targeted and organized defamation campaign against Palestinian NGOs, resumed their efforts, spearheading a months-long campaign aimed at pressuring the Dutch government to withdraw its funding of UAWC.

Ultimately the tactics were not all that different from those applied against Ma'an. In this case, Israeli groups lobbied the Dutch government, successfully, to freeze a $1 million grant to UAWC despite there being no evidence that linked UAWC as an organization to the bombing that killed Shnerb. Rather, the "guilt by association" tenet that has long underwritten US material support laws was mobilized to justify the aid cutoff. Unsurpris-ingly, the escalated attacks on UAWC came at a time when a global network of Israel-aligned advocacy groups—such as Shurat HaDin, UKLFI, the In-ternational Legal Forum, the NGO Monitor, and the Lawfare Project—had been lobbying European governments to cut funding streams to Palestin-ian NGOs, especially those giving support to Palestinian communities and farmers to cultivate and remain on their lands, on the one hand, and, on the other, to those institutions documenting violations of human rights and

FIGURE 9. Letter sent from UK Lawyers for Israel to UAWC.

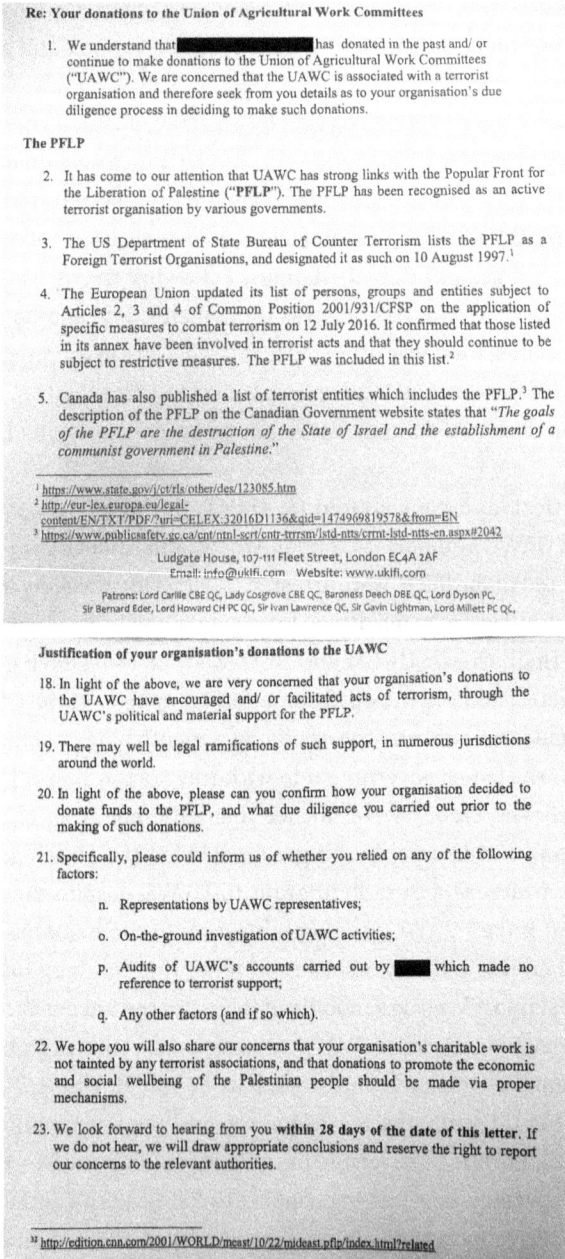

Re: Your donations to the Union of Agricultural Work Committees

1. We understand that ▮▮▮▮▮▮▮▮▮▮ has donated in the past and/ or continue to make donations to the Union of Agricultural Work Committees ("UAWC"). We are concerned that the UAWC is associated with a terrorist organisation and therefore seek from you details as to your organisation's due diligence process in deciding to make such donations.

The PFLP

2. It has come to our attention that UAWC has strong links with the Popular Front for the Liberation of Palestine ("**PFLP**"). The PFLP has been recognised as an active terrorist organisation by various governments.

3. The US Department of State Bureau of Counter Terrorism lists the PFLP as a Foreign Terrorist Organisations, and designated it as such on 10 August 1997.[1]

4. The European Union updated its list of persons, groups and entities subject to Articles 2, 3 and 4 of Common Position 2001/931/CFSP on the application of specific measures to combat terrorism on 12 July 2016. It confirmed that those listed in its annex have been involved in terrorist acts and that they should continue to be subject to restrictive measures. The PFLP was included in this list.[2]

5. Canada has also published a list of terrorist entities which includes the PFLP.[3] The description of the PFLP on the Canadian Government website states that *"The goals of the PFLP are the destruction of the State of Israel and the establishment of a communist government in Palestine."*

[1] https://www.state.gov/j/ct/rls/other/des/123085.htm
[2] http://eur-lex.europa.eu/legal-content/EN/TXT/PDF/?uri=CELEX:32016D1136&qid=1474969819578&ftom=EN
[3] https://www.publicsafety.gc.ca/cnt/ntnl-scrt/cntr-trrrsm/lstd-ntts/crrnt-lstd-ntts-en.aspx#2042

Ludgate House, 107-111 Fleet Street, London EC4A 2AF
Email: info@ukifi.com   Website: www.ukifi.com

Patrons: Lord Carlile CBE QC, Lady Cosgrove CBE QC, Baroness Deech DBE QC, Lord Dyson PC,
Sir Bernard Eder, Lord Howard CH PC QC, Sir Ivan Lawrence QC, Sir Gavin Lightman, Lord Millett PC QC,

---

Justification of your organisation's donations to the UAWC

18. In light of the above, we are very concerned that your organisation's donations to the UAWC have encouraged and/ or facilitated acts of terrorism, through the UAWC's political and material support for the PFLP.

19. There may well be legal ramifications of such support, in numerous jurisdictions around the world.

20. In light of the above, please can you confirm how your organisation decided to donate funds to the PFLP, and what due diligence you carried out prior to the making of such donations.

21. Specifically, please could inform us of whether you relied on any of the following factors:

    n. Representations by UAWC representatives;

    o. On-the-ground investigation of UAWC activities;

    p. Audits of UAWC's accounts carried out by ▮▮▮ which made no reference to terrorist support;

    q. Any other factors (and if so which).

22. We hope you will also share our concerns that your organisation's charitable work is not tainted by any terrorist associations, and that donations to promote the economic and social wellbeing of the Palestinian people should be made via proper mechanisms.

23. We look forward to hearing from you **within 28 days of the date of this letter**. If we do not hear, we will draw appropriate conclusions and reserve the right to report our concerns to the relevant authorities.

[32] http://edition.cnn.com/2001/WORLD/meast/10/22/mideast.pflp/index.html?related

Source: UAWC, 2019.

international law across the occupied territories. "There are usually two reasons behind [terrorism] allegations," the UAWC staffer remarked. "You are [either] working in Area C on the ground [or] you are a human rights organization," and Israel is concerned that you are collecting documentation for the International Criminal Court, he added.

Similar to Ma'an, the freeze in Dutch funds had an immediate impact, most notably across some one hundred communities in Area C that had relied on UAWC's Dutch-funded programs. UAWC warned that the loss of funds would severely dampen its ability to help farmers remain on their lands, especially as Israeli settlement expansion accelerated during the period of escalated aggression during the Netanyahu–Trump era. In the end, UAWC was unable to withstand the multiple waves of attacks. The Dutch freeze hampered its ability to continue its agricultural projects at the scale, and aggression against it only intensified. In July 2021, the IDF raided the offices of UAWC's Ramallah headquarters, breaking down the door and confiscating computers and documents, and subsequently shut it down. UAWC's fate was similar to almost every Palestinian NGO with whom I spoke that had, in the first instance, been alleged to have terrorist links. The validity of the allegations mattered not. Violence was set into motion by the speech act itself—from the slow, grating violence of attrition and unraveling of relationships shot through with loosely defined allegations of terror, to military raids, torture, and detention.

UAWC's story would be told again and again, though with slightly varying details, as I went down the list of organizations featured in the MSA report. Each time was a bit more harrowing, as with Defence for Children International–Palestine (DCI–P). DCI–P, like many featured in the MSA report, was among a number of Palestinian organizations long in the crosshairs of Israeli governmental and aligned lobby groups seeking to delegitimize and defund humanitarian and human rights organizations operating in Palestine. DCI–P, a Palestinian human rights organization that focuses specifically on the rights of children, has, since 1991, documented and investigated crimes committed by Israel against Palestinian children, represented Palestinian children in Israeli military courts, and supported the protection of children's rights in accordance with international standards.

Eerily similar to the case of Ma'an, DCI–P would first come under fire after one of its employees, Hashem Abu Maria, was shot and killed by the Israeli military in 2014 while attending a solidarity march for Gaza. As was the case with al-Adine, multiple political factions were represented at Maria's funeral, including the PFLP. Accordingly, DCI–P would soon thereafter be branded by the coterie of Israeli lawfare groups as being PFLP-affiliated. The mere accusation of the charge amounted to war, as the DCI–P employee described it. "The accusation," he stated, "freezes your work. Except you aren't doing work. You are just trying to manage disaster fallout."[74] Moreover, as with Ma'an, DCI–P was increasingly isolated from its partners and coalitions following the allegations. "They threatened our banks and partners," the employee stated. "We are now having problems with the Arab Bank, which has frozen our transfers." The Arab Bank has links to Citibank, and is therefore subject to US terrorism-financing laws and policies. So too did the UKLFI campaign of defamation result in the crowdfunding platform Global Giving removing DCI–P from its platform.[75]

Meanwhile, in New York, the NGO Monitor pressured the City University of New York (CUNY) Law School's Human Rights and Gender Justice Clinic to investigate its ties with DCI–P based on its well-worn allegation that the organization sustains links to the PFLP.[76] The charge came after CUNY and DCI–P submitted a fifty-seven-page report to the UN Commission of Inquiry documenting Israeli military and settler violence and killings of Palestinians. The NGO Monitor claimed the findings about Israel were tainted by DCI–P's ties to PFLP. Ultimately the charges were ruled as baseless;[77] however, not without considerable energy and resources expended, detracting from DCI–P's legal work with child detainees.[78] "They are attacking the networks of infrastructure on which we rely," the employee remarked. "They are coming from all points." The strategy, he underscored, now appears to be about sustaining pressure on Palestinian institutions through global networks into which they are integrated and supported, intermediaries, and financial means of subsistence, notably using tools honed over the decades-long global war on terror. "The attacks are coming more frequently," he lamented, "but so far they have not succeeded in shutting us down." "Right now, it's about attrition," he added.

When asked about his assessment as to why the escalated attacks are coming at this moment, he replied, "Maybe because we are trying to push a bill through Congress condemning Israel for war crimes against children and other human rights violations. We introduced the bill in 2018," he added. More broadly, he speculated, this is part of an attempt to eliminate human rights work. Concerns voiced by the UN echo his analysis. UN Special Rapporteur Michael Lynk expressed concerns that the hostile environment for Palestinian human rights organizations has "become even more overtly toxic and harsh since 2015" following Israel's 2014 military invasion of Gaza and subsequent "initiation by the International Criminal Court of a preliminary investigation, with the cooperation of a number of Palestinian human rights defenders, into possible war crimes and crimes against humanity" committed during Israel's military invasion and its West Bank settlement project.[79] Relatedly, Israeli officials and government-affiliated organizations have more systematically targeted European governments to end their funding of these institutions.[80] As a joint statement issued by the Palestinian NGO Network and the PNCRCF details,

> Israel's Prime Minister Benjamin Netanyahu has repeatedly called on European Government officials, most recently in a January 2018 meeting with the Norwegian Foreign Minister, to halt their funding of Palestinian human rights organization Al-Haq, accused of engaging in BDS activities or "lawfare" against the State of Israel. This followed a similar meeting between Prime Minister Netanyahu and the Danish Foreign Minister in May 2017, which led Denmark to reconsider its funding of Palestinian NGOs.[81]

"Right now, they are largely attacking those [of us] who work on advocacy," the DCI–P staffer lamented, "but it will spread. Everyone's turn will come." I couldn't help but think of this conversation, and his war metaphor, nearly two years later as I watched video surveillance footage of the IDF raiding DCI–P's headquarters in Al-Bireh's Sateh Marhaba neighborhood just after 5:00 in the morning, confiscating computers, hard drives, and files of Palestinian child detainee clients in Israeli military courts.[82] I looked down at the desk on which I had taken my notes. It had piles of paper, some neatly stacked under paperweights, some plants to the left, and soldiers pacing back and forth, carrying computers out the door, disassembling hard drives, dropping detainee files, and attempting, unsuccessfully for some time to cut the CCTV until 5:27 when video feed would be cut. Not "like a war" I thought. This *is* the war now.

COUNTERMOVEMENTS

The fates of the targeted chronicled here, among a range of others not discussed, at the hands of escalated lawfare and defamation campaigns by actors global in scope, should be understood as the outcome of accretive processes of securitization. The tactics and strategies set into motion by Bush's declaration of a "war on the financial foundation of terror" have metastasized and escalated to new heights. This is not to ascribe sole authorship to the United States; to the contrary, it is to point to the synergistic processes at play as states, and non-, quasi-, and hybrid-state actors, borrow, adapt, and evolve strategies of policing and securitization to create more finely tuned regimes of warfare and control. At the same time, these spiraling circuits of policing and counterinsurgency warfare have also birthed new kinds of openings, fissures, and political possibilities.

As greater numbers of Palestinian organizations and coalitions are targeted and shut down by terrorism financing allegations, conversations about divestment from foreign aid are emergent. Many interlocutors with whom I spoke in Palestine during the period of these escalated attacks, in 2018 and 2019, spoke of a revived boycott of foreign aid. This time however, the boycott would be directed not just at the United States, as was done in 2003 following the introduction of anti-terrorism certification (see Chapter 3 on the Palestinian NGO Network boycott), but more broadly, against an entire international aid regime that conscripts them foremost as threats to be managed and secondarily as humanitarian subjects to be administered by charitable donations, but rarely as political subjects endowed with rights.[83] Aid securitization, in other words was also infusing the emergence of a collective divestment in the status quo, and in turn, investment in possibilities for future horizons shaped not by settler–colonial anxieties and national security projects, but instead by questions of autonomy, justice, and collective liberation. These debates and strategies in Palestine and among Palestinians are ongoing. So too is the war enacted through the "point of the list" intensifying. Events roughly two years later brought this war to a critical escalation point.

Five
ASPHYXIATORY VIOLENCE

THE DESIGNATION

On October 16, 2021, a staff member of Al Haq contacted Mohammed al-Maskati, the digital protection coordinator at Front Line Defenders, regarding suspicious activity on a staffer's phone.[1] Upon conducting forensic analysis, al-Maskati determined the device had been infected with Pegasus, an exceptionally sophisticated spyware engineered by an Israeli technology firm, the NSO Group. Just weeks later, the NSO Group would be placed on the US sanctions list.[2]

Touted as among the world's most sophisticated spyware, Pegasus is capable of launching "zero-clicks" attacks, requiring no action on the part of the target for the spyware to be installed. The spyware can moreover obtain root privileges of the targeted device, enabling it to harvest all phone data, gain complete access to the phone's applications (including activation of the phone camera and microphone), and overtake primary functions of the device, including initiating calls and downloading material.[3] Given the sophistication of the software and the financial costs incurred for installation, it is often reserved for high-level targets (described as "whaling attacks").[4] On October 17, al-Maskati convened a meeting with representatives of Palestinian NGOs in the West Bank to inform them of the Pegasus discovery and subsequently ran forensic analysis on an additional seventy-five devices.

Pegasus spyware was found on the devices of five more human rights workers.[5] One of the six targets, Salah Hamouri, a lawyer for the prisoner support
group Addameer, had his Jerusalem residency ordered revoked by Israel the
next day.[6]

Two days later, on October 19, Israel's minister of defense declared six
Palestinian human rights organizations to be "terrorist organizations" (TOs)
under Israel's 2016 Israeli Counter-Terrorism Law, citing alleged links to the
Popular Front for the Liberation of Palestine (PFLP).[7] Under its terrorism law,
Israel can exercise extensive powers over organizations and residents of the
occupied territories, including blocking funds from reaching proscribed organizations, arresting staff and employees of such organizations, and criminalizing anyone providing professional services or expressing support for a
designated entity, carrying sharp echoes to US material support law.

On November 7, 2021, the day before Front Line Defenders released its
report of the Pegasus findings, Israel extended the designation to include the
occupied territories via military order, thus outlawing the six organizations
in the West Bank as well. The six groups designated by Israel[8] were the same
six organizations that had convened with al-Maskati just days earlier.[9] The
timing of the designation led some analysts to conclude that the ministry's
move was in part an attempt to legitimate the surveillance and infiltration
of the devices of Palestinian human rights defenders with Pegasus spyware
producing a kind of recursive logic wherein the spyware is somehow justi-
fied because the entities targeted were determined by Israel to be terrorist.[10]
The ministry's designation imposed severe penalties on the six organizations, their staff, and associates, constituting grounds for imprisonment, the
blockage of funding, and seizure of financial assets. Staff of the designated
organizations faced imprisonment for up to twenty-five years, the offices
were subject to military raids and closure, and organizational assets could
be seized. Meanwhile, supporters of the designated groups, "including those
who publish 'words of praise, support or sympathy,'" could face imprisonment.[11] The impactful violence of the designation was immediately felt by
staffers and leadership alike.[12]

The defense ministry's designation was widely condemned by human
rights organizations, with some calling it characteristic "of totalitarian regimes" and demanding its immediate revocation.[13] Described by UN Special

Rapporteur Fionnuala Ní Aoláin as a "civic death," the classification imposed a de facto ban on the designated entities, rendering those who associate with or finance the organizations potentially liable under a broad amalgam of terrorism financing laws, sanctions policies, and banking restrictions.[14]

Of even greater concern for those affiliated with the designated organizations were the transnational implications of the designation if endorsed explicitly or implicitly by foreign powers, which could yield the closure of bank accounts, blocks on fundraising platforms, and denials of visas for staff and affiliated persons among other punitive measures. As a director of one of the designated organizations remarked when we met in November 2021:

> If the US, even in a hidden way—and this is what worries me—starts silently to impose [the designation], if they start to question board members, if they deny visas for people to travel, if they try to do these actions, this means secretly they are buying the Israeli story—they just don't want to *publish* it. But on the practical level they will support shutting us down.

I met with five of the six designated groups shortly after the ministry's announcement,[15] and nearly all expressed grave concerns regarding the tacit acceptance of Israel's classification by foreign powers, most notably for the banking implications it would entail.[16] Even if foreign powers do not formally endorse Israel's designation, the classification nonetheless jeopardizes the financial flows on which the designated groups rely as it triggers various risk technologies embedded in international financial systems.[17] Accordingly, donors could elect (and have already begun) to end their funding of the organizations that they are seemingly too risky to fund.[18] Israel's designation, as one research analyst relayed, is intended to sever links between these groups and the outside world, to curb their financial flows and disconnect them from the networked relations that sustain them.[19] To date, Israel's designation remains in place barring any evidentiary proof for its basis.[20] When I met with the designated organizations in late 2021, many described experiencing what felt like a quiet, grating war slowly engulfing them. A passive non-challenge, as has been the case thus far with respect to Europe and the United States, coupled with the practices of censure, embargo, and blacklisting that the classification induces, has the potential to collapse these organizations through a slow suffocation of the financial networks on which they rely. In November, one of the six had already closed its doors.[21]

This chapter explores how Israel's designation enacts what I call asphyxiatory violence—a modality of violence that realizes its destructive effects through less spectacular means than a bomb or tank, and instead through a quieter, temporally stretched process of constriction, one that progressively erodes conditions of livability.[22] Here we can see parallels to Rob Nixon's theorization of the attritional lethality of environmental crises on the poor, what he calls "slow violence," or Jasbir Puar's account of maiming in the Gaza Strip wherein the population as an aggregate is progressively debilitated of life capacities.[23] Asphyxiatory violence is stretched across time—it is "uneventful" as Lauren Berlant might suggest, but no less potent in its effects.[24] The temporality of asphyxiation is one of a "slow death" wherein life capacities are gradually eliminated. There is no explosion, per se, but instead a gradual process of constriction. This is far from a new modality of violence and control—indeed the cordoning off and enclavation of subjugated peoples has long been a tactic deployed in colonial and imperial projects, as Laleh Khalili has detailed.[25] Such too is the logic built into contemporary sanctions policies imposed on regimes that violate international, and particularly political and economic interests, of powerful countries in the Global North. Asphyxiatory modalities of control have likewise been deployed by Israel throughout its nearly half a century of counterinsurgency warfare against the Palestinians and most notably in the Gaza Strip.

In the wake of Israel's disengagement from the territory in 2005, Israel deployed new tactics of biopolitical and spatial control that centered on the tight modulation of critical life-sustaining flows (food aid, medicine, etc.) and life-eliminating forces (bombs) into and out of the territory.[26] Controls necessarily tightened or loosened in accordance with Israel's counterinsurgency aims. In a similar vein, Omar Jabary Salamanca has explored how Israel's manipulation (and calculated destruction) of infrastructural networks and systems that sustain life (i.e., the bombing of systems that distribute water and electricity), what he calls "infrastructural violence," functions as a means of biopolitical control.[27] Such tactics, Salamanca contends, mark a shift "from a 'regulatory' to an 'asphyxiatory' application of power."[28] In the case of Israel's terrorist designation, we see a similar modality of power in effect: much like modulatory control of critical flows into and out of the Gaza Strip following Hamas's ascension into power, the designation facilitates a gradual process of collapse through targeting the flows and linkages that sustain these institutions (at least in their current form). Taking Salamanca's theorization as a point of departure, here I theorize how the ministry's terrorism designation functions as a technology of topological manipulation that facilitates a gradual process of collapse through the targeting of flows, linkages, and relationalities that sustain these entities. At the same time, as Jasbir Puar observes in her account of debilitation through the maiming of Palestinian bodies, the target of this asphyxiatory power is not necessarily life but rather resistance itself.[29]

While the ministry's designation might be novel in terms in the targets selected—among the six designated are some of the most prominent and well-respected institutions in Palestine—it is but one tactic within a longer arc of Israeli counterinsurgency. As Khalili's seminal work on counterinsurgencies demonstrates, tactics of colonial policing and engineering are in constant evolution and flux.[30] Indeed, the ministry's designation, while perhaps accelerated by the Pegasus spyware reveal, is itself part of the evolution of counterinsurgency warfare—a direct response to previous failed efforts on the part of Israel to curb the activities of the designated groups. As a legal researcher for Al-Haq put it, this designation is one tactic in a larger arsenal of strategies to silence and pacify. Pegasus was simply a trigger, not the cause for the designation. The real impetus for the designation, as he put it, is to silence and isolate those engaging the International Criminal Court (ICC) and human rights more broadly. To designate as a "terrorist organization," he stated, "is among the easiest of ways to destroy."[31] At the same time, the designation, he added, is but one tactic in a long, slow-grind war.

Four of the six targeted organizations conduct research on Israel's activities in the occupied territories and are actively collecting and transmitting data on human rights violations and potential war crimes to international organizations, including prosecutors at the International Criminal Court;[32] other targeted groups work on issues of land dispossession providing direct support to Palestinians to remain on their land, especially in Area C, despite intensifying tactics to remove their presence.[33] As an employee of the Union of Agricultural Work Committees relayed in December 2021, Israel has tried for years, albeit unsuccessfully, to convince the organization to modify its programmatic focus from land issues in Area C to something "more benign" through various tactics, including intimidation campaigns waged by Israel's Ministry of Strategic Affairs (MSA) and international Zionist groups such as UK Lawyers for Israel and NGO Monitor (see Chapter 4).[34] Evolving its strategy, Israel then pivoted its efforts to the transnational realm, directly targeting the global webs of financial support on which the six organizations rely to do their work. As many pointed out, Israel did not need the designation to exact violence on DCI–P, or any of the other designated five, though it did offer a useful pretext to intensify repression against them. It did, however, need the designation to effect processes that would, over time, isolate these entities and drain them of their means of subsistence and ultimately hinder their ability to leverage transnational mechanisms of accountability. The designation, put differently, functions as a mechanism of topological manipulation constricting transnational networks and pathways. This shift in strategy placed Europe at the center.[35]

As part of Israel's evolving strategy, in May 2021 Israeli emissaries sent a seventy-four-page classified Shin Bet dossier to representatives of European countries containing their allegations of "terrorist links" in hopes of persuading the European donors to stop funding the organizations.[36] The dossier relied primarily on discredited testimonies of Said Abdat and Amro Hamuda—two accountants affiliated with a seventh organization, the Health Work Committees.[37] The dossier failed to persuade European governments of the validity of terrorist designation, and European aid flows to the groups continued.[38]

In light of its failed effort, Israel then resorted, as human rights lawyer Michael Sfard suggests, to "unconventional warfare: declaring the organizations terrorist groups."[39] "It all starts and ends," he underscores, "with the fact that these organizations are seen as promoting a boycott of Israel and the investigation of war crimes at the International Criminal Court."[40] In 2015, the Palestinian Authority became a signatory to the ICC and the Rome statute governing it, and in 2021, the ICC ruled that it had jurisdiction in the occupied Palestinian territories, over Israeli objections, clearing the way for its chief prosecutor to investigate alleged war crimes committed by Israel and Hamas.[41] The court's ruling placed "hundreds of Israelis—including soldiers and senior political figures—at risk of prosecution."[42]

Within hours of the announcement, *Haaretz* reported that Israel was planning to "brief hundreds of senior security officials, past and present, over the risk of their exposure to prosecution."[43] Echoing Sfard's position, human and civil rights expert and lawyer Jamil Dakwar likewise asserted a relational link between Israel's targeting of the six groups and the ICC investigation.[44] As Dakwar argues, punitive measures ensue "once you cross that line"—that line being when efforts are waged to place personal and criminal liability on Israeli officials and military leaders and assist efforts to hold Israel to account in international fora.[45] It is precisely because these organizations have been especially effective in this regard, as Dakwar suggests, that Israel has escalated this case to this degree. The designation, Dakwar contends, sends multiple messages, including,

> messages against holding Israel accountable in international fora, messages to the funders, messages to politicians and policy makers particularly in the United States and in Europe and also messages to Israeli civil society organizations including international human rights organizations that have joined the effort to hold Israel accountable.[46]

A staffer at DCI–Palestine contended, "They tried to silence us through different means but they weren't able to. This was a message."[47] Similarly, as Al-Haq's director Shawan Jabarin suggested, "This [designation] is their last bullet."[48] Indeed, as Shawan underscores, this designation is the culmination of the "long war," as one interlocutor coined it, and as traced in this book; it also exposes its limits.

LONG WARS AND EXHAUSTION POINTS

Far from a novel tactic, Israel's recent designation builds on a longer history of banning Palestinian organizations both in the occupied territories and in Israel itself.[49] From 1967 to 1995, there was a "long and expanding list of proscribed groups issued by the Israeli military commander under 'emergency' regulations first put in place by the British in 1945."[50] Moreover, under Israeli military law, "virtually all political parties and movements are considered/classified as illegal."[51] Since the start of the 1967 occupation, Israel has "decreed more than 411 Palestinian organizations illegal," as Sahar Francis of Addameer points out, "including all the major Palestinian political parties."[52] Palestinians are then prosecuted by Israel for "membership and activity in an unlawful association," creating a kind of circular, punitive loop. The criminalization of Palestinian association, as Francis points out, constitutes a key tactic in the repression of Palestinian organizing and mobilization.

Evolving its strategy, Israel's tactics of banning now include relations of association, similar to the approach adopted in US material support law, which Israel has borrowed, evolved, and exploited.[53] As this most recent designation underscores, any association to a banned party is now considered illegal under Israeli law.[54] The anti-terrorism frame, which intensified significantly in the post–9/11 era and proves to be an especially useful tool for suppressing dissent, builds on this decades-long history of banning Palestinian political activity and organizational formations. However, even as the ministry's classification builds on this longer history of banning, this most recent escalation can be read more specifically as linked to the Goldstone Report.

On December 27, 2008, Israel began Operation Cast Lead, a twenty-two-day military offensive on the Gaza Strip that left some 1,400 Palestinians dead and hundreds more wounded. In the aftermath, the United Nations launched a fact-finding mission into the Gaza Strip, headed by Justice Richard Goldstone, to investigate violations of international humanitarian and human rights law. The mission published its findings in the Goldstone Report, which concluded that Israel had waged a "deliberately disproportionate attack designed to punish, humiliate and terrorize a civilian population, radically diminish its local economic capacity both to work and to provide for itself, and to force upon it an ever increasing sense of dependency and vulnerability"—asphyxiatory power par excellence—and opened the door, in turn, for criminal responsibility.[55] The report's findings were corroborated by two separate investigations undertaken by Human Rights Watch and Amnesty International.

Israel refused to cooperate with the fact-finding mission; meanwhile Palestinian groups participated in the UN investigation, including Addameer and Al-Haq—two of the six Palestinian human rights organizations targeted in the ministry's October 2021 designation. Israel and pro-Israel groups, such as NGO Monitor, soon launched an aggressive public relations campaign to undermine the credibility of the report and punish Palestinian groups that provided testimonies and participated in the investigation. Then–Israeli

Prime Minister Benjamin Netanyahu promised a lengthy diplomatic battle to delegitimize the UN findings.[56] "Israel must delegitimize the delegitimization," Netanyahu stated.

NGO Monitor reports published at the time of the Goldstone Report are instructive. In early September 2009, before the official release of the report, NGO Monitor had branded Palestinian NGOs participating in the fact-finding mission, including Al-Haq and Addameer, as "political" and "radical NGOs" bent on delegitimizing Israel.[57] The report furthermore recast NGO officials providing testimonies for the commission as "activists" and driven by ideology.[58] Roughly a month later, NGO Monitor placed European funders more centrally in the crosshairs, charging that the Goldstone Report was "made in Europe."[59] It argued that European funders were enabling delegitimization of Israel through the funding of organizations exposing war crimes as well as propelling forward what it termed the "Durban Strategy," birthed at the World Conference on Racism held in 2001, which spearheaded a transnational campaign to delegitimize Israel as " 'an apartheid regime' through international isolation based on the South African model."[60] The blueprint for the ministry's designation in 2021 was laid in the aftermath of Cast Lead. It is from this point on that Israel and state-affiliated organizations pivoted their tactics to undermine efforts aimed at holding Israel accountable in international fora, a strategy that included exacting punishment on human rights groups that partake in such efforts.

Israel's strategy to "delegitimize the delegitimization," as Netanyahu put it, continued with the establishment of an entire ministry dedicated to the realization of this mission. In 2015, the Ministry of Strategic Affairs (MSA) was established to coordinate an effort to counter the "delegitimization of Israel" especially within international media and through the growing Boycott, Divestment, and Sanctions (BDS) movement (see Chapter 4). In January 2019, the MSA published "The Money Trail," which argues that the European Union is funding Palestinian NGOs, deemed fronts for terror, that work to delegitimize Israel through BDS work "even if the EU funding has been granted for projects not directly related to promoting boycotts"— echoing the fungibility argument that underwrites US material support law (see Chapter 1).[61] It moreover calls for the EU to halt its funding of "organizations promoting boycotts against the State of Israel, and stipulate that any future funding will be contingent on a commitment not to promote such boycotts."[62] A month later the MSA published another report, "Terrorists in Suits" (discussed in Chapter 4), which continues on the theme that Palestinian NGOs are "fronts for terror" but further expands the argument to incorporate the BDS movement, making the claim that Palestinian NGOs that endorse or promote BDS have explicit ties to terror groups, with a direct link made in particular to the PFLP.[63]

Another MSA report, a kind of part two to "Terrorists in Suits," was published the following year. This report, "Terrorists in Suits: Blood Money," further accentuates arguments made in the previous two but explicitly targets Addameer, contending that Addameer constitutes "one of the best examples of the NGO-terror connection" with direct ties to the PFLP. "Addameer lay leaders and employees," it alleges, "play a dual role—human rights activists by day and PFLP terrorists by night."[64] The seeds of the ministry's designation were laid years before. Indeed, for the six organizations targeted by the ministry in October 2021, this was hardly a surprising move. As a staffer of Addameer noted, "We were expecting this thing to happen and especially because they failed in their campaign to attack main donors of the human rights sector."[65]

Equally, even as Israel's 2021 classification must be situated within a longer historical context dating back at least a decade earlier, this moment is nonetheless significant. This is the first time that Palestinian NGOs of this stature have been placed on Israel's terrorist registry.[66] This moment marks a critical escalation in the long war traced in this book—the methods, tools, and strategies of which have been developed, honed, and refined over the course of at least three decades—but it also marks a potential exhaustion point, one that arguably tests the limits of the discourse on terrorism: if the designation "sticks"—that is, if it is afforded value and legitimacy or even tacitly accepted—then the implications for human rights work in Palestine, and the world over, are grave.[67] At the same time, Israel has arguably traversed a critical threshold in terms of the credibility of its claims in mainstream liberal and international (i.e., Western) circles.[68] The majority of groups targeted in this latest round are highly regarded in this sphere—operating largely within European human rights discourses and frameworks they are rendered legible and credible within normative, mainstream human rights circles. That is, they conform to the bounds of acceptability. Here in this moment of heightened war we might also be seeing potential exhaustion points to the effective power of the terrorism discourse.

How this story will unfold remains to be seen. While Israel raided and shut down the six designated organizations, along with the Health Work Committees, in August 2022, most of the organizations continue to operate, albeit under constrained circumstances. The longer implications of this classification are still unknown. This chapter treads within this moment of heightened war and violence while dually exploring its productive effects in Palestine and beyond. In the wake of the ministry's designation, I met with five of the six designated organizations, the majority of whom I had been in years-long conversations (four of the six feature prominently in the previous chapter).[69] Drawing on interviews, formal meetings, and informal conversations with directors, leadership, and staffers of the designated groups—as well as lawyers, bankers, researchers, administrative personnel, and activists— this chapter examines how the TO classification enacts asphyxiatory violence on the designated entities, progressively severing them from the networks on which they are reliant and from the broader milieu within which are embedded. It also suggests this moment carries within it the potential to critically rupture the status quo: Israel has arguably pushed its own war to its limits.

Accordingly, this is an unfinished story—one of a long, protracted, even if largely silent, low-grade war, waged through the "point of the list" (Chapter 3). This moment lays bare the stakes of the legal, administrative, and political violence the terrorist classification enacts on its targets, their networks, and indeed ability to withstand the full force of settler–colonial dispossession.[70] At the same time, it simultaneously deposits us into an uncertain future, one wherein an arguably unprecedented escalation of the financial war on the "infrastructure of terror" as Bush put it, has too produced a new horizon of possibility: as international financial flows to the targeted organizations are rendered increasingly precarious, Palestinians are actively forging new pathways forward, those less reliant on international aid flows that have been overtaken by spiraling circuits of securitization and imperial policing, and instead on internal networks and systems of support and mutual solidarities. This chapter tracks this double move.

ASPHYXIATORY VIOLENCE

To designate as a "terrorist organization" is
among the easiest of ways to destroy.
Legal researcher, Al-Haq, Ramallah, December 2021

I had been to this building many times over in previous years. Four stories high, it houses Palestinian research institutes and NGOs and a smattering of other offices. One of the offices housed here belonged to one of the designated six. I entered the stairwell, which felt more eerie than times before. Maybe it was that the lights didn't turn on as I ascended the stairwell, but more so, I could only think of the military raids on this place that had occurred just weeks before, soldiers roaming the building and breaking down doors, apprehending files, notes, and computers, sifting through personal, private conversations. I was visiting a friend and interlocutor who worked for one of the organizations located here. His day was ending; I was jetlagged. He offered me the ritual Nescafé and invited me into the boardroom. "Should I leave my phone here?" I inquired. "It's not scanned yet." The Pegasus story had just broken, and everyone was operating under the general assumption that any phone could be infected with the spyware. There was a pause and I said, "I'm just going to leave it here by the coffeemaker." My friend laughed but didn't object. We entered the meeting room.

"How's it going?" I asked immediately realizing the ridiculousness of my question. He laughed. He worked for an organization that, while not included in Israel's latest designation, had previously been targeted by conjoined attacks of the now-defunct Israeli Ministry of Strategic Affairs, nationalist settler organizations, and international Zionist groups; it was also active in the Palestinian Non-Governmental Organization Network (PNGO), which had long been under attack by NGO Monitor and other Israeli-affiliated organizations and settler groups. "We just had a PNGO meeting here," he said. "We are trying to figure out what to do. . . . It keeps expanding." NGO Monitor had just released a new report charging that an additional 16 Palestinian NGOs, including PNGO—which contains within it some 135 organizations—had "ties to terrorist organizations."[71]

These reports from NGO Monitor, the MSA, and other Israeli-affiliated groups, have been more or less predictive in terms of identifying who would be targeted next. Given the ban on relations of association with a designated group, this essentially translated into nearly the entirety of the NGO sector in Palestine being at risk of targeting and potential collapse. He talked about how nearly every Palestinian NGO was in a state of heightened awareness, policing their activities to mitigate the chances that they might appear on the list. His organization had curbed its participation in projects relating to challenging Israel's expanding settlement enterprise. The power of Israel's designation permeated, as arguably intended, well beyond the distinctly targeted groups. I explained why I had returned to Palestine at this particular moment. People will probably talk, he told me, but they are nervous. However, "we need to speak," he added.

This contradictory moment in Palestine is one that challenged me in ways I had not anticipated. Varying degrees of risk and surveillance were always part and parcel of the research I conducted; however, this moment felt more foreboding, more insidious than anything I had previously encountered in some ten years of doing this research. I had to operate under the assumption that my mere presence in this meeting room with this interlocutor could be putting him at risk, and that every meeting I had hereafter with members of the targeted designations could be wielded against them or me. This weighed heavily on my mind. If the intention of this designation is to silence and isolate, then my presence violated both.

The ethics of research in this moment was one that challenged me in unforeseen ways. I knew well that the elasticity and fluidity of terrorism financing laws—how they could virtually be applied to the most mundane kinds of transactions—and the associational logic underwriting TO designations meant that any one of us could be caught in the dragnet, though with different degrees of vulnerability. Of course, the wide net of fear these terrorism technologies cast is precisely their intended function. In the end, the point, as Dima Khalidi rightly puts it, is not necessarily what evidence one might have but rather, "can you make this organization radioactive, can you suck their resources dry, can you intimidate other people from engaging on this issue."[72] Likewise, as Ubai al-Aboudi, director of Bisan, pointed out, "There's no evidence but we [Palestinians] also do not have a judicial system. There's no democratic process." Israel's speech act alone is the conviction.

Ultimately, I opted to continue this research, while undertaking all possible precautions, and with the full explicit consent of my interlocutors. They likewise underscored the importance of not retreating into silence at this critical juncture. Accordingly, I spent the next month talking and meeting with the targeted groups, gathering their testimonies, hearing their stories, to gain a better understanding of the modalities of violence that the terrorism designation unleashes on the targeted—but also how they navigate the conditions of precarity to which they had been subjected.

———

As I walked through Al-Bireh's Sateh Marhaba neighborhood, all I could think about is how this road, which wound through residential areas with small business scattered throughout, had also been populated, not long ago, by Israeli military forces who had raided the building to which I was headed, confiscating computers and confidential lawyer files, including conversations between attorneys and child detainees. The violence layered beneath the normalcy of the current moment—children riding bikes, laundry freshly hung, and people going about their daily routines—generated an eeriness I could not shake.

I arrived in front of the building that housed Defence for Children International–Palestine, one of the six designated just months earlier. As I walked up two flights of stairs, I passed the Health Work Committees— the organization at the center of Israel's dossier. In January 2020, the organization had been designated an "outlaw organization" by Israel, laying the groundwork for the escalated attacks that ensued.[73] The IDF subsequently arrested five employees of the Health Work Committees on suspicion of "misappropriating funds to PFLP activities using false financial reports of the organization."[74] Two former Health Work Committees accountants, Said Abdat and Amro Hamuda, previously fired from the organization for financial misconduct, testified in Israeli interrogation that the six organizations named in the ministry's October designation had links to the PFLP. Their testimonies, allegedly extracted under torture in Israeli interrogation, constituted the basis for the evidence Israel used to justify its designation. In June 2021, Israeli forces raided and closed the Ramallah office of the Health Work Committees. A month later, the IDF arrested Shatha Odeh, the organization's director and held her in Israeli administrative detention for a year. She was released in June 2022 without being charged with a crime. I paused for a moment in front of the door of Health Work Committees, where the placard still hung, registering the intricacies and relational webs underwriting this latest episode of a much longer story.

I entered the DCI–P office and facing me were two young staffers both hunched over a computer staring intently at the screen. I thought back to a conversation I had just days prior with a policy analyst regarding the impli-

FIGURE 10. Sign outside Defence for Children International–Palestine, Ramallah.

Photo by author, 2021.

cations of Israel's designation on the professional careers of young employees who work for these organizations. Google searches under their names, she pointed out, now associate them with terrorist organizations, a stigma that will follow them into their future careers.[75] As intended, the impacts of the designation reverberated far and wide. I looked around the main room as I waited for the director. To my right was the desk where Khaled Quzmar, the director of DCI–P, and I had talked two years previously and onto which the CCTV feed that had captured Israel's raid was centered. I noticed the plants by his desk were gone but most everything else looked the same. Routines carried on—lawyers sorted through case files; staffers fielded calls and replied to emails; at the same time, everyone braced for what might come. The designation had created a gray space of uncertainty: no one knew when a raid might occur, who might get arrested and when, what law, or whose law, would apply, and for how long the organization would be permitted to function. The production of chaos and uncertainty, as many underscored, was precisely the point; meanwhile work carried on.

Khaled greeted me, and we retreated to a separate room. I remarked on developments since our last interview roughly two years prior. At that point, DCI–P had been sustaining attacks by the MSA and UK Lawyers for Israel, among other groups. It was speculated at the time that the attacks were motivated in large part by DCI–P's participation in a bill introduced in US Congress to prevent US tax dollars from being used to violate the rights of Palestinian children in Israeli military detention. DCI–P had also worked openly in support of the BDS movement. Much like the latest designation, the attacks sought to progressively strain and constrict their relations and networks of connection among funders, banking, allies, and partners. As a precautionary measure, Arab Bank, concerned about past lawsuits waged by Zionist groups, froze DCI–P's bank transfers, while PayPal blacklisted them entirely. They were also subjected to extensive auditing, which consumed the greater part of their organizational labor and time. The strategy, then as now, appeared to be centered on exerting pressure on DCI–P's networks of connections, intermediaries, financial means of subsistence. The seeds of Israel's designation were planted years before—this was part of the long war.

Discontented with the argument that the discovery of Pegasus was the motivating factor behind the ministry's designation, I asked Khaled to share with me his thoughts on the "why now" question. DCI–P, like most of the organizations targeted, had been around since before the start of Oslo; it had, in fact, just celebrated its thirtieth anniversary. For the first fifteen years, Khaled told me, the Israelis did not intervene in their work. This was due, in his analysis, to the fact that at that time DCI–P focused primarily on documenting human rights violations on the part of both Israel and the Palestinian Authority. It was when the organization moved to demand accountability at the international level that Israel began to intervene.[76] In 2014, DCI–P started to build a case against Israel in the ICC for its violations of international law, including the Geneva Conventions and the Conventions on the Rights of the Child. It had also started advocating in Washington for the passage of a bill prohibiting US taxpayer funding for the military detention of children the world over, including in Israel.[77]

In Khaled's analysis, it was DCI–P's turn to the international sphere, combined with sensitivity surrounding the issue of child detention specifically, that made it a target for Israel. As he pointed out, "Human rights violations against children are universally condemned. Israel does not want a trail of its violations of the rights of Palestinian children following it to the ICC." "Israel," he added, "is trying manage the field of visibility for its crimes." Indeed, as a liberal settler–colonial power, Israel has long invested in performing adherence to international legal norms and ethical compliance. As Talal Asad observes, what distinguishes liberal from illiberal violence is not the violence itself but rather performances around that violence.[78] As he argues, "moderns believe that unlike barbarians and savages, civilized fighters act within a legal-moral framework."[79] Ayca Çubukçu points out that violence enacted by liberal modern states is framed as "virtuous and caring," counterposed to terrorist violence framed as "vicious and cruel." "Liberal violence is 'rule bound,' whereas terrorist violence is lawless."[80] Indeed, Israel seeks to gain legitimacy by counterposing its violence (ethical, regulated, rule bound) to that of the Palestinians (horrific, irrational, lawless). In creating a trail to the ICC, Al-Haq and DCI–P, among other organizations, effectively undermine the very narrative Israel promulgates about itself and projects to the world.

The story of Al-Haq is similar to that of DCI–P. Among the oldest of Palestinian human rights organizations, Al-Haq, founded in 1979, has garnered respect both within Palestine and internationally for its longstanding record of human rights advocacy. Like DCI–P, it serves as a crucial conduit through which information regarding Israel's activities in Palestine is channeled to the outside world. Many international agencies and organizations rely on the information Al-Haq provides. In recent years, Al-Haq has played a pivotal role in providing evidence to the ICC for its investigation of potential war crimes committed by Israel in the occupied territories.[81]

I had the opportunity to speak with Al-Haq's director, Shawan Jabarin, just hours before I was due to leave Palestine. Shawan had just returned from Europe where he was meeting with donors to discuss Israel's latest designation. We met on a cold, rainy day in Ramallah. As I ascended the stairwell to Al-Haq's office, I came upon a placard hung outside the entrance that read:

> Established in 1979 to protect and promote human rights and the rule of law in the occupied Palestinian territory (OPT). Al-Haq documents violations of the individual and collective rights of Palestinians in the OPT, irrespective of the identity of the perpetrator, and seeks to end such breaches by way of advocacy before national and international mechanisms and by holding the violators accountable.

I wondered how this designation might impact Al-Haq's ability to continue this legacy.

Our last meeting had taken place in 2019. The signs leading to this moment were already present. The MSA's "Terrorists in Suits" had recently been published, in which Al-Haq and Shawan in particular had been profiled. The list of Al-Haq's offenses included participation in the UN fact-finding mission for the Goldstone Report, leading the legal effort against Israel in The Hague, and coordinating with international groups and coalitions to promote BDS. In the report, Shawan, coined "Dr. Jekyll and Mr. Hyde" (by Israel's Supreme Court), was alleged to have a "dual identity," one part human rights activist, one part "terror operative."[82] Shawan then, just as now, seemed largely unfazed by the allegations made against him. He had long been engaged in human rights advocacy in Palestine and had suffered the consequences for it. He had been arrested multiple times by Israel, held in administrative detention, and placed under a travel ban for seven years, yet he remained undeterred in his work.[83] As one of his colleagues relayed, even when held inside an Israeli prison in the 1980s and 1990s, Shawan continued to document Israel's human rights violations.[84]

Shawan wasted no time putting this moment in its proper context. "I think it's a continuum," he began. This process started fourteen years ago, he noted, echoing Dakwar's analysis, when Al-Haq, along with Al Mezan, had come under attack by Israel for participating in the fact-finding mission for the Goldstone Report. Al-Haq also played a key role in encouraging PA president Mahmoud Abbas to pursue non-member observer status in the United Nations, which was granted by the General Assembly in 2012, a move that paved the way for Palestinians to pursue a case in the ICC. So too had Al-Haq adopted a lead role in building a case against Israel in the ICC, which brought reprisals on the organization, Shawan in particular, and the lawyer representing Al-Haq in The Hague.[85]

In leveraging international mechanisms of accountability, Al-Haq, like the other designated groups, had "crossed the line," as Shawan put it, and were to be policed back into place. The designation, as per Israel's calculations, would function as a counterinsurgency tactic to rein these groups back into "acceptable" modalities of behavior—or to simply eliminate them. As a legal researcher at Al-Haq contended, "To designate as a terrorist organization is among the easiest of ways to destroy."[86] Of considerable concern to Israel, Shawan suggested, was the growing resonance between what Palestinians have long asserted—in his words, that Israel's occupation is one of apartheid and colonialism—and analyses put forward by mainstream human rights organizations, such as Amnesty International and Human Rights Watch.[87] "International, regional, and local organizations now [have] the same language; [they have] reached the same conclusion. This is what concerns Israel," Shawan asserted, and the designation, in his view, was aimed at isolating those Palestinian groups at the center of these developments.

Yet this counterinsurgency tactic on the part of Israel, he asserted, would ultimately fail. Even as the TO designation rendered Al-Haq and the others exceptionally vulnerable to escalated attacks and violence and put them at risk of institutional collapse, it would not achieve, in his analysis the desired aim of rendering them silent and passive. "They can raid [us], arrest us, [and] freeze our funds . . . penalize anyone who works with, helps, or partners with [us]," but these measures, he contended, would not deter them from continuing with this work; the designation, he argued, has in fact had the oppositive effect: it has rejuvenated and infused new energy into the human rights work these groups undertake in Palestine, a point further explored later on this in this chapter. "We are operating on different principles," he said. "This is not just a salary for us."

Even as the designation, in Shawan's view, would not dissuade them from their larger vision, many have remarked on the distinct challenges the designation imposes on the very inputs—the financial flows—on which these organizations depend, at least in their current form, due in no small part to how Oslo transmuted Palestinian politics from grassroots, popular mobilizations and movements to institutionalized, donor-dependent forms. Remarking on the asphyxiatory processes the classification activates, one Al-Haq staffer contended that the main concern right now is about the war of attrition that would ensue through the domain of finance and funding.

WAR THROUGH FINANCE

In January 2022, the Dutch government announced it was rescinding its funding to UAWC despite its admission that the group had no organizational ties to the PFLP.[88] The Dutch had been UAWC's lead funder since 2013. Soon thereafter, a Finnish Christian missionary group, Felm, cut its financial ties to Defence for Children International–Palestine. Similar to the Dutch, Felm confirmed there was no evidence of misused funds. "We have actively monitored the use of the money and it has been used for work advancing children's rights," stated Rolf Steffansson, Felm's executive director.[89] However, Steffansson expressed concern about the potential banking implications if it continued to fund the organization. "The Israeli designation had made it impossible to maintain ties," Steffansson explained. "It could have impacted the work we do in thirty countries through banking services for example."

Other European funders have echoed Felm's concerns surrounding the implications of funding entities encoded as "high risk" in financial systems and networks. The European Union likewise suspended its funding to two of the designated organizations.[90] Concerns surrounding the impact of Israel's designation on the financial flows on which these organizations rely preoccupied many within the designated groups and their supporters. As Fuad Abu Saif, UAWC's director, relayed to me in late December 2021:

> [With] this designation, I think we will have financial problems. We know the purpose from this designation is to scare the donor and they

more or less succeeded in that. . . . They are asking themselves how are they going to fund these six organizations? And they are waiting for their capitals to answer. I think we are in front of a new financial crisis as six organizations with this designation. . . . [We tell the donors] even if slow down your funds, it's like a kind of sending a message to them [Israel] that they are succeeding, and they will expand the designation to others. Recently NGO Monitor report mentioned sixteen members, including PNGO which means it's not sixteen organizations; it's all Palestinian civil society. They want to silence us and all. And that's the problem. That's the problem actually.[91]

A banker in Ramallah who agreed to speak with me anonymously relayed the game at play. As he explained, within the global financial system, monetary flows are regulated in relation to a perceived risk calculation.[92] He explained how if, as a banker, he opens an account for someone later found to be connected to a terrorist network, then he and the institution for which he works can be held accountable. Accordingly, financial institutions, much like the aid contractors and intermediaries discussed in Chapter 2, have adopted a risk-averse position to avoid potential liability for terrorist financing and the trafficking of other illicit flows. The designation casts its imprint far and wide. In the shadows of his statement is the story of Arab Bank, sued twice, once in US courts and a second time by Israel, for maintaining accounts of Hamas members.[93] The operative logic here, the banker described, is that of risk aversion.

The banker's remarks index a growing trend in the global financial system in the post–9/11 world wherein financial institutions, including donor agencies, adopt a defensive positioning vis-à-vis entities perceived as high risk—a practice known as "de-risking"—often refusing them financial services to avoid running afoul of terrorism financing laws, sanction regimes, and other compliance measures, including Financial Action Task Force standards.[94] Responsibility for compliance with task force and other policymaking bodies—including the UN Security Council, the European Union, and the US Treasury, among others—is effectively offloaded onto financial institutions, conscripting them in turn to act as "monitoring and enforcement arms" enlisted to "identify, track and stop illicit money flows."[95] Banks are moreover required to ensure they are not in breach of multiple national and supranational sanctions lists, including perhaps the most influential in the global sanctions regime, the US Treasury OFAC list.

The adoption of a risk-averse posturing has meant that banks increasingly refuse financial services to clients perceived as too risky on account of any number of factors, including geographic location, presumed proximity to or involvement in criminal/terrorist networks, or inclusion on any number of sanctions lists.[96] A similar logic has permeated the donor world, as donors too have adopted a risk-averse position for fear of reprisal by their own financial institutions, and have accordingly severed financial ties with partners perceived as too great a risk to fund. Donors, like banks, do not require evidence of a criminal or terrorist link to sever a financial relationship. Mere allegation, as with the ministry's designation, carries with it the power to shift an entity into the suspect category. As per donor calculations, entities carrying a high-risk factor are often deemed not worth the risk of maintaining financial ties. Felm's retraction of funding to DCI–P and the Dutch rescinding support for UAWC, alongside EU suspension of funds to two designated groups, demonstrate the operative logic of de-risking at work.

The Palestinians sit at the intersection of multiple factors that render them particularly suspect in global financial systems and networks. The discursive power Israel has wielded to construct the Palestinian subject as always potentially terrorist, combined with the inclusion of Palestinian groups on terrorism lists, alongside a coordinated campaign waged on the part of Israel and affiliated organizations to eliminate funds to Palestinian NGOs (see Chapter 4), has meant that Palestinians have long been discriminated against within the global financial system. When I met with Sahar Francis, the director of Addameer, in 2019, she spoke about ongoing complications that Addameer, DCI–P, and other Palestinian institutions had faced in the financial system. European funds to Addameer had been frozen by the Bank of Palestine on account of undisclosed security concerns, while DCI–P had their entire PayPal account frozen.[97] The Health Work Committees also had their accounts shut down. Other Palestinian NGOs not included in the ministry's 2021 designation had transfers blocked and accounts frozen. A senior staffer at the Applied Research Institution in Bethlehem relayed that the organization's funds had been frozen on account of a bank hold.[98] Stories of blocked transfers and frozen accounts abounded. Israel's designation

intensified trends already in motion, trends that lead us back to developments set in motion by Bush's declared "war on the financial infrastructure
of terror." The tools to squeeze Palestinian organizations, one staffer at Addameer remarked, have been in formation for some time.[99]

However, the ministry's designation adds a further layer of complica-
tion to the continued flow of funds. National lists and sanctions lists are
embedded into global financial flows. Any transaction, for instance, conducted through the US dollar (USD) requires a US-based correspondent
bank through which the transaction must take place, even if the transaction occurs between two non-US entities. Accordingly, the correspondent
financial institutions fall under US Treasury jurisdiction—"all transactions
that pass through them . . . come under the OFAC jurisdiction and must be
blocked if they are in violation of OFAC Sanctions."[100] As a joint report by
NYU and the EU Public Interest Clinic explains,

> The importance of the US dollar internationally—and the fear other
> banks may have of losing access to risk-averse US correspondent banks
> and potentially violating OFAC's material support provisions—means
> that most major financial institutions around the globe integrate com-
> pliance with OFAC in their due diligence work, even in transactions in
> which there is absolutely no connection to US dollars, US persons, or US
> jurisdiction.[101]

In this way, the OFAC sanctions regime is embedded into global financial flows, transporting, in effect, the US national security apparatus into
sites and transactions that may never, and often do not, take place within the
United States. This has potentially dire implications for the designated six
if the United States opts to "silently impose" Israel's designation, as Francis
put it—or donors might opt to cut ties with the designated groups for fear
of losing access to risk-averse US corresponding banks. If the United States
opts to silently enforce Israel's designation, transactions converted into US
dollars—the global reserve currency—could be frozen or blocked, the ramifications of which would be dire for the designated six. As Francis noted, a
silent endorsement from the United Sates would "allow these restrictions to
take place and at the end, we will not be able to work. . . . This is why we are
pushing that they should have a clear position," she added. A similar prob-

lem emerges vis-à-vis transactions trafficking through any Israeli financial institution, which for Palestinians constitutes most transactions. given that the Palestinian economy is structurally tied to the New Israeli Shekel (NIS).

A topological technology that fragments, disassembles, and reorganizes sociopolitical formations and relationalities, the designation sets into motion a gradual process of severing these organizations from the financial networks on which they rely; it mobilizes, à la Salamanca, an asphyxiatory modality of power that may carry the potential to collapse, or at the very least, damage the ability of these organizations to keep functioning. This is the "slow but long game," as the director of one of the designated groups put it.[102] She further underscored that the UN and other international legal bodies depend on the information and reports these organizations generate. "If they are collapsed," she pointed out, "there will be "virtually no information coming out [of Palestine]."[103] The designation, in other words, institutes a kind of double constriction of both financial and information flows. Indeed, as Diana Buttu argues, Israel's designation is an attempt "to silence these organizations by making it impossible for them to be funded."[104] This process of slow suffocation hardly garners global attention—it is not "Shock and Awe," nor Cast Lead. It nonetheless sets into motion a protracted, "uneventful" destruction that is perhaps most insidious because it hardly registers as violence at all.

EXHAUSTION POINTS

Israel's latest designation must be understood within a longer history of counterinsurgency warfare in Palestine:[105] from British attempts to pacify the Arab Revolt of 1936–39; to Israel's "iron wall of bayonets" predicated on the belief that colonization can only develop in the context of "an iron wall which the native population cannot break through";[106] to the development of a sophisticated closure regime, permit system, and tiered citizenship; to the Oslo Accords, which resulted in the unprecedented fragmentation of the Palestinian movement, the production of an aid-dependent population, and the conditioning of that aid in accordance with settler–colonial prerogatives. This designation, as one staffer at Al-Haq argued, is part and parcel of a "broader colonial policy" with the aim being to "silence and curb our work."[107] "They are now resorting to authoritarian technologies like the terrorist classification" to achieve these ends, asserted another staffer at Al-Haq.[108]

And yet—even as this war might feel all-encompassing, especially for the designated, this most recent escalation might also be pushing the war to its limits. For example, it has failed, thus far, to silence and collapse these institutions, and has instead, effected the opposite. It has infused new life into solidarity politics among Palestinians predicated on mutual aid and exchange. It has also compelled a critical discussion about the authoritarian nature of the terrorist organization designation, as one interlocutor put it.[109] "Israel did not expect this kind of a response," he added. The absolute power of terrorism discourse, in this moment, might be seeing its limits. I explore these productive effects in turn.

———

I was sitting in the living room of an apartment turned makeshift office. The main office of the Union of Agricultural Work Committees had been raided a few months prior and closed under Israeli miliary order. For now, UAWC was renting a flat in a residential neighborhood in Ramallah, the kitchen serving as a coffee station, the dining room now cluttered with desks and laptops, a bedroom now the director's office. UAWC's director, Fuad Abu Saif, was running late from another meeting. The designation had made everyone frantic, operating in a kind of permanent crisis management mode.

Fuad and I had last spoken in 2019, shortly after they had started experiencing an escalating series of attacks from Zionist groups charging UAWC with being "terrorist affiliated." UAWC had in 2013 made Area C a principal focus of its work and not heeded warnings by Israel to change focus. Its Dutch-funded land development programs in Area C provided direct support to Palestinian farmers to help them remain on their lands in the face of threats by settlers backed by the army. Since this point, UAWC had sustained escalating attacks from the MSA, UK Lawyers for Israel, Regavim and other state-affiliated organizations, which targeted both the organization itself and its funding sources. As Fuad relayed,

> From 2013 we launched a large land development program in Area C. That was a milestone. [At this point] we started feeling that it [the attacks] was becoming more systematic, planned, bigger. It started with letters to donors. UK Lawyers for Israel sent I don't know how many letters to all of our donors, but that had no consequences on our work. There's no evidence; we know what's behind it. We didn't care about it

in the beginning. We even decided not to respond to any of these allegations. Over the years, the Israelis kept saying things to us like, "Area C,
if you keep going you'll have problem." . . . We explained, look there's no
way to compromise here. We are an agriculture organization. We protect
the land. . . . On October 19th they designated us a terrorist organization.
[This is] a dangerous escalation—declaring us terrorist according to the
2016 law in Israel. It's like no other law.[110]

At the time of this conversation, the Dutch had put UAWC under investigation, carried out by a third party, Proximities Risk Consultancy. The Netherlands would soon terminate financial ties to the group despite Proximities
having found no organizational ties to the PFLP. Despite the blows to the
organization, Fuad saw this moment as productive. He shared how after the
raid of their offices in July, which in his words, "destroyed and affected everything, [including] the farmers and employees," the farmers, whom they
had been supporting for decades, were now asking UAWC how they could
support them. In this moment of heightened precarity and violence, different relationalities and solidarities were emergent. As Fuad explained,

> We've received messages from the farmers and the representatives of
> farmers in different areas is that they are ready to support, in different
> ways. In some areas, in Salfit, for example they offered us houses; in
> Hebron they offered us some materials in Area C where they have some
> facilities. . . . This is a different solidarity message.

Al-Haq shared similar experiences to that of UAWC in the wake of the
designation. As Shawan Jabarin described:

> This is one of the things that we discovered. We discovered that the
> people and the power that maintain our society is high; it is very high.
> We felt this from the actions of the people. We felt this from the action
> of the municipalities. We felt this from the action of victims and every-
> one. They came here, people came to the office to show their solidarity
> and they are standing behind us. The people said, "We are ready. We will
> work voluntarily for you." This is the action of our people. . . . Organiza-
> tions said to us: "If they close your office, come here to our offices; our
> offices are open. If they close your accounts, our accounts are open, and
> we will channel you your money.

He added, "To be honest with you, I haven't discussed the banking system and how it will work. Let that happen." This line struck me. Shawan's comment indexes the limits of Israel's power. It can make Al-Haq (and the other five organizations) "radioactive" as Dima Khalidi put it, most notably at the international scale, yet within Palestine there are different forces at play. Even as the designation might have made these organizations "radioactive" for funders and international institutions, it has *within* Palestine fostered different kinds of solidarities and relationalities that notably depart from the dominant Oslo model of politics (or anti-politics), which transformed a broad-based popular movement into fragmented, foreign donor-dependent, professionalized institutions. Under this model, an urban middle class driven by a "individualistic ethos" sought social mobility—what Lisa Taraki describes as the rise of a "new normal politics."[111] It has created, in a sense, a radical rupture in the Oslo-induced normalized order of things, and is breathing new life into the reactivation of a community-based, grassroots solidarity politics that has long been part and parcel of the Palestinian historical tradition.[112]

It is still unclear how this story will play out; however, what is clear is that this moment a significant something otherwise is emerging[113]—hyper aid securitization is perhaps surfacing the very limits of aid. While Israel's terrorist designation has animated a different kind of politics within Palestine, it has also propelled significant developments on the global stage. Israel's branding of some of the most reputable Palestinian human rights groups as "terrorist organizations" has provoked widespread international condemnation. Prominent human rights organizations have charged Israel with deploying tactics utilized by "totalitarian regimes."[114] In a statement released shortly after the ministry's announcement, the Israeli human rights organization B'Tselem asserted that Israel's designation "is not merely declarative. It is an act characteristic of totalitarian regimes, with the clear purpose of shutting down these organizations."[115] In a similar vein, Human Rights Watch and Amnesty International contextualized the designation within a longer historical trajectory, arguing that while Israeli authorities have for decades "systematically sought to muzzle human rights monitoring and punish those who criticize its repressive rule over Palestinians," this designation constitutes an "alarming escalation" that directly threatens to "shut down the work of Palestine's most prominent civil society organizations."[116] Meanwhile, UNHCR and other international bodies charged that the designation signals a dangerous escalation in the deepening entanglement of counterterrorism infrastructures and aid.[117]

Suffice it to say that international condemnation of Israeli violence absent any real pursuit of accountability for that violence has long been part of the Palestinian experience. This moment may prove to be no different. There is, though, something productive in this yet-again moment of international condemnation. In this moment we are arguably seeing a weakening of the absolute power of the terrorism discourse. That terrorism designations ultimately rest on executive decisionism, coupled with the violence that the classification itself enables, has, for increasing numbers of people, laid bare the authoritarian nature of the terrorist designation itself. And while Palestinians have long argued that the discourse on terrorism functions as a colonial technology of policing and counterinsurgency, this analysis, in more diluted form, is now circulating within mainstream human rights circles. In short, Israel's designation—even as it exacts violence on these organizations, their staff, and beneficiaries—has not achieved the desired effect: it has not only emboldened the work of the designated groups, but it has also laid bare what Shawan Jabarin called the "fascist nature of the TO designation itself." Power trips up over itself, he added. "Power is leaky." Israel did not expect this outcome, as another staffer at Al-Haq noted.[118]

Israel's designation has propelled a critical discussion about the authoritarian nature of the terrorist designation itself. As an Al-Haq staffer contended, Israel's embrace of authoritarian tools to manage the optics of its global image, most especially in the ICC, has undermined its own claim to adhere to liberal principles, the rule of law, and other liberal precepts. Likewise, for the director of Bisan, Israel's conflation of human rights with terrorism is instructive. As he argued, this designation lays bare how the charge of terrorism is used to police and manage Palestinian life, politics, thought. "This is the kind of state [Israel] is," he asserted. "This is really important for people to understand."[119]

In a rare move, a resolution (HR 751) has been introduced in the US House of Representatives condemning the "repressive designation by the Government of Israel of six prominent Palestinian human rights and civil society groups as terrorist organizations" and calling on the president and State Department to "publicly condemn this authoritarian and antidemocratic act of repression." The global discourse on terrorism law and designations, as one

Al-Haq staffer contended, is finally shifting. "Israel cannot control the narrative anymore despite its efforts. It is resorting to authoritarian technologies like the TO classification to silence [us]. It won't work," he proclaimed.[120]

Thus far, Israel has yet to accrue public support from any foreign power for its designation. This, of course, does not mean that states will not, over time, tacitly endorse Israel's designation—but it does indicate that Israel's power to manage the "field of visibility for its crimes," as Khaled put it, is arguably in decline. How the state will recalibrate to remedy this problem is unclear; however, suffice it to say that this heightened moment in the "long war" traced in this book might too be exposing its very limits.

ASPHYXIATION AS WAR

The economic practice of sanctions is generally conceived as a "prophylactic against war."[121] However, even as sanctions are oft framed as an alternative to war, early architects of the economic weapon were more clear-eyed in their analysis. For many internationalists of the interwar period, Woodrow Wilson for one, sanctions were understood as the "very essence of total war"[122]—"something more tremendous than war," as Wilson put it.[123] For Wilson, the power of sanctions is that it,

> brings a nation to its senses just as suffocation removes from the individual all inclinations to fight. . . . Apply this economic, peaceful, silent, deadly remedy and there will be no need for force. It is a terrible remedy. [It] is an infinitely more terrible instrument of war.[124]

The engineering of societal collapse via the forced economic strangulation and material isolation, as Wilson underscores (even as he promoted the tactic), is a particularly cruel modality of warfare due in no small part to the slow, temporally stretched and largely concealed violence such practices bring about. There is no spectacular violence to condemn, no tank to demand be withdrawn; rather populations are subjected to progressive but largely concealed debilitating destruction that manifests in the gradual evisceration of critical life-sustaining systems, in degraded health, malnutrition, and the collapse of civilian infrastructures. Indeed, as Nicholas Mulder contends, the economic weapon of sanctions "cast[s] a long-lasting socioeconomic and biological shadow over targeted societies, not unlike radioactive fallout."[125]

The asphyxiatory violence exercised through the terrorism classification operates within a similar economy of violence—a violence of forced disconnection, of ban, a violence embedded in the stroke of a pen rather than a bomb and exercised in the supposed absence of war—that is, war waged in the absence of *war*. At the same time, processes of debilitation that the terrorism classification facilitate presents us with a different temporality of war—one wherein violence is stretched over time—and a different optics of violence—there is no bomb to condemn nor troops to demand come home. It is arguably precisely because of the visual and temporal registers that slow, debilitating processes of asphyxiation evade that make blacklisting practices, sanctions regimes, and seemingly mundane financial restrictions an increasingly preferred method of warfare,[126] most notably for liberal imperial and settler–colonial powers that, as Khaled astutely put it, desire to manage the field of visibility for their crimes. So too then must we reframe our analysis to understand Bush's "stroke of a pen" some two decades ago and the ever-expanding architectures of "counterterrorism" that have proliferated in its wake, as manifestations of perpetual war in the absence of war.

Conclusion

WAR IN A LANDSCAPE OF RECEDING WAR

"I [am] not going to extend this forever war," Joe Biden announced from the White House briefing room on the heels of the US withdrawal from Afghanistan in August 2021. The United States, he contended, has "ended twenty years of war in Afghanistan—the longest war in American history."[1] Both on the campaign trail and upon assuming office, Biden pledged that he would depart from previous administrations and shrink the US military footprint, citing troop withdrawal from Afghanistan as among the most significant accomplishments towards this end. As Biden's press secretary Jen Psaki remarked just months before the US withdrawal from Afghanistan, the Biden administration is committed to ensuring it "can protect Americans from terrorist threats while ending the forever wars."[2]

While the Biden administration, journalists, and pundits alike have focused on the spectacular event of the US pullout from Afghanistan, alongside the assassination of Ayman al-Zawahiri (successor to Al-Qaeda leadership after Osama bin Laden) by a US drone one year later as evidence that the US global war on terror was coming to an end, the United States has done little to curb its war-making capacities and counterterrorism powers. It has instead further proliferated and redistributed these capacities through more opaque arrangements, legal regimes, and proxy forces rendering the operations of US power even more difficult to track.[3] The 2001 Authorization for Use of Military Force (AUMF), which was signed just weeks after September 11, 2001, and undergirds most US counterterrorism operations, remains in place; large-scale ground troops have been replaced by highly mobile and largely covert special operations forces; drone wars—what Biden prefers to call "over-the-horizon capabilities"—across Africa and Asia continue apace; terrorism lists expand (as does the list of groups with which the United States is at war[4]); US secret detention centers and black sites remain fully operational while securitized arrangements formed under the banner of the global war on terror persist. Notably, as Biden ordered the withdrawal of US troops from Afghanistan, the CIA quietly expanded a secret base in the Sahara, from which it runs drone flights to monitor activity in Libya, Niger, Chad, and Mali.[5]

While the optics of US wars have changed—brazen displays of US war power may have receded from view (at least within the United States)—the infrastructures, laws, and practices that enable the continuation of US forever wars remain fully ensconced.[6] The mechanics and manifold distributions of contemporary warfare and empire, it could be said, defy metrics. They work instead through securitized arrangements that persist in "postwar" theaters, in sprawling surveillance and intelligence infrastructures developed over the last two decades, and in emergency laws now normalized and global in scope. It is within this context of receding, persistent war that this book is situated. *Elastic Empire* foregrounds a little-known but ever-expanding war within this broader terrain of proliferation: war wrought through the securitization of aid.

LAW IN A SHADOW WORLD OF WAR

The counterterrorism legal regime examined within these pages is an ideal technology of contemporary warfare and empire in two senses. First, predicated on state decisionism and exceptionalism, this legal regime renders liberal protections and the rule of law obsolete.[7] Once an individual or organization is charged under material support laws or placed on a terrorism list, there is virtually no recourse to challenge the designation. Moreover, as per the speculative and associational security logics that underpin material support and counterterrorism laws, there need not necessarily be evidence of a crime committed (one can be targeted based on relations of association or on the presumption of what one *might* possibly do in the future) for this legal regime to apply.[8] The counterterrorism legal regime produces, in Agambenian terms, the paradoxical space of the exception: subjects targeted by it remain in a relationship with sovereign power yet are often not afforded rights, due process, or other constitutional protections, as in the case of Muhammad Salah discussed in Chapter 1.

Second, and arguably of greater utility to liberal powers, this body of law and its attendant infrastructures of surveillance and policing do not constitute exceptionally sensational displays of state power and violence, thus rendering them largely unknowable to domestic publics at large. There were no large-scale protests, for instance, after Bush's signing into force Executive Order (EO) 13224, as there were broad-based mobilizations to the US invasion of Iraq. Without implying any parity between the two actions, I nonetheless draw attention to the reality that sensational displays of state violence and power are more easily recognizable and, accordingly, more susceptible to challenge and protests. By contrast, the violence of this legal regime is concealed in mundane texts and clauses of bills virtually no one reads and embedded in humanitarian aid flows and emergency relief, rendering this legal-war technology exceptionally difficult to recognize, characterize, and challenge. So too is its violence most often enacted on racialized bodies and populations "over there" or on those othered within domestic space. These laws are selective, not sweeping, in their instrumentalization. As such, the violence that these laws enact through their attendant lists and designations, the practices of ban they activate, and the technologies of policing and surveillance they mobilize are concealed for most of us. It is precisely this unknowability that makes this legal-war infrastructure such an effective tool of liberal war and empire. Shrouded in secrecy and mundane in its application, the violence it inflicts takes place in a shadow world unknown to most of us.

Imperial formations, as Ann Stoler reminds us, are adaptive and elastic forms of rule, and she insists that we must consider why "representations surface in the *form* they do."[9] Indeed, as more spectacular forms of US warfare are in decline in the supposed "post" era of US forever wars, this legal-war regime continues to intensify and proliferate through new domains both domestically and internationally. Just months after Biden announced the withdrawal of US troops from Afghanistan and declared an end to the US forever war, the Biden White House released the first-ever National Strategy for Countering Domestic Terrorism (NSCDT), which called for new US domestic terrorism legislation in the wake of the January 6 riot at the Capitol.[10] The NSCDT argued that enhanced counterterrorism capabilities are necessary to counter the growing threat of white supremacist violence and restore exalted US values of multiculturalism, liberal democracy, and freedom. In so doing, the Biden administration capitalized on January 6 to further embolden counterterrorism powers of the US security state through narratives of liberal progress and redemption.[11] So too did the Biden administration deploy a similar liberal ethos to embolden US counterterrorism powers at the global scale and in Palestine specifically.

_____

Appealing to liberal precepts of humanitarianism, peacebuilding, and global engagement said to be lost by the isolationist, illiberal, revanchist policies of Washington policy under Trump, the Biden administration announced the restoration of US humanitarian funding to the United Nations Relief and Works Agency (UNRWA) for Palestine refugees. Prior to Trump, the United States had been UNRWA's largest donor, providing nearly a quarter of its $1.24 billion budget.[12] On July 14, 2021, the US Department of State and UNRWA signed the "Framework for Cooperation Between the United Nations Relief and Works Agency for Palestine Refugees in the Near East and the United States 2021–2022" (hereafter, Framework) in which Washington pledged to restore $135.8 million (a portion of its previous $235 million annual donation) of US funding to UNRWA for the 2021–2022 fiscal year.[13]

UNRWA Commissioner-General Philippe Lazzarini celebrated the restoration of US funds, contending that the agreement signals that UNRWA "once again [has] an ongoing partner in the United States that understands the need to provide critical assistance to some of the region's most vulnerable refugees."[14] The Framework also establishes a particular set of conditions upon which the resumption of US aid to the agency is contingent. UNRWA must ensure compliance with US counterterrorism law to resume the flow of funds cut under the Trump Administration. As outlined in the agreement,

> The Department of State seeks to ensure that none of its funds are used, directly or indirectly, to provide support to individuals or entities associ-

ated with terrorism.... In furtherance of [the] international fight against terrorism, including terrorism financing, consistent with section 301(c) of the Foreign Assistance Act of 1961 ... it is fully understood and agreed that by accepting this contribution, UNRWA certifies that it is taking all possible measures to ensure that no part of the United States contribution is being used to furnish assistance to any refugee who is receiving military training as a member of the so-called Palestine Liberation Army, or any guerilla-type organization or anyone who has engaged in any act of terrorism.[15]

It goes on to note that UNRWA commits to take "all possible measures to ensure funding provided by the United States to UNRWA does not provide assistance to, or otherwise support, terrorists or terrorist organizations." Accordingly, the Framework directly activates the US counterterrorism legal regime examined in this book, embedding it into humanitarian and emergency relief flows administered through a UN agency, the ramifications of which are significant. UNRWA, as a UN agency, had previously been protected, in part, by agreements to which it is bound under international humanitarian law. The agency is required to adhere to UN Security Council resolutions and other international counterterrorism instruments.[16] UNRWA does not, however, as per UN policy, vet against individual national lists.

The Framework arguably changes that. As per the agreement, UNRWA is required to ensure compliance with US counterterrorism regulations rather than simply the UN sanctions list, as required for every other UN agency to determine eligibility criteria.[17] Accordingly, the agreement effectively conscripts a UN humanitarian agency to uphold US terrorism measures, resulting, in turn, in the supplanting of international law with national terrorism regulations. In so doing, it arguably modifies UNRWA's mandate. UNRWA was established by UN General Assembly Resolution 302 (IV) in December 1949 to administer relief for Palestinian refugees, defined as "persons whose normal place of residence was Palestine during the period 1 June 1946 to 15 May 1948, and who lost both home and means of livelihood as a result of the 1948 conflict"—eligibility for relief is based on these criteria, not on the subjective calculations of foreign states concerning who is and who is not deemed a terrorist.

Sara Pantuliano and Victoria Metcalfe note that international humanitarian law "regulates the behavior of all parties in equal fashion," irrespective of their political, religious, and other personal beliefs and affiliations (while still distinguishing between civilian and combatant), whereas counterterrorism legislation begins with the premise that one party of a conflict is (or may be) criminal.[18] There is a marked difference between being a

> combatant under clearly defined criteria established in international humanitarian law, and being designated on a sanction list for a broad range of reasons, often based on individual states' interests, many of which would not affect a person's civilian status under international humanitarian law.[19]

Moreover, even if one is deemed a combatant and thus excluded from receiving aid under international humanitarian law, the relation of exclusion would not expand to the combatant's family or dependents. This is not the case with US counterterrorism legislation, which would necessarily exclude entire families from UNRWA's services and assistance if the head of a household is designated under the US determination of terrorist.

Thus the imposition of counterterrorism criteria on UNRWA's programming effectively creates new forms of exclusion within the registered UNRWA refugee pool. Under US law, those excluded from receiving assistance would include, but are not limited to: any refugee with perceived connections to a US-designated group; those who are deemed to have engaged in "terrorist activity," which as the Palestinian refugee rights organization BADIL points out, invariably translates into any activity that Israel perceives as a threat to its settler–colonial rule; as well as broad categories of refugees who, for any reason, are believed to be associated directly or indirectly with someone belonging to a designated group.[20] The expansive associational logic on which US terrorism law is predicated could easily translate into the exclusion of entire families from UNRWA's services and assistance if the head of a household is deemed to have connections to a designated group, or if a family member has been imprisoned by Israel.

Chapter 2 explored how these associational logics and banning practices have translated with respect to USAID flows, especially in Gaza, wherein the material support ban cast a net so wide that any relation with the governing authority—Hamas—was prohibited. Similarly, we saw how water pipes in the Bethlehem Municipality could not be funded with any portion of US assistance given that members of a US-designated FTO served on the municipal council. Notably, Hamas, while listed by the United States as an FTO, and thus sanctioned by the United States, is not listed in the UN Consolidated List, to which UNRWA was bound prior to the Washington-brokered agreement. "It is thus clear," as BADIL notes, that "this regulation, if applied rigorously, would exclude a large number of UNRWA beneficiaries," thus directly threatening "Palestine refugee status and other persons eligible for UNRWA's services."[21] It could also result in the considerable loss of employment, as UNRWA staffers, many of whom are refugees, would be prohibited from working on any US-funded portion of UNRWA projects.

The infusion of US counterterrorism law into UNRWA's humanitarian programming not only redefines UNRWA's field of operability, but it also conscripts UNRWA to undertake policing and surveillance functions on behalf of the United States among the refugee population it serves. Pursuant to the agreement, UNRWA arguably must ensure refugees, UNRWA employees, and vendors do not run afoul of US counterterrorism laws and policies and is required to transmit key information to the US government. This obligation not only erodes trust in the refugee population UNRWA is mandated to serve but it also transforms UNRWA into "a security proxy" for the United States.[22] As Salah Abdulatti, a Gaza-based lawyer, argues, "The agreement will transform the agency from a service agency to an intelligence agency whose goal is to provide security information."[23]

Just as Palestinians foresaw the implications of Bush's little-known order signed in the immediate aftermath of September 11, 2001, resulting, in turn, in a boycott of USAID in subsequent years, the implications of this latest Washington-brokered agreement are not lost on Palestinian refugees, most especially in the Gaza Strip.[24] Soon after the Framework signing, Palestinians in the Gaza Strip organized a conference in Al-Shati refugee camp to call for the rescinding of the Framework. A statement released by the Joint Refugee Committee asserted the Framework affords "donors, especially the US, the right to oversee UNRWA's overall work, allowing its performance to be judged based on the US concept and not according to international law" and called on UNRWA Commissioner-General Lazzarini to retract the deal in an official letter.[25] UNRWA has not, at the time of this writing, issued a response. While the Biden administration might have departed from its predecessor, opting to resuscitate (a portion of) humanitarian assistance to the Palestinians, it has simultaneously amplified and expanded the tentacles of the US security state into new domains—not through formally declared wars and spectacular violence, but instead through more opaque arrangements, muted and mundane in their application and underwritten by an appeal to humanitarian intent.

The expansion of this "little known war" has been a throughline of the US security state over consecutive decades, irrespective of whether centrists, liberals, or conservatives sit at the helm of power. (In fact, key legal infrastructure of this body of law, as Chapter 1 details, was established under Bill Clinton in the 1990s.) From the International Emergency Economic Powers Act in the 1970s, to EO 12947 and the Antiterrorism and Effective Death Penalty Act in the 1990s, to EO 13224 in 2001, counterterrorism law compounds layer upon layer, rarely ever being rescinded or scaled back. This body of law, as Lara Friedman puts it, is "like zombie legislation. It lives forever."[26]

In the era of the supposed eclipse of US forever wars, this law further entrenches expands, and amplifies US war-making and counterterrorism powers into ever-expansive domains and notably, in this case, embeds itself in refugee relief and emergency aid. Moreover, as we saw with the case of USAID, processes of aid securitization spearheaded by Washington metastasized across and were normalized within nearly all donor streams (Chapter 4). There is ample evidence to suggest the infusion of national counterterrorism laws into UNRWA aid streams as stipulated by the Washington-brokered Framework will not be limited to US donations. UNRWA's top government donors, other than the United States, are European (barring Japan and Canada). As Chapter 5 demonstrated, Israel and Israel-supporting NGOs have concentrated their efforts on curbing inbound aid flows to the Palestinians from Europe.

If indeed asphyxiatory violence aims to slowly erode conditions of livability, then we will likely see, in the coming years, more concentrated and intensified efforts on the part of Israel and settler organizations to force European donor states to emulate the Washington–UNRWA agreement. This would ultimately transform UNRWA into foremost an enforcement agency of foreign terrorism laws while creating massive exclusions in the Palestinian refugee pool. The infusion of this counterterrorism regime into UNRWA's aid flows could ultimately, if fully enforced, collapse UN-administered relief to Palestinian refugees, making relief contingent not on the loss of "both home and means of livelihood" during the founding of Israel but instead on the highly subjective distinction of terrorist/non-terrorist, itself an ambiguous and elastic distinction, as determined by foreign capitals.

Many speculated the decision by the Trump administration to withdraw US contributions to UNRWA was part of a broader strategy to dissolve the agency itself. The Biden administration has opted for a different tactic—to repurpose the agency into a securitized medium wherein it is primarily accountable to the policing and counterinsurgency dictates of a far-flung, yet intimately embedded, capital. Given that UNRWA lost nearly a quarter of its annual aid revenue with the loss of US donations in 2018, it is unlikely it will rescind the Framework and risk the withdrawal of US funds again. This is not the stuff of spectacular warfare, which is precisely the point. Headlines surrounding Biden's resumption of US flows to UNRWA abounded—hardly mentioned was the inclusion of this little-known (outside of Palestine) counterterrorism stipulation. The work this body of law performs on the bodies, spaces, and institutions it touches and into which it embeds, as this book aims to show, matters—both in Palestine and beyond.

———

When I sat across from Yousef some years ago at Yasmeen café in Nablus, an important story about the workings of the US security state presented itself. While few outside of Washington had heard of Bush's little-known order, Palestinians had not the fortune of ignorance. This little-known order, and the larger counterterrorism regime to which it is connected, presented itself in their lives in innumerable ways—in their material landscapes and urban infrastructures, in their greenhouses and in preschool programs, in their local councils and municipal halls and in sites of post-bomb reconstruction. For some, like Sami, who had found a way to return to Palestine through employment with a USAID-funded institution, it presented a seemingly impossible set of options: to either police other Palestinians or forgo an opportunity to access Palestine, his home. For others, compliance with US counterterrorism dictates (and an acceptance of the exclusions they invariably produce—i.e., not being able to serve populations in certain geographical zones or with certain kinds of associations, perceived or otherwise) was part and parcel of the "aid game"—it created merely another set of conditions within an already deeply compromised structure. For others still, such as for Samira, who had played a key role in organizing the boycott of USAID, the enrollment of Palestinians into enforcing the counterterrorism dictates of Washington, effectively transforming them into serving as their own counterinsurgency force, had to be challenged and refused.

Equally this story exceeds Washington. Processes set in motion by the global war on terror have established a new normal for aid practice that will be exceedingly difficult to roll back. It is unlikely that foreign donors will disembed terrorism lists and sanctions regimes from their aid flows or that foreign capitals will rescind counterterrorism legislation and adjacent legislation that criminalizes the Boycott, Divestment, Sanctions movement. To the contrary, blacklists and terrorism laws have only multiplied; vetting has intensified, now engulfing greater swaths of the aid-receiving population and aid-administering staff; financial flows are even more securitized. The global war on terror has given rise to enhanced security infrastructures, policing mechanisms, and surveillance practices that are fundamental to the way aid works in Palestine today. As one NGO worker put it, hyper aid securitization, he asserted, "is now normalized. The US paved the way for this trend."[27] This is not to afford an all-consuming power to the workings of the US counterterrorism regime, but it is to say this little-known legal-war architecture and its embedding into aid flows and life-sustaining systems halfway around the world, stitching together Palestine and Washington in intimate though asymmetrical ways, presents to us an important story about how US empire works.

Empire, as Catherine Lutz has rightfully argued, is "in the details."[28] Indeed, a different story about the intimacies of Washington in the world emerges when we reorient the sites from which we theorize empire and warmaking from imperial capitals to the landscapes and bodies on which this power operates. As Tom Engelhardt pointed out over a decade ago, while it might be difficult for Americans to conceive that "Washington is a war capital . . . and that the norm for us is to be at war somewhere at any moment,"[29] for those situated in the playlands of US war lawyers, security strategists, and weapons contractors, these wars are hardly obscured. Indeed, for Palestinians living with the death-producing implications of US military aid to Israel, or for Yemenis with mass starvation, or those living with the toxic legacies of US militarism and colonialism in the Philippines, Japan, Guam, or Iraq, the US security state is intimately *there*, embedded in the daily textures of their lives, in the cells of their bodies, in their hunger and premature death even as it professes post-intervention, a declared "end" to war, or denies its presence altogether.

This is not to assign an all-consuming, totalizing power to the United States, for to do so would be both to ignore a primary modality of how US empire works—that is through contracted relationships and indirect controls, in "hazy" liminal spaces, and through blurred genres of rule. It would dually be to erase the agency and power of those living with the legacies and ongoing presence of US war and militarism. At the same time, and precisely because of the increasingly opaque nature of US wars as these operate across global space, it is necessary to think critically about the sites from which we analyze US war power and empire. What do we miss when we theorize empire (exclusively) from within centers of global power? How might this politics of location ultimately reproduce a story about the West even if it remains critical of it? Moreover, if indeed, imperial formations, as per Stoler, operate through diffuse, mobile technologies and opaque arrangements that render the tracings of imperial power difficult to track, what is omitted when we focus primarily on debates and developments within imperial capitals?

Samar al-Bulushi, Sahana Ghosh, and Madiha Tahir argue, we must "grapple more concretely with transnational entanglements and the question of empire," an intervention I take seriously.[30] The global war on terror is more than a set of policy documents; it is more than the distantiated view of a drone operator. It is more than charged debates among political camps in Washington pertaining to whether the AUMF should be repealed or not (though this is not inconsequential). For many across the Global South, war and empire, as Carol McGranahan and John Collins suggest, are not simply an aspect of foreign policy; they are "a way of life."[31] As I began conducting the research for this book over a decade ago, it is telling that I learned more about the US security state sitting in Nablus with Yousef where I encountered "the paper," that seemingly innocuous object that had fractured the humanitarian field and embroiled Palestinian subjects into the "security" world of

Washington, than I had in nearly three decades of living in the United States.

Responding to the call made by lowercase al-Bulushi and coauthors, *Elastic Empire* pivots our engagement with US warfare to a site where no war is declared per se, but Washington's power is nonetheless intimately present. Moving beyond representation—whether the long view from Washington or the optic of the drone operator, and critiques thereof—*Elastic Empire* employs a topological approach to US empire and war-making to consider the connectivities, embeddings, and relationalities that render Washington's punitive counterterrorism regime intimately present in the lifeworlds of those in Palestine, notably through the aid flows on which they are largely reliant. This bundling and dispersion of the US security state into humanitarian aid flows is perhaps an archetypal example of the workings of American empire. It is one where the presence of the United States, despite having no de jure claim to sovereignty or territory, is nevertheless viscerally felt, through its military aid and weapons contracts, its exertion of diplomatic pressure via supranational bodies, and the projection of regimes of sanction and punishment through financial and transnational aid flows. In turning our attention to the intimate embeddings of Washington's counterterrorism regime in the lifeworlds of Palestinians, *Elastic Empire* constructs a different theoretical apparatus of war and empire. Reorienting the view of Washington's wars from within Palestine, it tells a story about the obscured and shape-shifting manifestations of late modern empire and war, its intimate embeddings in opaque arrangements, its coupling of intimacy and denial, the continuation of war in a context of *non*-war.

The US global war on terror, ongoing for two decades, has taken over 800,000 lives, disappeared countless others, and wrought incalculable violence on racialized populations, their communities and social worlds. Despite recent pronouncements that the "longest US war" is ending, the global war on terror, and its multiple manifestations and iterations the world over, are hardly *over*. While the United States prefers to frame its interventions as temporary and limited, it has dispersed its capacities for violence and war-making within ever-evolving and elusive arrangements, mediated relationships and, as this book shows, within architectures putatively intended to ameliorate the deleterious effects of occupation and war. In turning our attention to the manifold distributions of late modern war and empire, the norms they constitute, and the social worlds they indelibly transform well after their declared end, if they are ever formally acknowledged to begin with, *Elastic Empire* puts these wars ongoing in Palestine and elsewhere back on the map, most notably because their very "unknowability" is precisely the point.

Acknowledgments

Acknowledgments are necessarily a declaration of debts. This book is a product of the people and places that have gone into its making across continents and over the course of many years. My greatest thanks goes to those in Palestine who opened their homes, workspaces, and social worlds to me and shared, at times with considerable risk to themselves, their insights, perspectives, and critiques. There are many who must remain anonymous, among them countless aid workers whose analysis and insights are all over these pages and especially those working in organizations designated as "terrorist" by Israel in 2021 and who are especially vulnerable to violence and backlash. Among those I am able to publicly name, special thanks go to Sami Khader and Wahbeh Asfour, with whom ongoing conversations helped this project grow in more ways than I am sure they realize. Nora Murad and the Dalia Association graciously opened their doors to me in the very early stages of this project and introduced me to the worlds that aid is making and unmaking in Palestine. Colleagues at the Center for Development Studies at Birzeit University also helped me cultivate a deeper understanding of critiques and analyses circulating in Palestine regarding the manifold problems inherent in foreign aid interventionism. I am especially indebted to Penelope Mitchell and Mandy Turner who provided ongoing support over the course of many research trips and integrated me into social networks that helped this project evolve into what is presented here. Thanks too are extended to Aid Watch for inviting me to present my research-in-progress to aid practitioners in Palestine for feedback and critique. Immense gratitude goes to Ubai al-Aboudi, Sahar Francis, Shawan Jabarin, Khaled Quzmar, and Fuad Abu Saif who welcomed me into their workplaces and shared crucial insights in times of great uncertainty and vulnerability.

Over the course of my many stays in Palestine and beyond in Amman and Cairo respectively, I was fortunate to have forged a rich and nurturing community of colleagues, scholars, and friends who provided intellectual support, sustenance, and friendship along the way. Special thanks goes to Nasser Abourahme, Sa'ed Atshan, Nadia Awad, Ala Alazzeh, Lori Allen, Hazem Alnamla, Nora Awaki, Tareq Baconi, Khulood Badawi, Samira Barakat, Ryvka Barnard, Najwan Berekdar, Emilio Dabed, Falastine Dwikat, Lara Friedman, Sophia Goodfriend, Neve Gordon, Jeannette Greven, Toufic Haddad, Leena Hasan, Yara Hawari, Saed Abu-Hijleh, Riham Hussein, Khaled Jarrar, Rania Jawwad, Hazem Jamjoum, Raja Khalidi, Abdullah Khalifeh, Peter Lagerquist, Jenny Kelly, Gabi Kirk, Shadi Mahmoud, Sandy Marshall, Mazen Masri, Penelope Mitchell, Nora Lester Murad, Sufian Mushasha, Tahani Mustafa, Nithya Nagarajan, Nicola Perugini, Omar Qasis, Kareem Rabie, Inès Abdel Razek, Rafeef Abdel Razek, Laura Ribeiro Rodrigues Pereira, Beesan Ramadan, Omar Jabary Salamanca, Sobhi Samour, Diala Shamas, Reem Shilleh, Jake Silver, Sophia Stamatopoulou-Robbins, Linda Tabar, Osama Tanous, Fiona Tarazi, Omar Tesdell, Mandy Turner, Shaira Vadasaria, Eyal Weizman, Allison West, and Rayya El Zein. I would also like to thank those who have helped me navigate through borders and across space, including Nirit Ben Ari, Haim Yacobi, Emily Schaeffer Omer-Man, and Noga Kadman.

The research and writing of this book were supported by fellowships and grants from the American Council of Learned Societies, Palestinian American Research Center, National Science Foundation, Mershon Center for International Security Studies at Ohio State University, and multiple fellowships from the Maxwell School of Citizenship and Public Affairs at Syracuse University. Arabic training was supported by fellowships and grants from Middlebury College Arabic Language School, Sijal Institute for Arabic Language and Culture, and the Maxwell School at Syracuse University. I am equally indebted to the many Arabic teachers I had along the way spanning Damascus, Cairo, Amman, Ramallah, and Middlebury.

Faculty and colleagues in the Department of Geography at Syracuse University, including Don Mitchell, Alison Mountz, and Jennifer Hyndman, and Osamah Khalil in the Department of History, were instrumental in pushing my thinking in expansive ways; they encouraged me to ask questions to which I did not have answers, to follow threads in the field and see where they lead, and to think more reflectively about the relationship between theory and method. At Ohio State University, Mat Coleman provided mentorship and support as the conceptual foundation for this project evolved and whose writing and thinking on the topological feature centrally. I am also indebted to two research assistants—Pádraigín O'Flynn and Nemet Alrawajfeh—who helpfully transcribed interview materials and provided invaluable research support during the final stages of this project.

A number of conferences, workshops, and working groups expanded how I think about imperiality, violence, empire, ethics, and justice. Among them: the Sovereignty and Space Working Group at Ohio State University, which brought me into conversation with Noah Tamarkin, Juno Salazar Parreñas, and Katherine Marino, among others; the Race and US Empire working group at the University of Illinois–Chicago, in which I was fortunate to think alongside Nadine Naber, Ronak Kapadia, Chandni Desai, Andy Clarno and Nicole Nguyen, and Atef Said; the Insecurity Conference at the Center for 21st Century Studies at the University of Wisconsin–Milwaukee, which entailed generative discussions with Naomi Paik, Jenna Loyd, Andrea Miller, Gloria Kim, and Richard Grusin; the Imperial Decline Conference in Florence, Italy, which included invaluable and ongoing discussions with Laleh Khalili, Lisa Hajjar, Abdullah al-Arian, Madiha Tahir, Don Mitchell, Jennifer Fluri, Sara Koopman, and Jim Tyner, and a special issue co-organized with Patricia Lopez and Léonie S. Newhouse on the question of humanitarian violence.

For commenting on earlier drafts and chapters and for offering insights to which I hope to have done some justice, I wish to thank Wadie Said, Andrea Miller, Alexis Salas, Jenna Loyd, and Elizabeth Ault, alongside anonymous reviewers at Stanford University Press and Duke University Press for helping me sharpen the conceptual framework of this project. I am especially indebted to Abigail Rosenthal for her critical, compassionate feedback and instrumental role in supporting the development of this book over the course of multiple drafts. Kate Wahl has been a steadfast supporter of this project from the outset. I am especially indebted to her, Marie-Catherine Pavel, and the production team at Stanford University Press for materializing this book into the world.

Alongside those already named, many have supported and sustained me over the years with their ideas, camaraderie, care, mentorship, and accountability, and most often a fusion thereof. Among them, I would like to thank Jenna Abell, Nora Akawi, Abdullah al-Arian, Mona Atia, Danya al-Saleh, Sophia Azeb, Kate Chandler, Charmaine Chua, Andy Clarno, Mat Coleman, Gavriel Cupita-Zorn, Chandni Desai, Meiver De la Cruz, Emily Mitchell Eaton, Joe Farag, Kristen Gerali, Lisa Hajjar, Maha Hilal, Jennifer Hyndman, Tarek Ismail, Craig Jones, Kate Kennedy, Laleh Khalili, Molly Kraft, Darryl Li, Patricia Lopez, Jenna Loyd, Rhys Machold, Monami Maulik, Andrea Miller, Andres Montoya-Montes, Nada Moumtaz, Alison Mountz, Rish Nisa, Dana Olwan, Rupal Oza, Juno Salazar Parreñas, Sharri Plonski, Linda Quiquivix, Ziad Abu Rish, Bob Ross, Anna Secor, Sherene Seikaly, Johanna Sellman, Josh Stacher, Madiha Tahir, Noah Tamarkin, Corrine Teed, Mandy Turner, Melody Wechsler, Sujith Xavier, and Rayya El Zein. Alexis Salas provided unwavering support and sustenance as I wrote much of this book in Los Angeles during the early stages of the pandemic. Sam Cohen has seen this book through to completion providing support and care as it rounded out. Finally, I would like to thank my parents, Holly and Amar Bhungalia, and sister, Amy Bhungalia, for their unfailing support and love over the many years of this book's development and for always providing a space of home. My late father did not live to see this book come to fruition, but his imprint is infused throughout. This book is dedicated to all those bound up in the messy, beautiful processes of building the decolonial futures we so desperately need now.

Notes

Introduction

1. Conversation with a senior policy analyst at a Palestinian policy think tank, Ramallah, June 2019.

2. Rabbani, "Rabbani on Israeli Annexation."

3. Rabbani, "Rabbani on Israeli Annexation."

4. Bhungalia, Greven, and Mustafa, "Shifting Contours of US Power."

5. Feldman, "Trump's Full Spectrum Assault."

6. See BADIL, *European Union Conditional Funding*; PNCRCF, "Against Terrorism and Against Conditional Funding."

7. Interview in Ramallah, July 2019.

8. Interview with an NGO director, Ramallah, July 2018.

9. Oft-touted is the statistic that Palestinians are among the highest recipients of nonmilitary foreign aid (per capita) in the world. Some $40 billion has been channeled into the West Bank and Gaza Strip since the start of the Oslo peace process in 1993. See Wildeman and Tartir, "Political Economy of Foreign Aid"; and OECD, "Qwids Query Wizard."

10. All amounts in US dollars (USD).

11. Sharp, "U.S. Foreign Aid to Israel."

12. Khalil, "At the Crossroads of Empire."

13. This is not to suggest that aid was somehow previously distinct from broader war aims (certainly the Cold War would prove otherwise) or that aid has not long served as a mechanism of pacification and control. But it is to say that the global war

on terror and the discourse of terrorism more generally has further securitized it through the concept of "terrorist financing."

14. The last time Congress officially declared war was in 1942. Since this point, US wars have been sanctioned by congressional authorizations for the use of military force. The 1964 Gulf of Tonkin Resolution authorized President Lyndon B. Johnson to use military force in Southeast Asia, constituting the basis for the Vietnam War and other anti-communist Cold War insurgencies. Likewise, two authorizations form the (domestic) legal basis for the global war on terror. Just a week following September 11th, President George W. Bush signed into law the 2001 Authorization for Use of Military Force (AUMF), which not only authorized war on Afghanistan but so too a broad array of military operations whose spatial and temporal horizons had no limits. The 2001 AUMF continues to undergird most other US counterterrorism operations to date. The AUMF of 2002, which authorized war in Iraq, likewise constitutes the principal domestic legal authority for the United States' past twenty years of post–9/11 conflict. It is the seemingly "boundless nature of the war that the AUMF helped to unleash," as Craig Jones and Michael Smith write, that has "prompted critics [such as Derek Gregory] to write of the Forever War and the Everywhere War." See Jones and Smith, "War/Law/Space," 582.

15. The deployment of elite forces under the Obama administration increased 123 percent with special operations deployments taking place in nearly 70 percent of the world's nations by 2013. Likewise, by that same year, the Obama White House oversaw an exponential rise in the US drone war. See Turse, "America's Secret War."

16. See ACLU, *Establishing a New Normal*.

17. It is important to qualify that I am referring specifically to notions of visibility and spectacularity in relation to a US audience. Indeed, for those on the receiving end of US wars, the violence experienced and lived within is hardly unseen or covert. For critiques of the militaristic temporalities and frames often deployed in Global North narratives about war, see Butler, *Frames of War*; Al-Bulushi, Ghosh, and Tahir, "American Anthropology, Decolonization, and the Politics of Location"; and Griffiths, "Geontological Time-Spaces."

18. Bush, "President Freezes Terrorists' Assets."

19. EO 13224 broadened the scope of those targeted under the material support law from individuals directly belonging to a Treasury-designated FTO to those deemed "otherwise associated" with an FTO, and it nullified the humanitarian exemption in terrorism-related cases. It moreover expanded the list of sanctioned entities from those specifically related to the Middle East peace process to a list of global entities and actors. EO 13224 created the Specially Designated Global Terrorist blacklist, consisting at the time of 27 organizations and individuals, which has

since grown to thousands of entries. And finally, EO 13224 established the ability to block US assets and deny access to US markets of foreign banks that refuse to freeze terrorist assets, which has had especially grave implications for global aid flows, as many transactions flow through US banks.

20. See Elden, *Terror and Territory*.

21. See Khalili, *Time in the Shadows*; Bell, "Civilianising Warfare"; Slim, "With or Against?"; Duffield, *Global Governance*; Bachmann, Bell, and Holmqvist, *War, Police and Assemblages of Intervention*.

22. See Weizman, *Least of All Possible Evils*; Fassin and Pandolfi, *Contemporary States of Emergency*.

23. See Bell, "Civilianising Warfare," 311–312; see also Foucault, *Security, Territory, Population*.

24. See Barkawi, "Pedagogy of 'Small Wars'"; Gregory, "The Everywhere War"; Khalili, *Time in the Shadows*; Parks and Kaplan, *Life in Age of Drone Warfare*.

25. Allen, "Powerful Assemblages?".

26. Agamben, *Homo Sacer*; Agamben, *State of Exception*; Serres and Latour, *Conversations on Science, Culture and Time*; Deleuze, *The Fold*; Deleuze, *Foucault*.

27. Law and Mol, "Situating Technoscience"; Bigo, "The Möbius Ribbon"; Martínez, "Topological Twists in the Syrian Conflict"; Law, "After ANT"; Moreira, "Surgical Monads."

28. Allen, "Powerful Assemblages? "; Allen, *Topologies of Power*; Martin and Secor, "Towards a Post-Mathematical Topology"; Gregory, *The Colonial Present*; Dixon and Jones, "Tactile Topologies of Contagion"; Lata and Minca, "The Surface and the Abyss"; Secor, "Topological City"; Cockayne, Ruez, and Secor, "Thinking Space Differently"; Joronen, "Politics of Being-Related"; Harker, *Spacing Debt*; Harker, "Debt Space."

29. Martin and Secor, "Towards a Post-Mathematical Topology," 420

30. Serres and Latour, *Conversations on Science, Culture and Time*.

31. Paasi, "Geography, Space and Topological Thinking."

32. Secor, "Topological City," 431. The "topological turn" in geography has also garnered critique among those who contend topology, with its emphasis on relationality, does not posit a conceptual framework or vocabulary that necessarily enriches our understanding of spatiality. John Allen's query of the topological, for instance, while proving generative for understanding contemporary spatial forms and complexes, has also been critiqued for his framing of the topological reworkings of power as *new*, a newness which he contrasts with an assumed topographical past. Geography has long approached space (and time) relationally, and likewise, theorized space-making as an iterative process of "taking-on-form" that is relational

and iterative rather than constituting any kind of *essence*, geometric or otherwise. See Coleman, "Topologies of Practice," 311; see also Dodge and Kitchin, "Code and Transduction of Space."

For an overview of debates concerning both the merits and shortcomings of what a topological analysis can lend to our understandings of spatialities and contemporary spatial forms, see Coleman, "Topologies of Practice"; Elden, "What's Shifting?"; Martin and Secor, "Towards a Post-Mathematical Topology"; Paasi, "Geography, Space and Topological Thinking." On Allen, see "Topological Twists"; "Three Spaces of Power"; "More Than Relational Geography?"; and *Topologies of Power*.

33. Secor, "Topological City." Breaking with linear or geometric conceptions of space, the spatiality at play in a topological arrangement is often described as one of twists and turns, folds, deformations, torsions, and severations. See Martin and Secor, "Towards a Post-Mathematical Topology," Allen, "Topological Twists," and Martínez, "Topological Twists in the Syrian Conflict."

34. Callon and Law, "Introduction: Absence," 6.

35. We could turn to the classic example offered by Michel Serres, for instance, of the crumpling a handkerchief wherein two points formerly distant are now "close, even superimposed." Conversely, if you tear the handkerchief in particular places, "two points that were close can become very distant" (Serres and Latour, *Conversations on Science, Culture and Time*, 60).

36. Likewise, we can look to the space of an operating room, as Tiago Moreira does, as another kind of topological formation constituted by a series of sociotechnical processes and relationships organized well beyond the contours of the room itself that bind it to the "'global' on which it depends [and] in which it is included." Moreira finds a turn to the topological generative for making sense of the different connections and circulations at work, from electricity flows to radiographic prints, medical technology, and specialized knowledge, which produce the space of the operating room and the activities that cohere within. The dynamics between topologies "are generative of the event" (Moreira, "Surgical Monads," 53). Likewise, we could turn to the topological relations at play in contagion, as Deborah Dixon and John Jones have done, to consider "material connections among mobile bodies," what they call "tactile topologies" of contagion. Contagion, they show, is fueled by the interplay of "materials and forces that grab onto each other, interpenetrating and reassembling at various speeds and intensities, such that diverse proximities and distances, contacts and connections, are made and remade" (Dixon and Jones, "Tactile Topologies of Contagion," 223), with COVID a befitting example. Topology, it could be said, provides a spatial lexicon to help account for the interplay of different relations, circulations, and "points of contact," which in turn produce a

"multiplicity of space-times resulting through their various intersections"—akin to the Deleuzian virtual of immanent potentialities. See Lata and Minca, "The Surface and the Abyss," 441.

37. Agamben, *Homo Sacer.*

38. See Coleman, "Immigrant Il-Legality"; Bigo, "Globalized (in)Security"; Gilbert, "Elasticity at the Canada–US Border"; Maillet, Mountz, and Williams, "Exclusion Through Imperio"; Mountz and Hiemstra, "Spatial Strategies."

39. Coleman, "Geopolitics of Engagement"; Coleman, "U.S. Statecraft"; Coleman, "Immigration Geopolitics."

40. Mountz, "The Enforcement Archipelago"; Mountz, "Where Asylum-Seekers Wait"; see also Loyd, Mitchell-Eaton, and Mountz, "The Militarization of Islands and Migration Control."

41. Mountz, "The Enforcement Archipelago," 123; italics in original.

42. Border work, as Bialasiewicz suggests, highlights the role of proxy forces, mechanisms, and neighboring states in the policing of Europe's borders. These actors, sites and mechanisms are central to European securitization strategies—they make the EU's "border-work possible." See Bialasiewicz, "Off-Shoring and Out-Sourcing," 845.

43. Lahav and Guiraudon, "Comparative Perspectives," 55; see also Coleman, "Geopolitics of Engagement."

44. Drawing on the topological interplay between interiority and exteriority, Didier Bigo deploys the topological figure of the Möbius strip as a means of grasping how the lines of internal and external security blend, blur, and merge across different realms and mediums of security practice. The Möbius strip represents for Bigo a way to chart a relationship of linkage and continuity, what he calls "the transversal dispositif" that weaves together internal and external security, war and policing, and crime and delinquency, See Bigo, ""The Möbius Ribbon"; Bigo, "Globalized (in) Security," 30.

45. Harker, *Spacing Debt*, 4.

46. For literature on contemporary imperialisms and late modern war and empire, see Li, *The Universal Enemy*; Khalili, "Utility of Proxy Detention in Counterinsurgencies"; Al-Arian, "Political Islam and Endurance of American Empire"; Kaplan, "Where Is Guantánamo?"; Li, "From Exception to Empire"; Stoler, "Degrees of Imperial Sovereignty"; Stoler with Bond, "Refractions Off Empire."

47. Li, "From Exception to Empire."

48. Al-Arian, "Political Islam and Endurance of American Empire," 3.

49. Al-Arian is referring here to Lebanese electoral law containing a "curious provision" in its governing election guidelines to allow Hizballah an opportunity

to participate in Lebanese elections while still adhering to "international banking regulations that prohibit local banks in Lebanon from granting accounts to members of a movement deemed by the United States to be a 'terrorist organization'"; Al-Arian, "Political Islam and Endurance of American Empire," 7; see also *Daily Star*, "Lebanese Electoral Law 2017."

50. Li, "From Exception to Empire"; Li, *The Universal Enemy*; Li, "Khaled el-Masri"; Khalili and Hajjar, "Torture, Drones, and Detention"; Hajjar, *Torture*; Hajjar, "Grave Injustice"; Hajjar, "The Afterlives of Torture: Global Implications of Reactionary US Politics"; Hajjar, "The Afterlives of Torture: Putting the US War on Terror in Historical and Global Context"; Khalili, "Utility of Proxy Detention in Counterinsurgencies"; Loyd and Mountz, *Boats, Borders, and Bases*.

51. Li, "Khaled el-Masri"; Li, "From Exception to Empire."

52. Li, "From Exception to Empire," 457–458.

53. Stoler, "Degrees of Imperial Sovereignty."

54. It is critical to demarcate this chapter in the history of US empire as one taking shape following the colonization of Indigenous lands in what became the settler colony of the United States.

55. Lutz, "Empire Is in the Details."

56. While this book foregrounds an analysis of the topological workings of US power, the analysis developed herein is not limited to the United States. Instead, it points to a broader refashioning of security and enforcement regimes as states extend across and embed into geographically disparate sites, bodies, and spaces.

57. Maillet, Mountz, and Williams, "Exclusion Through Imperio"; Coleman, "Immigrant Il-Legality"; Mountz and Hiemstra, "Spatial Strategies."

58. Coleman, "Immigrant Il-Legality," 418.

59. Mountz and Hiemstra, "Spatial Strategies"; Coleman, "Immigrant Il-Legality"; Gilbert, "Elasticity at the Canada–US Border"; Benton, *A Search for Sovereignty*.

60. Mountz and Hiemstra, "Spatial Strategies"; see also Loyd and Mountz, *Boats, Borders, and Bases*.

61. Coleman, "Immigrant Il-Legality," 418–419.

62. Coleman, "Immigrant Il-Legality," 419.

63. Maillet, Mountz, and Williams, "Exclusion Through Imperio."

64. Gilbert, "Elasticity at the Canada–US Border," 425.

65. The many deaths along the US–Mexico border are a testament to elastic empire at work, with the killing of Sergio Hernández Guereca as but one example. Hernández Guereca, a fifteen-year-old Mexican national, was shot and killed by US border guard Jesus Mesa Jr. while playing on the culvert of the Rio Grande, which separates El Paso and Ciudad Juárez, Mexico. The US Department of Justice deter-

mined that Mesa would not be charged with Hernández's murder. US federal criminal civil rights statutes did not apply, it argued, because Hernández "was neither within the borders of the United States nor present on US property, as required for jurisdiction to exist under the applicable federal civil rights statute" (Department of Justice, "Federal Officials Close Investigation"). Mesa was charged with Hernández's murder in Mexico, but the Obama administration refused to extradite him. Hernández's parents then brought a lawsuit against Mesa in US federal court, which ultimately made it to the Supreme Court. The Supreme Court corroborated the Justice Department's determination that Mesa would not be held accountable for Hernández's murder. The Court argued that Hernández's position when he was shot, some sixty feet from the US border on the Mexican side, precluded punitive actions be taken against the guard. Justices sympathetic to Hernández expressed concern that to "extend constitutional protections beyond the nation's borders" would set a dangerous precedent (Liptak, "Justices Weigh Agent's Cross-Border Shooting").

    66. Coleman, "Immigrant Il-Legality."

    67. Gilbert, "Elasticity at the Canada–US Border," 426–427.

    68. Gilbert, "Elasticity at the Canada–US Border," 426.

    69. See Weizman, *Hollow Land*. While Weizman tends to view Israel's frontier as anarchic, consisting of both chaos and resistance, Gilbert contends that "elasticity is also structured in and through law" ("Elasticity at the Canada–US Border," 425).

    70. Weizman, *Hollow Land*, 6.

    71. Weizman, *Hollow Land*, 7.

    72. Weizman, *Hollow Land*, 8.

    73. Immigration enforcement and counterterrorism regimes are invariably linked to and co-constituted by one another, but they also cannot necessarily be reduced to one another. In addition to the differential evolution of immigration and counterterrorism regimes within and across states, there is, one could argue, a different economy of risk at play within each respectively. While both immigration and counterterrorism regimes are both governed foremost by security logics that purport to manage and contain threat, the former retains, at least theoretically, the possibility that some subjects might be good/worthy for inclusion for their value/labor. Counterterrorism measures, however, do not hold open that possibility. The "terrorist" (which includes the potential terrorist) is constituted as a purely threatening object to be stamped out. At the same time, parallels between these two distinct regimes remain (see the case of Muhammad Salah in Chapter 1). The figure of the terrorist, like the non-citizen deemed never-to-have-arrived, is equally not afforded due process, rights, or protections within domestic space.

    74. This book focuses predominately on the global workings of the US counter-

terrorism regime (processes of externalization). Considerable work has been done on how the terrorist exception, when applied domestically and to US citizens, functions to relax, if not render inapplicable, generally applicable legal standards and protections. See, for example, Akbar, "Policing 'Radicalization'"; Aziz, "Countering Religion or Terrorism?"; W. Said, "Coercing Voluntariness"; W. Said, "Sentencing Terrorist Crimes;" W. Said, *Crimes of Terror.*

75. Elden, *Terror and Territory*; Elden, *The Birth of Territory.*

76. See also Maillet, Mountz, and Williams, "Exclusion Through Imperio."

77. Amar, "Turning the Gendered Politics."

78. Mountz, "Political Geography I."

79. Gregory, "The Everywhere War."

80. Lutz, "Empire Is in the Details."

81. Weizman, *Hollow Land*, 8.

82. See Jabri, *War and Transformation of Global Politics*; Jabri, *The Postcolonial Subject.*

83. Stamatopoulou-Robbins, "In Colonial Shoes," 74.

84. Bhungalia, "Managing Violence."

85. Jabri, *The Postcolonial Subject*, i.

86. Jabri, *The Postcolonial Subject*, i.

87. Jabri, "War, Government, Politics," 55.

88. Jabri, "War, Government, Politics," 55.

89. This point too has been made elsewhere. See Turner, "Peacebuilding as Counterinsurgency" and Tartir, "Criminalizing Resistance" as but two examples.

90. Bhungalia, "Managing Violence."

91. Weizman, *Least of All Possible Evils.*

92. Weizman, *Least of All Possible Evils.*

93. Bhungalia, "Managing Violence."

94. Strachan and Scheipers, "The Changing Character of War."

95. See Khalili, "Utility of Proxy Detention in Counterinsurgencies"; Barkawi, "Pedagogy of 'Small Wars' "; Gregory, "The Everywhere War"; C. Jones, "Lawfare and Juridification of Late Modern War"; Khalili, *Time in the Shadows;* Tahir, "Life in Age of Drone Warfare"; Weizman, *Least of All Possible Evils*; Jabri, "Global War and Government of Populations"; Griffiths, "Geontological Time-Spaces"; Grove, *Savage Ecology*; Gregory, "War and Peace. " "Late modern" connotes an epochal shift from the Cold War doctrine of deterrence to an anticipatory, prefigurative logic of preemption whereby potential threats are intercepted and eradicated before they materialize. "Late modern warfare" refers to a technologically driven mode of warfare that utilizes advanced systems of aerial sensing, surveillance, and targeting and is oriented around this anticipatory figuring of time.

96. See Fassin, "Humanitarianism as a Politics of Life"; Feldman and Ticktin, *In the Name of Humanity*; Ticktin, "Where Ethics and Politics Meet"; Feldman, "The Humanitarian Condition"; Feldman, *Life Lived in Relief*; Reid-Henry, "Politics of Our Humanitarian Present."

97. See Coulthard, *Red Skin, White Masks*; A. Simpson, *Mohawk Interruptus*; Gregory, *The Colonial Present*; Salamanca, "Assembling the Fabric of Life."

98. Khalili, *Time in the Shadows*. See also Weizman, *Least of All Possible Evils*.

99. Whittall, "Treating Terrorists"; Slim, "With or Against?"; Weizman, *Least of All Possible Evils*.

100. Whittall, "Treating Terrorists," see esp. para. 1.

101. Research began in Amman in 2009 where I undertook archival, policy, and interview-based research on the United Nations Relief and Works Agency's (UNRWA) role in managing Palestinian displacement. To gain a better sense of the policy, planning, and institutional oversight that go into refugee management and administration, interviews were conducted with UNRWA officials at the agency's headquarters, aid workers, scholars, and displaced Palestinians living in Jordan. Archival research and policy analysis was also carried out at the French Institute of the Near East to gain further insights into the institutional history of UNRWA and its changing role and function over the course of six decades. Arabic language study further expanded the geographic scope of this project to include Damascus, Syria (2008), Cairo, Egypt (2009), and Middlebury College (2010, 2011) in the United States where I completed two intensive Arabic programs at the Middlebury Arabic Language School.

102. Palestinians in the West Bank are not permitted entry into Israel or Gaza, and Palestinians in Gaza are not permitted entry into Israel or the West Bank. Many Palestinians now reside outside of the territories and have obtained citizenship in other countries. If a Palestinian holds a West Bank or Gaza *huwyieh* (Palestinian identity card), she is restricted to the West Bank or Gaza, respectively, and is not permitted entry into Israel. Her identity as a Palestinian, in other words, "trumps" her foreign citizenship. Additionally, within the West Bank, Palestinians are not permitted to enter sites designated "Area C" (places containing Israeli military bases or settlements and their surrounding areas), nor are they permitted to drive on settler roads. The elaborate bureaucratic regime that has been created by Israel is one among a number of instruments that serves to divide and isolate the Palestinian population into disconnected geopolitical spaces controlled by Israel.

103. USAID headquarters are based in Tel Aviv. Due to US-imposed security restrictions, USAID officials are not permitted to travel into the West Bank without extensive security protocols in place.

104. There is no shortage of critical works on the foreign aid regime in post–Oslo Palestine: Atshan, "Prolonged Humanitarianism"; Challand, "Evolution of Western

Aid"; Feldman, "Gaza's Humanitarian Problem"; Haddad, *Palestine Ltd*; Hanafi and Tabar, *Emergence of Palestinian Globalized Elite*; Keating, Le More, and Lowe, *Aid, Diplomacy and Facts*; Khan, Giacaman, and Amundsen, *State Formation in Palestine*; Nabulsi, "State-Building Project"; Rabie, *Palestine Is Throwing a Party*; Roy, "De-Development Revisited"; Stamatopoulou-Robbins, *Waste Siege*; Tartir, Dana, and Seidel, *Political Economy of Palestine;* Tartir and Seidel, *Palestine and Rule of Power*; Turner, "Peacebuilding as Counterinsurgency."

This scholarship has developed loosely along four lines. First, there has been a burgeoning interest in the intersection of foreign aid, settler colonialism, and the built environment. A number of scholars have offered empirically grounded and theoretically rich accounts of how international aid is contributing to the production of material landscapes that have further entrenched Israel's control over (and removal of) the Palestinian population: Gordon and Ram, "Ethnic Cleansing"; Petti, Hilal, and Weizman, *Architecture After Revolution*; Salamanca, "Assembling the Fabric of Life"; Tabar, " 'Urban Redesign' "; Weizman, "Military Operations"; Weizman, *Hollow Land*.

A second strand of scholarship has focused on the role of international donors, primarily American and European, in consolidating an ever-sophisticated infrastructure of security coordination between Israel and the Palestinian Authority through "security sector reform" initiatives: Clarno, "Securing Oslo"; Clarno, *Neoliberal Apartheid*; Mustafa, "Damming the Palestinian Spring"; Tartir, "Criminalizing Resistance"; Tartir, "Securitised Development"; Usher, "Politics of Internal Security."

A third strand of scholarship has focused on the role of aid in neoliberal peacebuilding, with attention in particular to how neoliberal economic and governance strategies have been deployed as a response to the fundamentally *political* problem of Palestinian statelessness and displacement: Haddad, *Palestine Ltd*; Tartir, "Securitised Development"; Turner and Shweiki, *Decolonizing Palestinian Political Economy*; Wildeman and Tartir, "Can Oslo's Failed Aid?"

Finally, scholars drawing on long-term, ethnographic fieldwork in Palestine and beyond have crucially attended to the politics of life and Palestinian subjectivity under conditions of protracted humanitarian crisis and relief: Atshan, "Prolonged Humanitarianism"; Feldman, "The Humanitarian Condition"; Feldman, *Life Lived in Relief.*

This book is conversant with but also further develops this rich body of literature through ethnographic attention to the intensifying trend of aid securitization in donor interventionism. While some scholars have attended to how aid functions as a technology of colonial pacification (Tartir, "Criminalizing Resistance"; Turner, "Peacebuilding as Counterinsurgency"), this book specifically examines the trend of aid securitization within the broader ambit of colonial counterinsurgency.

Chapter 1

1. For a detailed account of Salah's time in Israeli custody, including allegations of torture, see a two-part report authored by Salah's lawyers, Michael Deutsch and Erica Thompson, in the *Journal of Palestine Studies*: "Secrets and Lies: The Persecution of Muhammad Salah (Part I)" and "Secrets and Lies: The Persecution of Muhammad Salah (Part II)." See also *US v. Salah*, 462 F.Supp.2d 915 (2006) for disclosure of interrogation methods authorized by the Israel Security Agency during Salah's interrogation. Salah underwent two years of intense Israeli interrogation before pleading guilty in an Israeli military court in 1995.

2. See B'Tselem, "The Mass Deportation of 1992," xxi–xxii; Chesney, "The Sleeper Scenario."

3. Deutsch and Thompson, "Secrets and Lies: Part I," 40; Silver, "Unjust Fate."

4. D. Hoffman, "Israel Holds U.S. Men."

5. D. Hoffman, "Israel Holds U.S. Men."

6. The charge came a time when Israel needed political leverage against the United States. The day following the expulsions, the UN Security Council passed Resolution 799, which "strongly condemned" the deportations and demanded that Israel allow the safe and immediate return of the deportees back into the occupied territories in accordance with the Fourth Geneva Convention (1949). In contravention to its usual exercise of veto power pertaining to resolutions critical of Israel's actions, the United States had signed on to Resolution 799.

7. Stampnitzky, *Disciplining Terror.*

8. Brulin, "Defining 'Terrorism' "; Stampnitzky, *Disciplining Terror*; E. Said, "The Essential Terrorist."

9. Kumar, "Terrorcraft," 34.

10. See also Ismail, "Palestine and the US 'War on Terror.' "

11. The 1968 battle of Karameh on the east of the Jordan River, wherein 300 Palestinian PLO guerilla fighters aided by the Jordanian military maintained a fifteen-hour standoff against 15,000 Israeli soldiers, would mark a pivotal year in Palestinian history, demarcating a new epoch in the long arc of the Palestinian resistance movement. It was also at this time, as Loubie Qutami points out, that a legal and discursive apparatus emerged that criminalized Palestinian resistance under the banner of terrorism (Qutami, "Palestine and the US 'War on Terror' ").

12. Stampnitzky, *Disciplining Terror*, 21. Some twenty years passed before Palestinians picked up arms. After nearly two decades of Palestinians being ignored and disregarded in international fora and after exhausting nearly every option to achieve a just solution to their dispossession to no avail, certain factions turned to more spectacular, violent tactics. On September 5, 1972, eight members of the Pal-

estinian Black September Organization (BSO) entered the Munich Olympic Village compound, took nine Israeli athletes hostage, and killed two others in the process. In exchange for the hostages, the BSO demanded the release of 236 Palestinians imprisoned in Israel, as well as several members of the Red Army Faction imprisoned in West Germany. Their demands were not met. In a failed rescue attempt by West German police, all nine Israeli hostages, five of eight members of the BSO, and a German policeman were killed in a gun battle. The events, aired to a global audience of some 900 million viewers, is oft-referenced as "the premier example of terrorism's power to rocket a cause from obscurity to renown" (B. Hoffman, *Inside Terrorism*, 68).

13. United Nations Security Council, *Letter from the Permanent Representative*.

14. The PLO was recognized by the Arab League in 1964 as the "sole and legitimate representative of the Palestinian people." A decade later, the UN General Assembly recognized the PLO as the "representative of the Palestinian people" with UN Resolutions 3210 and 3236 and granted the PLO observer status with Resolution 3237 on November 22, 1974. The PLO was moreover recognized as the Palestinians' representative body of among the Movement of Non-Aligned Countries and the Organization of the Islamic Conference, among others. The United Stated designated the PLO a terrorist organization in 1987—though in 1988, a presidential waiver was issued that permitted PLO contact. The waiver system remains in place to date. Israel also designated the PLO a terrorist organization until the Madrid Conference in 1991.

15. Stampnitzky, *Disciplining Terror*, 23

16. Brulin, "Defining 'Terrorism.'"

17. Brulin, "Defining 'Terrorism'"; Kumar, "Terrorcraft"; Naftali, *Blind Spot*.

18. Naftali, *Blind Spot*, 52

19. Naftali, *Blind Spot*, 52. See also the work of Remi Brulin ("Defining 'Terrorism,'" "Compartmentalization") on this point.

20. Szulc, "US Moves for World Campaign."

21. Stampnitzky, *Disciplining Terror*, 25.

22. Stampnitzky, *Disciplining Terror*. See also Wagner-Pacifici, *The Moro Morality Play* and *Discourse and Destruction* for an analysis of terrorism as "social drama."

23. See Stampnitzky, *Disciplining Terror*.

24. Stampnitzky, *Disciplining Terror*, 113.

25. Quoted in Netanyahu, *International Terrorism*, 6.

26. Netanyahu, *Terrorism: How the West Can Win*, 113.

27. See Stampnitzky, *Disciplining Terror*, for a detailed account of how the discourse of terrorism first began to take shape in its contemporary form in the early

1970s. Predating this period, political violence was most often seen as legitimate (often termed "insurgency") and was generally understood to be rational and purposeful. With the emergence of the discourse of terrorism in the 1970s, however, such acts came to be understood as "fundamentally immoral, and [entailed] a complicated relationship to the political realm" (*Disciplining Terror*, 66).

28. Ismail, "Palestine and the US 'War on Terror.'"

29. Li, "A Jihadism Anti-Primer."

30. The construction of the essential terrorist itself, as Edward Said argues, is necessarily predicated on a selectivity that obliterates history and temporality. If "you can show that Libyans, Moslems, Palestinians and Arabs, generally speaking, have no reality except that which tautologically confirms their terrorist essence as Libyans, Moslems, Palestinians and Arabs, you can go on to attack them and their 'terrorist' states generally, and avoid all questions about your own behavior or about your share in their present fate" ("The Essential Terrorist," np).

31. Cited in Stampnitzky, *Disciplining Terror*, 116

32. Kumar, "Terrorcraft," 49

33. Brulin, "Compartmentalization," 113.

34. Brulin, "Distorting Justice?".

35. Brulin, "Distorting Justice?". Throughout the 1970s and 1980s, American policymakers viewed Israel through the prism of the Cold War. Having demonstrated its decisive military advantage in the 1967 war, Israel was seen as a strategic asset in a region viewed as susceptible to communist influence on the one hand and pan-Arab nationalism on the other. During the Nixon administration, US military aid and diplomatic support to Israel rose sharply after Israel assisted King Hussein of Jordan in repressing the Palestinian rebellion in 1970 at the expense of the PLO, viewed in Washington as a Soviet proxy. Nixon also airlifted armaments to Israel to ensure it prevailed over Soviet-aligned Egypt and Syria in the 1973 Arab–Israeli War.

36. Khalil, "Pax Americana," 9.

37. The Oslo Accords established an interim governance arrangement between Israel and the PLO, intended to last five years. The Declaration of Principles (Oslo I) signed in 1993 established that Israel would withdraw from the Gaza Strip and Jericho (in the West Bank) and that responsibility for civil administration (e.g., taxation, health services, social welfare, education) and policing within these designated autonomous zones would be delegated to the PLO (see Khalil, "Pax Americana"). Oslo II, which included the 1994 Cairo Accord and the Paris Protocols, created a similar graduated sovereignty arrangement in the West Bank dividing the West Bank into three differentiated political zones: Areas A, B, and C. Key permanent-status issues such as Jerusalem, the fate of Palestinian refugees, Israeli settlements, and

borders were relegated to final status talks, which never occurred. Oslo effectively institutionalized ultimate Israeli control over Palestinian territories while relegating policing and administrative duties over the Palestinian population to the newly established Palestinian Authority.

38. E. Said, "The Morning After."

39. Clinton's issuance of EO 12947 closed a loophole within the first material support statute, §2339A, passed in 1993, which forbids the provision of material support or resources "to anyone, regardless of the identity of the recipient," so long as the provider "know[s] or intend[s] that [the aid is] to be used in preparation for, or in carrying out, a violation" of any of more than two dozen crimes of violence specified in the statute (Chesney, "The Sleeper Scenario").

40. Clinton resolved an issue that had plagued the US government since the late 1970s. The executive and legislative branches had been locked in a battle over which branch should have the power to designate entities to be included on the list. Invoking executive authority with EO 12947, Clinton resolved the stalemate and set the stage for one of the key material support statutes that remains in force today. It was also at this time that the Clinton administration announced a new counterterrorism initiative that would strengthen the ability of the United States to prevent terrorist acts through US law. Passed in 1996, this would become a centerpiece of US counterterrorism law and policy following September 11, 2001.

41. IEEPA specifically notes that the declared threat to the national security, foreign policy, or economy of United States can be entirely or partially outside of the United States. The oldest declaration under IEEPA dates to the Iranian hostage crisis of 1979.

42. Ruff, "Scared to Donate."

43. ACLU, *Blocking Faith, Freezing Charity*, 34.

44. This list includes, among others: the National Liberation Army (ELN), Democratic Front for the Liberation of Palestine, Hizballah, Islamic Gamaat, Islamic Resistance Movement (Hamas), Kahane Chai, Palestinian Islamic Jihad-Shiqaqi faction, Palestine Liberation Front-Abu Abbas faction, Popular Front for the Liberation of Palestine, and the Popular Front for the Liberation of Palestine-General Command. EO 12947 also authorized the secretary of state, in coordination with the secretary of the treasury and attorney general, to designate further foreign entities and individuals the United States believed to pose a risk for undermining the Middle East peace process (USAID 2002). Certification Regarding Terrorist Financing, USAID Acquisition and Assistance Policy Directive.

45. "The President's New Counterterrorism Initiative [Cable]."

46. The Antiterrorism and Effective Death Penalty Act (AEDPA), passed on the one-year anniversary of the Oklahoma City bombing, created a new regime

of listing foreign terrorist organizations (maintained by the State Department) and deemed material support to FTOs as criminal activity punishable under US criminal law.

47. Classifications of the designated change with each new law and executive order passed: under EO12947 listed entities are called specially designated terrorists or SDTs; under the Antiterrorism and Effective Death Penalty Act of 1996, they are called foreign terrorist organizations or FTOs; while under Executive Order 13224, passed in 2001, they are called specially designated global terrorists.

48. This same classification would later be applied to others such as Anwar al-Awlaki who was assassinated, along with his son, by a targeted US drone attack in Yemen in 2012.

49. W. Said, *Crimes of Terror.*

50. Sabin, *Testimony of Barry Sabin.*

51. Peterson, "Addressing Tomorrow's Terrorists, " 320.

52. 18 USC §2339B inserted a broad material ban that had been struck out of an earlier material support statute, 18 USC §2339A. The latter, passed roughly a year after the 1993 World Trade Center bombing, prohibited material support when the provider "knows or intends it will be used to commit one of the crimes specified in the statute" (Chesney, "The Sleeper Scenario," 18). §2339B however bans material support irrespective of intent.

53. Peterson, "Addressing Tomorrow's Terrorists."

54. Peterson, "Addressing Tomorrow's Terrorists"; W. Said, *Crimes of Terror.*

55. Peterson, "Addressing Tomorrow's Terrorists," 326.

56. Sinnar, "Separate and Unequal."

57. Whidden, "Unequal Justice"; Sabin, *Testimony of Barry Sabin.*

58. Wilcox, *Testimony of Philip Wilcox Jr.*

59. Lansner, *Testimony of Ruth Lansner.*

60. Ismail, "Palestine and the US 'War on Terror.' "

61. See Shirin Sinnar's "Separate and Unequal" for an incisive account of the operation, origins, and effects of the legal divide between domestic and international terrorism.

62. See ACLU, *Blocking Faith, Freezing Charity.*

63. de Goede, *Speculative Security.*

64. For analysis on the admission of confessions obtained by foreign agencies into evidence in US courts, see W. Said, "Coercing Voluntariness."

65. Deutsch and Thompson, "Secrets and Lies: Part I," 39.

66. See Deutsch and Thompson, "Secrets and Lies: Part I"; Deutsch and Thompson, "Secrets and Lies: Part II."

67. Deutsch and Thompson, "Secrets and Lies: Part I," 52.

68. de Goede, *Speculative Security*, xxii.

69. de Goede, *Speculative Security*, xx.

70. *9/11 Commission Report*, 132; italics in original.

71. W. Said, *Crimes of Terror*, 51.

72. Miller and Bhungalia, "The Fungible Terrorist."

73. Miller, "(Im)Material Terror."

74. Amoore, *Politics of Possibility*.

75. Akbar, "Policing 'Radicalization' "; W. Said, *Crimes of Terror*; de Goede, *Speculative Security*; Massumi, *Ontopower*; Foucault, *Security, Territory, Population*; Miller, "Shadows of War"; Miller, "(Im)Material Terror."

76. de Goede, *Speculative Security*, xxvi.

77. Amoore, *Politics of Possibility*.

78. de Goede, *Speculative Security*, xxii.

79. Miller, "(Im)Material Terror," 114.

80. Massumi, *Ontopower*.

81. Similarly, the National Security Strategy of 2002 underscored the central importance of preemptive, anticipatory action, noting that the Cold War doctrine of deterrence was inadequate in the face of emerging, imminent threats.

82. Bush, "Remarks by the President."

83. Akbar, "Policing 'Radicalization' "; Howell and Richter-Montpetit, "Is Securitization Theory Racist?"; Khalili, *Time in the Shadows*; Miller, "(Im)Material Terror."

84. Akbar, "Policing 'Radicalization.' "

85. Shamas and Arastu, *Mapping Muslims*.

86. Miller and Bhungalia, "The Fungible Terrorist."

87. Miller, "(Im)Material Terror," 92.

88. Bush, "Fact Sheet on Terrorist Financing Executive Order." Most accounts of the Bush doctrine of preemption mark its first enunciation in his 2002 West Point speech, wherein he emphasized the need to "take the battle to the enemy, disrupt his plans and confront the worst threats before they emerge." However, I contend the first articulation of this strategy can be found in EO 13224, which directly targets the "infrastructure of terrorism" to preclude the materialization of unknown but always potentially emergent threats.

89. Atia, "In Whose Interest?"; W. Said, *Crimes of Terror*.

90. Eaton, "U.S. Prosecution of Muslim Group."

91. Charity & Security Network, "USA v Holy Land Foundation."

92. W. Said, "Material Support Prosecution."

93. See Deutsch and Thompson, "Secrets and Lies: Part I" and Deutsch and Thompson, "Secrets and Lies: Part II."

94. W. Said, "Material Support Prosecution," 585.

95. A central tenet of §2339b—predicated on the "money-is-fungible theory"—has shielded it from numerous constitutional challenges surrounding the intrinsic link it creates between humanitarian aid and FTOs. See W. Said, *Crimes of Terror*, 62–64.

96. W. Said, *Crimes of Terror*.

97. Miller, "(Im)Material Terror," 118.

98. Similarly, in *Holder v. Humanitarian Law Project* (2010), "material support" was deemed to encompass otherwise constitutionally protected speech acts if they were deemed to provide "legitimacy" to FTOs.

99. Cited in de Goede, *Speculative Security*, xviii.

100. de Goede, *Speculative Security*, xxii.

Chapter 2

1. On March 20, 2002, USAID issued Acquisition & Assistance Policy Directive (AAPD) 02–04 to ensure compliance with EO 13224. The directive stipulates that it is the legal responsibility of the contractor and recipient of USAID monies to ensure full compliance with US law and executive orders, which prohibit "transactions with, and the provision of resources and support to, individuals and organizations associated with terrorism." The directive mandates the inclusion of this provision in all USAID-issued subcontracts and subawards. Soon thereafter, on December 31, 2002, USAID issued AAPD 02–19, which stipulated applicants for USAID assistance certify that they do not provide material support of terrorism nor have links to those who commit terrorist acts. AAPD 02–19 was revised twice in 2004 with AAPD 04–07 (March) and AAPD 04–14 (September), and then further with Mission Order 21, first introduced in 2006 and then updated in 2007. EO 13224 is but one of the referenced EOs and statutes to which USAID-administered monies must comply. Other relevant statutes, although not an exhaustive list, include §2339A and §2339B of USC 18, which prohibit material support to designated foreign terrorist organizations, and Executive Orders 12947 and 13099, both passed during the Oslo period, which prohibit transactions with those who "threaten to disrupt the Middle East peace process." The recipient of US funds must also verify that the individual or entity has not been designated by the UN Security Council sanctions committee as per UNSC Resolution 1267 (1999).

2. R. Jones et al., "Interventions on Sovereignty at the Border," 5.

3. R. Jones et al., "Interventions on Sovereignty at the Border," 5.

4. Coining what he calls the "territorial trap," John Agnew argues that conventional thinking across international relations, political science, and cognate disciplines has relied on three misguided geographical assumptions: (1) states as

fixed units of sovereign space; (2) the domestic/foreign polarity; and (3) states as containers of people, administrative and economic systems, cultural practices, and military power ("The Territorial Trap," 54). Undercutting these theses, Agnew argues territoriality "has been 'unbundled' by all kinds of formal agreements and informal practices" ("The Territorial Trap," 54). Pushing Agnew's thesis further, Alexander Murphy ("The Sovereign State System") has argued that de jure sovereignty should not only be seen as falling prey to geographical assumptions of the "territorial trap" but that it also serves to reinforce a "sovereign-territorial ideal" that while never fully realized nevertheless retains ideological and practical significance. The "sovereign-territorial ideal," as Fiona McConnell ("De Facto, Displaced, Tacit") has demonstrated, remains a "potent fiction" particularly for those conventionally excluded from statehood.

5. McConnell, "De Facto, Displaced, Tacit."

6. Murphy, "The Sovereign State System." Indeed this is a configuration that rarely exists. See Agnew, "The Territorial Trap"; Sharma and Gupta, *The Anthropology of the State*; R. Jones et al., "Interventions on Sovereignty at the Border"; McConnell, "Sovereignty"; Mountz, "Political Geography I"; and Trouillot, "The Anthropology of the State."

7. De facto sovereignty is defined by the "ability and capacity to exercise power" and can be disentangled from the notion of bounded territory; see McConnell, "Sovereignty," 113; Agnew, "Sovereignty Regimes." We might think, for example, about George Bush's November 13, 2001, military order, which authorized the indefinite detention of non-US nationals anywhere in the world so long as they had been designated by the president to be suspected terrorists or to have aided and abetted suspected terrorists.

8. See also Lauren Benton's novel accounting of the "spatially elastic" nature of European imperial sovereignty, which relied on dynamic and fluid relations between law and geography. Benton, *A Search for Sovereignty*.

9. Latour, *Reassembling the Social*, 39.

10. Harker, *Spacing Debt*, 4.

11. Conversation with a Palestinian aid activist and director of a grassroots organization, Ramallah, August 2015.

12. This NGO, like many in Palestine, began operating in the West Bank and Gaza Strip at the start of the Oslo period and had since established a prominent presence throughout the region. It ceased its operations following US aid cuts under the Trump administration.

13. Interview with the director of a US NGO, Ramallah, March 2010.

14. This interlocutor here highlighted two pivotal elements that shape much of

the NGO's work in the West Bank and Gaza Strip. First, "you have the law—no material support directly or indirectly to any terrorist entity," she stated. Second, you have the "no-contact policy," which prohibits contact with any entity considered a terrorist entity by the United States. Flowing from each of these mandates, she further explained, is a dizzying array of oversight and compliance mechanisms that agencies handling US monies are obligated to enforce.

15. I conducted meetings and interviews with roughly twenty intermediary bodies (contractors and NGOs) from 2009 to 2019, totaling over seventy interviews.

16. See also Bruno Latour's discussion of "immutable mobiles" or objects that circulate but also hold their shape allowing for the reproduction and standardization of actions across space; see Latour, *Science in Action*.

17. Latour, *Reassembling the Social*, 39.

18. These bodies consist of (1) private contracting firms, such as Chemonics, ARD, Tetra Tech, DAI, and IRD, among others; and (2) international NGOs, which usually have an established presence in Palestine and deeper connections with the communities they serve. Some of the most prominent NGOs operating on US funds include Save the Children, CARE, Relief International, ANERA, and CHF/Global Communities.

19. Guinane, "19 Years Later."

20. USAID, "ADS Chapter 319 Partner Vetting."

21. USAID, "Supporting the USAID Mission." A similar order, Mission Order 201.5, was introduced into the USAID Afghanistan Mission in 2011.

22. This includes those listed as Specially Designated Nationals and Specially Designated Global Terrorist or as belonging to a foreign terrorist organization (FTO).

23. Individuals vetted include non-US personnel of organizations and contracting bodies, non-US recipients of assistance instruments, non-US trainees, and some direct recipients of cash or in-kind assistance. The personal information collected includes the name and pseudonyms, date and place of birth, citizenship, gender, government-issued photo identification number and country of issuance, address of residence, email, occupation, employer and job title, organizational affiliation, and rank or title in the organization for each key individual.

24. See CHE Project, "Partner Vetting." While USAID maintains that it is "not a law enforcement or intelligence agency," it has asserted that its mandate to ensure USAID funding is not "purposefully or inadvertently used to provide support to entities or individuals deemed to be a risk to national security necessarily requires coordination with law enforcement and intelligence agencies as well as use of their information"; see https://www.govinfo.gov/content/pkg/FR-2007-07-17/pdf/07-3330 .pdf

25. CHE Project, "Partner Vetting," 1.

26. See Rhys Machold, "Reconsidering the Laboratory Thesis" for a critique of the laboratory thesis.

27. This includes any facility that has *shuhada* in its name, which is commonly used by Palestinians to refer to those arrested or killed by the state of Israel.

28. Interview with a staff member working for an international NGO, West Bank, 2009.

29. Interview with the director of a US NGO, Ramallah, March 2010.

30. The interviewee then went on to list a range of municipalities in the West Bank—including Nablus, Jenin, and Ramallah—with which they were prohibited from having relations, given that these cities contained municipal council members belonging to groups the United States had designated as foreign terrorist organizations. Interview with the director of a US NGO, Ramallah, March 2010.

31. Interview with the director of a US NGO, Jerusalem, May 2010.

32. Interview with the Gaza director of a US NGO, Jerusalem, May 2010.

33. Interview in Jerusalem, May 2010.

34. Ultimately, the NGO ended up contracting an OFAC-cleared local Gaza organization to implement construction projects for explicitly *non*-government infrastructures, including the expansion of water pipelines to outlying areas lacking adequate water infrastructure. The local body with which they partnered could have undertaken necessary coordination, and as such, the local NGO was not technically in violation of US policy. Yet this strategy also had definitive limitations: it could not be used with large-scale projects, like the USAID-funded project they had been awarded, which required close coordination with engineers and technical experts in the municipalities.

35. Amoore, *Politics of Possibility.*

36. Interview in Jerusalem, May 2010.

37. Interview with a US contractor, Jerusalem, October 2011.

38. Gisha, *Red Lines Crossed*; Amnesty International, *Israel/Gaza.*

39. Bhungalia, "Im/Mobilities."

40. Oxfam, "Gaza Strip."

41. Oxfam, "Gaza Strip."

42. OCHA, "Farming Without Land."

43. Amnesty International, *Israel/Gaza*, 63.

44. Amnesty International, *Israel/Gaza,* 63.

45. Interview with a US contractor, Jerusalem, October 2010.

46. This is USAID's slogan, which is branded on all of its projects, infrastructures, and equipment.

47. Weizman, *Hollow Land*, 5.

48. Weizman, *Hollow Land*, 8

49. Bhungalia, "Managing Violence."

50. Interview with a Palestinian working for a US contractor, Ramallah, August 2009.

51. Khalili, *Time in the Shadows*.

52. I do not claim here that these local staff members are "informants," a term that carries a particularly charged valence in this context given that Israel often coerces Palestinians, and especially Palestinian prisoners, to become informants.

53. Interview with the Gaza director of a US NGO, Jerusalem, May 2010.

54. Interview with a Palestinian staffer formerly employed by a US contractor, Ramallah, October 2009.

55. Interview with a Palestinian staffer formerly employed by a US contractor, Ramallah, October 2009.

56. Interview with a Palestinian staffer formerly employed by a US contractor, Ramallah, October 2009.

57. Interview with the director of a Palestinian mental health organization, Jerusalem, February 2010.

58. Interview with a Palestinian formerly employed by a US contractor, Ramallah, October 2009.

59. "Mohammad El Halabi Trial Overview."

60. Interview with a Palestinian NGO worker, Ramallah, November 2009.

61. Interview in Ramallah, July 2015.

62. Interview with a Palestinian aid worker formerly contracted to work on the USAID-funded West Bank greenhouse program, Jerusalem, July 2018.

63. Interview with the chief of party of a US contractor, Jerusalem, May 2010.

64. Interview with the country director of a French humanitarian organization, Ramallah, September 2009.

65. Tamari, "In League with Zion," 41.

66. Prior to 1976, Israel sought to delegate the management of civil services to locally elected Palestinian figures, assuming that Palestinian elites voted into power would establish a Palestinian leadership that would not challenge the status quo. Palestinian municipalities, working in collaboration with other social institutions such as the Red Crescent Society among others, provided institutional leadership and filled gaps in service provision and distribution for Palestinians living under Israeli military occupation (see Makky, "The Role of Local Government"; Mukhimer, *State Building Process*).

67. Mukhimer, *State Building Process*; Tamari, "In League with Zion"; Litani,

" 'Village Leagues.' " During this period, Israel also took over water sources in the occupied territories and denied municipalities any power to manage electricity and water.

68. Mustafa Dudin of Dura in the Hebron District emerged as a key figure and liaison between the Leagues and the military government. See Litani, " 'Village Leagues.' "

69. Tamari, "In League with Zion," 42, 45.

70. Tamari, "In League with Zion," 45.

71. Tamari, "In League with Zion," 46–47.

72. Signoles, "Local Government in Palestine."

73. Tamari, "In League with Zion," 47.

74. Much of this failure was written into Israel's hardfisted approach. While the Leagues were designed to be a repressive instrument of control, they were also supposed to foster a political alternative to the PLO. This latter requires, at the very least, a "respectable link to the national movement," as Salim Tamari points out. The Leagues fulfilled the first function to the detriment of the second. The Village Leagues were officially disbanded in 1984. See Tamari, "In League with Zion," 55.

75. Litani, " 'Village Leagues.' "

76. ARIJ, "PPI & Palestinian Local Authorities."

77. World Bank, "West Bank and Gaza Local Government"; ARIJ, "PPI & Palestinian Local Authorities."

78. Signoles, "Local Government in Palestine"; World Bank, "West Bank and Gaza Local Government."

79. Interview with the former head of Aid Management and Coordination Directorate at the Ministry of Finance and Planning, Ramallah, July 2017.

80. Abed-Alnaser Makky has also pointed to the importance of municipalities, both prior to the existence of the PA and throughout periods when the PA came under systematic attack by Israel, in providing services and critical functions in the absence of a central authority. See Makky, "The Role of Local Government."

81. Local elections held from December 2004 to December 2005 were supposed to be carried out over the course of five phases. The fifth phase however did not take place due to fragmentation of the Palestinian political process following the Hamas victory in the January 2006 Palestinian parliamentary elections, caused in part by punitive actions undertaken by Western states and Israel in the immediate aftermath.

82. Since the Oslo Accords were signed in 1993, the US government committed an estimated $1.8 billion in economic assistance to the Palestinians channeled through contractors and NGOs (Sharp and Blanchard, "U.S. Foreign Aid to the Palestinians").

83. In Nablus, Hamas won thirteen seats on the fifteen-member council, more than 70 percent of the vote. In Jenin, Hamas garnered eight municipal seats while the remaining seven went to a coalition of Fatah and the PFLP. In Ramallah, the home of the Fatah-controlled Palestinian Authority, Hamas garnered 73 percent of the electoral vote, while in the Ramallah suburb of Al Birah, Hamas secured nine spots of the fifteen-member council; Fatah took four, and the remaining two seats went to the Popular Front and independents.

84. The Bethlehem Governorate consists of Bethlehem, Beit Jala, and Beit Sahour. Following the 2005 local election, Bethlehem was boycotted by the United States; Beit Jala and Beit Sahour were not.

85. Weizman, *Hollow Land*, 6.

86. Salamanca, "Assembling the Fabric of Life."

87. Many of these roads would be part of an alternative road system proposed by Israel to foreign donors in 2004 with the intention of filtering Palestinian traffic into a separate transportation network that, like the Wadi al-Nar route, effectively normalized Israeli settlement development, both past and future, and its accompanying infrastructure (see Salamanca, "Assembling the Fabric of Life"). The road on which we were traveling was part of an alternative route being constructed to prevent Palestinians from entering Jerusalem or from using Road No. 1 that passes through E-1 (land allocated for expansion of Ma'ale Adumim) and Road 60 that passes through East Jerusalem. When the road program was first proposed in 2004, it was rejected. However, according to calculations by the Applied Research Institute in Jerusalem, some 30 percent of those roads originally housed in the plan were funded and implemented by USAID.

88. My trips to Bethlehem spanned the period during which Bethlehem was placed under sanction by the United States and followed the subsequent mayoral term of Vera Baboun, who was elected into office in 2012.

89. Batarseh did not appear on the US OFAC list of Specially Designated Nationals and Blocked Persons as of October 2011.

90. Interview with the director of a US contractor in the West Bank, May 2010.

91. Executive Order 13224 required the US Treasury and State Departments to "develop a list of persons or entities whose assets will be subject to blocking under the Order, including persons or entities" (Lakatos and Blöchliger, "The Extraterritorial Reach," 3).

92. Interview in Bethlehem, March 2010.

93. I made a series of trips to Beit Jala, Bethlehem, and Beit Sahour to meet with the respective mayors and see the material geographies created by the US boycott.

94. Interview with the mayor of Beit Sahour, Beit Sahour, April 2010.

95. Interview with the mayor of Beit Jala, Beit Jala, April 2010.

96. Interview with a Bethlehem municipal staffer, July 2018.

Chapter 3

1. de Goede, Leander, and Sullivan, "Introduction: The Politics of the List," 3.

2. Bedford, "Letting the Right Ones In"; Leander, "The Politics of Whitelisting."

3. de Goede and Sullivan, "The Politics of Security Lists," 71. Lists are grounded in a logic of preemption. Listed subjects, as Gavin Sullivan notes, are "not targeted for acts they have done but for things designating states believe they might do in the future;" Sullivan, *The Law of the List,* 2.

4. Law, "Collateral Realities."

5. de Goede and Sullivan, "The Politics of Security Lists," 70; see Li, "A Jihadism Anti-Primer" for a parallel discussion of jihad

6. Interview in Ramallah, July 2019.

7. Stäheli, "Indexing," 14.

8. Stäheli, "Indexing," 14.

9. de Goede and Sullivan, "The Politics of Security Lists," 67; italics in original; see also Latour, "Visualization and Cognition."

10. de Goede and Sullivan, "The Politics of Security Lists."

11. Hussain, "One Man's No-Fly List Nightmare"; Devereaux, "Secret Terrorism Watchlist"; Scahill and Devereaux, "Blacklisted."

12. Hussain, "One Man's No-Fly List Nightmare."

13. See National Counterterrorism Center, "Watchlisting Guidance."

14. Devereaux, "Secret Terrorism Watchlist."

15. Devereaux, "Secret Terrorism Watchlist"; Hussain, "One Man's No-Fly List Nightmare."

16. Sullivan, *The Law of the List.*

17. Charity & Security Network, "World-Check."

18. de Goede, Leander, and Sullivan, "Introduction: The Politics of the List"; de Goede and Sullivan, "The Politics of Security Lists"; Amicelle and Jacobsen, "The Cross-Colonization of Finance"; Sullivan, *The Law of the List*; Leander, "The Politics of Whitelisting"; Stäheli, "Indexing."

19. Scahill and Devereaux, "Blacklisted."

20. Terrorism lists, as discussed here, are embedded in a broader global legal-security architecture discussed at length in Chapter 1. "The list," as I use it here, is an index of, a shorthand for, this broad legal-security assemblage and the technologies that flow from it.

21. Aid flows and recipients alike in Palestine are subject to screenings against

terrorism lists. Each national government hosts their own list, such as the OFAC list in the US case, or the Proscribed Terrorist Organizations list in the UK. State lists are often cross-checked with private firm and supranational lists, including the United Nations Security Council Consolidated List and the Thomson Reuters World-Check, which consolidates sanctions, counterterrorism watchlists, law enforcement lists, public sources and media sites (including sites publishing false and misleading information such as *Jihad Watch*) into a "master list," which is sold to financial institutions and charitable organizations.

22. Interview with a staffer of a Palestinian NGO, Ramallah, July 2019.

23. Sullivan, *The Law of the List,* 3.

24. de Goede, Leander, and Sullivan, "Introduction: The Politics of the List," 10.

25. On January 25, 2006, candidates from the Hamas movement secured seventy-four seats in the PA's 132-member parliament. By virtue of obtaining a majority vote over the ruling Fatah party, Hamas was the only party constitutionally able to form a government. For many Western donor states, funding could no longer be channeled to the PA, as it now contained within its composition a foreign terrorist organization, resulting in near total aid cutoff. Aid to the PA was only restored once Palestinian Authority President Mahmoud Abbas dissolved the parliament, purged Hamas ministers from its internal ranks, and instituted emergency law.

26. Interview with a Palestinian staffer of a US contractor working in health sector reform in the West Bank, Ramallah, February 2010.

27. The US material support statute prohibits support in both tangible and intangible forms, including "training" to individuals affiliated with designated FTOs.

28. Interview with a former Palestinian employee of a US contractor, Ramallah, October 2009.

29. Interview in Jerusalem, February 2010.

30. Interview with a financial manager of Arab Bank, Ramallah, July 2018.

31. See Jamal, *The Palestinian National Movement,* for a more extensive account.

32. Hammami, "NGOs." While having a fairly expansive reach across the West Bank, containing some forty-two member organizations by 1995, PNGO was not entirely inclusive. Islamist groups, such as Hamas, were preemptively excluded by virtue of the secular position adopted by PNGO in principles of declaration. In 1995, a sister network formed in Gaza, comprised of a small steering committee of eight Gaza-based NGOs.

33. Interview in Jerusalem, February 2010.

34. PNGO, "The Palestinian Non-Governmental Organizations."

35. PNGO, "The Palestinian Non-Governmental Organizations."

36. Bowker and Star, *Sorting Things Out,* 137.

37. Interview in Jerusalem, February 2010.

38. Interview with a PNGO member, Ramallah, August 2015.

39. Information relayed during an interview with a PNGO member, February 2010.

40. Information relayed during an interview with a PNGO member, August 2015.

41. Interview with the director of a Palestinian development NGO, Ramallah, July 2019.

42. Interview with the director of a US NGO, Ramallah, March 2010.

43. Interview in Jerusalem, December 2009.

44. While PNGO did officially pass a measure to boycott USAID, the decision to do so did not come easily. Approval of the boycott could only be obtained with full consensus (as opposed to a majority vote) of all members on the steering committee. At the time of the boycott deliberations, a number of organizations on the PNGO steering committee were receiving USAID funding. An interview conducted with one member active in the committee deliberations revealed that a number of these organizations contested the boycott even if they supported the politics and the principles behind it. This tension resulted in a number of internal splits, and in at least one case, defection from the network.

45. Interview in Jerusalem, February 2010.

46. PNGO, "The Palestinian Non-Governmental Organizations."

47. Interview in Jerusalem, February 2010.

48. Interview in Ramallah, March 2010.

49. E. Said, "The Essential Terrorist."

50. Interview in Jerusalem, March 2010. The dire situation in Jenin to which this activist refers pertains to the period following Israel's military offensive on Jenin Refugee Camp in April 2002. Following the siege, other aid agencies joined UNRWA to assist those in need. The United States Agency for International Development sent shipments of tents, food, and other relief supplies. Once the trucks carrying the US goods arrived, however, the camp's residents refused the aid on the grounds that US foreign policy, it was argued, and most notably US military aid to Israel, had much to do with their current predicament (see BADIL, "Statement Issued"). Underscoring the role of US military aid in contributing to Jenin's widescale destruction, the Popular Committees in the Palestinian Refugee Camps argued: "The crime committed is large and extensive. Its traces cannot be erased by the aid and assistance which is now being provided." The military dimensions of US aid, Jenin's residents insist, cannot be erased by gestures of humanitarian support. It is only by separating US military aid from its humanitarian and development counterparts that discourses of benevolence and charity gain force. By way of their refusal, the residents of Jenin demand we consider these dual facets of US aid relationally.

51. On refusal see A. Simpson, *Mohawk Interruptus*; A. Simpson, "On Ethnographic Refusal"; Coulthard, *Red Skin, White Masks*; Alfred, *Heeding the Voices*; L. Simpson, "The Misery of Settler Colonialism."

52. Resistance to the terrorism certification also prompted the United States in 2007 to undertake minor revisions with respect to the document language, though in terms of content, nothing changed.

53. Interview in Jerusalem, February 2010.

54. Interview with a staffer of the Palestinian Popular Art Center, Ramallah, March 2010.

55. Interview with a PNGO staffer, Ramallah, August 2015.

56. Interview in Jerusalem, February 2010.

57. Interview in Ramallah, March 2010.

58. Some, however, have argued the boycott was only ever symbolic. Even within PNGO, a number of organizations continued to receive funds from USAID while also maintaining their membership within the network. Other organizations simply devised ways to receive US funds without signing the anti-terrorism clause. Especially since the Fatah–Hamas split in 2007, which resulted in the emergence of two distinct governing authorities—the West Bank and Gaza, respectively—many organizations, especially in the West Bank, have come to accept US funding.

59. Sullivan, *The Law of the List*.

60. Sullivan, *The Law of the List*, 3.

61. Sullivan, *The Law of the List*, 3.

62. Interview conducted in Ramallah, August 2018. Some of the specific security and counterterrorism instruments and practices being referenced here are the anti-terrorism certification, introduced by USAID in 2003, rigorous vetting of recipient entities, and prohibitions on relations with entities not cleared by donor intelligence systems.

63. Gyeney, "US Aid Freeze."

64. Unsleber, "Destroying Belief."

65. Gyeney, "US Aid Freeze."

66. Interview in Jerusalem, July 2018.

67. Interview with the mayor of Birzeit, Yousef Nasser, Birzeit, April 2010.

68. One staffer involved in the organization during its formative years noted, during an interview, that a main impetus for the transformation of Sharek from an initiative of the UN into an independent NGO was a desire among a number of youth organizers to create "an official body that would represent the youth in Palestine." UNDP helped to facilitate this transformation. It assigned a number of UNDP volunteers to assist in building the institutional capacity and internal systems to sustain

Sharek as an independent body, and in 2004, after registering with the Ministry of Interior, Sharek gained official status as an independent NGO. Sharek's first years as an independent organization were sustained in large part by funding from the Swiss Agency for Development and Cooperation.

69. The decision to refuse USAID funds, while supported by much of the staff, came from Sharek's board of directors.

70. Interview in Ramallah, May 2010.

71. The Youth Shadow Local Council initiative was first piloted in four West Bank municipalities in 2008 by CHF, in partnership with Al-Mawrid. In 2010, funded by the USAID-funded Local Democratic Reform program in partnership with Sharek, the program was expanded to nine additional municipalities. In 2013, the initiative was expanded to an additional seven municipalities resulting in a total of twenty included municipalities.

72. Interview in Ramallah, May 2010.

73. Interview with a Sharek staffer, Ramallah, March 2010.

74. Debates within Sharek revealed that by 2010, when Sharek was considering this project, the difference between USAID and other large-scale donors such as the EU was effectively nil. As one staff member argued, accepting USAID money is not dissimilar from the EU or any number of other foreign donors. The language of the ATC clause is different, the staffer noted, but the vetting that takes place is essentially the same. The economic stipulations, the staffer further noted, in practice are also similar with a name change, however: "With US money you have to buy American instead of buying European; [likewise] if you do a project with the EU, you have to buy a computer that is European . . . I just had to stick an EU flag sticker on my computer today because it was paid for by the EU." Interview in Ramallah, March 2010.

75. At the same time, understandably, many among Sharek's constituency and staff remarked on the curious contradiction between the stated objective of increasing youth democratic practice in local politics and then excluding significant numbers of youth from participation based on US determinations of unacceptability. Moreover, youth participating in the councils were told that they must remain apolitical. In the words of one staff member, "It's a requirement for participation in the youth councils that the youth will not represent any political party. In order to run, they have to agree that they do not represent any political party. They represent themselves." But certain political parties, she went on to note, are preemptively eliminated, as well as Gaza in its entirety. "There are a lot of ironic isolations in the democratic project." Interview in Ramallah, March 2010.

76. Interview in Ramallah, May 2010.

77. Interview with a former Sharek staffer, Ramallah, August 2015.

78. Interview with a former Sharek high-level staffer, Jerusalem, July 2018.

79. Interview in Ramallah, March 2010.

80. Birzeit Municipality had a long-standing relationship with CHF that began near the end of 2005. However, the US boycott of Hamas and transition to emergency projects resulted in a reconfiguration of this relationship until US aid flows resumed to relatively normal levels.

81. Interview with Birzeit mayor, Yousef Nasser, Birzeit, April 2010.

82. Interview with Birzeit mayor, Yousef Nasser, Birzeit, April 2010.

83. Additionally, among the most severe issues facing the municipality were concerns that the water meters had been installed during the period of Israeli administration. The water meters installed by Israel were built for conditions where you have a continuous flow of water. As Nasser explained, this is not the case for Palestinians writ large or in Birzeit specifically. "The meters work on pressure," Nasser explained. If the pressure goes too low, as it oft-does during water cutoffs, the meters stop working. The Israeli-installed meters need a minimum amount of pressure to function, which resulted in significant water loss. At the time of this interview, Birzeit was in the process of trying to procure ample funds for the purchase of volumetric water meters, which did not require minimum pressure to function.

84. Even as Birzeit was required to sign the ATC as part of the 2009 Sharek-administered LDR project to "enhance municipal capacities," the ATC, Nasser remarked, had not had a significant impact on their broader relationships. "We aren't stupid," he said. "We don't sell out that easily. Signing the ATC doesn't mean that we sold out, but it opens you to political accusation. No one advertises that they've signed the clause."

85. Interview in Ramallah, March 2010.

Chapter 4

1. Zanotti, "U.S. Foreign Aid."

2. Elgindy, *Blind Spot*; see also Bhungalia, Greven, and Mustafa, "Shifting Contours of US Power."

3. Rabbani, "Team Trump's Magical Thinking."

4. Friedman, "Anatomy of the ATCA."

5. Kurd, *Polarized and Demobilized*.

6. Interview with high-level PA intelligence official, Ramallah, July 2018.

7. Shushan, "Congress Must Move Quickly."

8. In *Waldman v. PLO*, a district court awarded the plaintiff $655.5 million; however, a circuit court ruled on appeal that the court lacked personal jurisdiction over the PLO (Shushan, "Congress Must Move Quickly").

9. Friedman, "Surprising New Battleground"; see also Chapter 1.

10. As a further repercussion of ATCA, Washington defunded the Bureau of International Narcotics and Law Enforcement Affairs office in the US consulate, cutting off the US security coordinator's official stream of support. It also accelerated the closure of the Jordan International Police Training Centre, host to trainings for regional partners in America's global war on terror, including the Palestinian Authority Security Forces since 2008.

11. Memo sent from the Office of the Prime Minister of Palestine to US Secretary of State, Mike Pompeo, December 26, 2018.

12. Friedman, "Anatomy of the ATCA."

13. Friedman, "FMEP Legislative Round-Up"; see also Charity & Security Network, "Congress Enacts Partial Fix."

14. Charity & Security Network, "Congress Enacts Partial Fix." It also subjects to US jurisdiction anyone who conducts activities in the United States on behalf of the Palestine Liberation Organization or the Palestinian Authority as well as any entity with an office or headquarters in the United States.

15. Friedman, "FMEP Legislative Round-Up."

16. Friedman, "Anatomy of the ATCA."

17. Friedman, "Anatomy of the ATCA."

18. Reports at the time estimated that over 1 million people in Gaza face dire food insecurity if UNRWA's budget crisis is left unresolved. The agency was also forced to slash mental health and short-term employment programs, cutting lifelines to a population under a decade-long siege (Rankin, "One Million Face Hunger").

19. Estrin, "Palestinian School and Sewage Projects."

20. Released in January 2020, Trump's "Deal of the Century," touted as offering a resolution to the Israeli–Palestinian conflict, consisted of a political and economic framework. The political framework included plans to redraw political boundaries in the West Bank to incorporate the majority of Israeli settlements into Israel and to annex the Jordan Valley. It also recognized Jerusalem as the "undivided capital" of Israel, while dually recognizing al-Quds as the capital of a future state of Palestine. The political framework also denied Palestinians' internationally recognized right of return and required that the state of Palestine be fully demilitarized. The economic framework promised $50 billion in new investment over the course of ten years, an artificial island off the coast of Gaza for an airport, and construction of a tunnel between the West Bank and Gaza Strip.

21. Interview in Ramallah, July 2018.

22. Feldman, "Trump's Full Spectrum Assault."

23. The Biden Administration resumed, in part, US aid to the Palestinians, which

is examined in the Conclusion. This chapter focuses specifically on the period of formal US withdrawal from the aid landscape in Palestine under the Trump administration.

24. Gordon, *Ghostly Matters,* 195; see also Stoler, *Imperial Debris.*

25. Stoler, "Introduction: 'The Rot Remains.' "

26. Stoler, "Introduction: 'The Rot Remains.' "

27. Belcher, "The Afterlives of Counterinsurgency."

28. Rubaii, "Birth Defects."

29. See also Rubaii, "Counterinsurgency and the Ethical Life."

30. Hajjar, "The Afterlives of Torture: Putting the US War on Terror in Historical and Global Context"; Hajjar, "The Afterlives of Torture: The Global Implications of Reactionary US Politics."

31. Hajjar, "The Afterlives of Torture: The Global Implications of Reactionary US Politics," 171. Likewise, Simone Browne traces how contemporary surveillance regimes are the product of a long history of racial formation. Disrupting the conventional temporality of modern surveillance, Browne locates the birth and genesis of contemporary surveillance in transatlantic slavery showing how racialized practices of "seeing" and their attendant technologies of tracking, policing, and social control that were indispensable to making and sustaining slave society animate the logics and practices of present-day surveillance regimes and systems of social control. See Browne, *Dark Matters.*

32. Gordon, *Ghostly Matters.*

33. The EU sanctions list contains a list of states placed under EU sanctions and a list of entities and individuals that the EU has designated as terrorist. EU restrictive measures consist of a set of restrictive practices and procedures imposed on states, entities, and individuals designated in the EU sanctions list. Much like in the US system, these measures include rigorous vetting and screening procedures before, during, and after the completion of an EU-funded project to ensure that funds are not channeled, directly or indirectly, to EU-classified terrorist entities or individuals.

34. PNCRCF, "Against Terrorism and Against Conditional Funding"; see also BADIL, *PNGO & PHROC Position Paper.*

35. PNCRCF, "All You Need to Know," 11.

36. Dana, "Criminalizing Palestinian Resistance," 2.

37. Dana, "Criminalizing Palestinian Resistance," 1.

38. Interview with the director of a Palestinian human rights organization, Ramallah, July 2019.

39. Interview with the director of a Palestinian NGO, Ramallah, July 2018.

40. Interview with the director of a Palestinian NGO, Ramallah, July 2019.

41. The director of a well-known Palestinian human rights organization interviewed in the summer of 2019 echoed this point. Over the last two years, she asserted, European donors were more forcefully adopting an "anti-terrorism" framework, incorporating terrorism clauses and instituting more extensive vetting. Prior to this period, she noted, "European donors did vet but *they* did it. They didn't make the NGOs do it. They just asked for the information and then ran it against their databases." Interview in Ramallah, July 2019.

42. MSA, "Terrorists in Suits: The Ties Between NGOs Promoting BDS and Terrorist Organizations."

43. Interview with the director of a Palestinian human rights organization, Ramallah, July 2019.

44. The report opens with the following proclamations:

(1) Over the past several years, an organized and well-coordinated campaign to delegitimize the State of Israel and promote the BDS campaign against it has been taking place around the world, primarily in Western countries; (2) The campaign involves a network of non-governmental organizations, a number of which have close ties to designated terrorist organizations . . . ; (3) This approach is an evolutionary development in the tactics of the terror organizations against the State of Israel."

See MSA, "Terrorists in Suits: The Ties Between NGOs Promoting BDS and Terrorist Organizations," 4.

45. "Terrorists in Suits" is one among a series of publications from the MSA flanked by "The Money Trail" published one month earlier, which focuses specifically on European Union aid streams to Palestinian and European NGOs that support BDS, and "Blood Money," focusing on European-funded Palestinian NGOs and their terror operatives, published in May 2020, which homes in on the Palestinian prisoner rights organization Addameer (about which I wrote in the Introduction). "Blood Money" furthers the thesis set out in its two predecessor reports, arguing that European money is funding terror operatives under the guise of human rights work.

46. MSA, "Terrorists in Suits: The Ties Between NGOs Promoting BDS and Terrorist Organizations," 4.

47. MSA, "Terrorists in Suits: The Ties Between NGOs Promoting BDS and Terrorist Organizations," 4.

48. See Policy Working Group, *NGO Monitor: Shrinking Space.*

49. Quoted in BADIL, *PNGO & PHROC Position Paper*; see also NGO Monitor, "NGO Monitory Annual Report 2017."

50. Conversation with a policy analyst at a Palestinian policy think tank, Ramallah, June 2019.

51. Funding for the third phase of AMENCA was routed through four intermediary organizations: Oxfam, Care, Union Aid Abroad-APHEDA, and Cardno Emerging Markets.

52. Interview with Sami Khader, Ma'an director, Ramallah, July 2018.

53. United Nations, "Two Years On." As Jasbir Puar has argued, Israel's policy of maiming in the Great March of Return marks an evolution of Israel's settler–colonial rule wherein rather than outright killing and death, which too are perpetuated, debilitation of the native through maiming constitutes a primary aim in a broader policy of slow dispossession. Israel's response to the Great March of Return in Gaza has historical parallels with the first *intifada*, when Yitzhak Rabin ordered Israeli army commanders to "break the bones" of Palestinian protestors. Today, this policy has evolved to specifically target the limbs of Palestinians to disable them. See Puar, *The Right to Maim*.

54. Eid, "Why I Marched."

55. At the time of al-Adine's assassination, he had not been employed by Ma'an for two months.

56. Markson, "Our West Bank Deposits."

57. Markson, "Our West Bank Deposits."

58. Levin, "Tax Dollars" charged that Australian aid was also being funneled to terrorists via World Vision in Gaza and through the UN Palestinian refugee program, UNRWA.

59. The consortium included Asala (the Palestinian Businesswomen's Association) and the Institute for Community Partnership of Bethlehem University.

60. de Goede, *Speculative Security*, 228.

61. The team was instructed to investigate across three areas, including (1) Ma'an links to political parties designated as "terrorist organizations"; (2) the presence of oversight systems to ensure monies are not diverted to terrorist entities; and (3) the allegations about al-Adine specifically.

62. Ma'an had also agreed to allow me to conduct longer-term research with the organization for a period of four months to track more comprehensively the impacts of the terrorism financing investigation on the organization's capacities and broader relations. However, this possibility was soon precluded with the outbreak of the COVID pandemic.

63. Interview with Sami Khader, Ma'an director, Ramallah, July 2018.

64. Interview with Sami Khader and Ma'an employee, Ramallah, July 2019.

65. Interview with Ma'an employee, Ramallah, July 2018.

66. Interview with Ma'an employee, Ramallah, July 2018.

67. Friedman, "Anatomy of the ATCA."

68. Interview with Ma'an employee, Ramallah, July 2019.

69. Interview with the director of a Palestinian human rights organization, Ramallah, July 2019.

70. Kane and Barghouti, "How an Israeli Smear Campaign"; BADIL, *PNGO & PHROC Position Paper.*

71. Letter addressed to the Union of Agricultural Work Committees from UK Lawyers for Israel in 2019. Portions of the letter were redacted when sharing the document, including the exact dating of the letter.

72. Interview with a high-level staffer of UAWC, Al-Bireh, July 2019.

73. UAWC was later designated a terrorist entity by Israel in 2018.

74. Interview with high-level staffer at DCI–P, Al-Bireh, July 2019.

75. Kane and Barghouti, "Israeli Smear Campaign."

76. Touré, "CUNY Investigates."

77. Mary Lu Bilek, dean of the CUNY School of Law, issued a statement affirming that "DCI–P is not, as alleged, a terrorist organization. It is not on the United States State Department's Foreign Terrorist Organizations List. DCI–P is identified by the State Department as a 'human rights organization' "; see Touré, "CUNY Investigates."

78. In June 2019, DCI–P issued libel proceedings against UK Lawyers for Israel (UKLFI) for publishing "blog posts on their website and sending letters to institutional donors alleging DCI–P had strong 'links' to a designated terrorist group"; see DCI–P, "Israeli Forces Raid DCI–P Office." UKLFI had also alleged that " 'donations to DCI–P have encouraged and/or facilitated acts of terrorism' and threatened to report donors to relevant authorities if they did not cease providing DCI–P with financial support." In March 2020, a settlement was reached and UKLFI claimed that it "did not intend to suggest that the organization has close current links, or provides any financial or material support to any terrorist organization"; see DCI–P, "UK Lawyers for Israel Recants."

79. UNGA, "A/HRC/34/70: Report of the Special Rapporteur," 10; see also BADIL, *PNGO & PHROC Position Paper.*

80. BADIL, *PNGO & PHROC Position Paper.*

81. BADIL, *PNGO & PHROC Position Paper,* 5.

82. DCI–P, "Israeli Forces Raid DCI–P Office."

83. Feldman, *Police Encounters.*

Chapter 5

1. Headquartered in Dublin, Front Line Defenders is an international organization that provides support and protection for human rights defenders and journalists at risk.

2. The NSO Group was placed on the US entity list after it was determined that the firm had acted "contrary to the foreign policy and national security interests of the United States." The designation was made just months after a network of journalists working with the NGO Forbidden Stories revealed multiple instances where journalists, activists, and diplomats, including American citizens, had been hacked by foreign governments using the NSO spyware. See Kirchgaessner, "Israeli Spyware Company."

3. This allows for the surveillance of not only the target but also anyone with whom the target has contact via the infected device. See Front Line Defenders, "Six Palestinian Human Rights Defenders."

4. The spyware costs nearly half a million US dollars to install on a smart device.

5. Front Line Defenders shared the collected data with Citizen Lab and Amnesty International's Security Lab to ensure the accuracy of their findings. Both corroborated that the phones had been hacked with the Pegasus spyware. See Front Line Defenders, "Six Palestinian Human Rights Defenders."

6. In June 2021, the Israeli Ministry of the Interior announced the adoption of recommendations to revoke the permanent residency of Hamouri on account of a breach of allegiance to the state of Israel. Israel deported Hamouri to France in December 2022.

7. The designation was made by Israel's Counter-Terrorism Bureau, created in 2018 with the goal of "coordinating activities against the financial infrastructure of terror groups" and which acts under the power of authorities vested in Israel's 2016 Counter-Terrorism Law. Authority for the ministry to outlaw groups in the occupied territories is granted under the 1945 Emergency Regulations, inherited from the British Mandate, which continues to be legally binding. For an organization to be declared a "disallowed association" in the West Bank, the IDF commander must issue a military order (rather than apply Israeli law). The Israeli newspaper *Haaretz* reported that as of November 1, 2021, no such order had been issued. See Shezaf, "The NGOs Israel Designated" and National Bureau for Counter Terror Financing of Israel, "The Minister of Defense Designated Six Organizations."

8. The six groups designated are: Addameer—Prisoner Support and Human Rights Association; Bisan Center for Research and Development; Al-Haq; Defense for Children International–Palestine (DCI–P); Union of Agricultural Work Committees (UAWC); and Union of Palestinian Women's Committees (UPWC).

9. Half of the organizations designated had discovered Pegasus spyware on staffers' phones.

10. Remarking on the sequence of events, Front Line Defenders contends that Israel's timing of the designation suggests that not only is this move part of a longer alarming trend designed to stymie the work of human rights organizations and human rights defenders but it is also an "effort to legitimate the surveillance and infiltration of the devices of Palestinian human rights defenders using Pegasus spyware, as discovered by a Front Line Defenders forensic investigation"; see Front Line Defenders, "Six Palestinian Human Rights Defenders"; Al-Haq, "Side Event"; Shezaf, "The NGOs Israel Designated"; Front Line Defenders, "Press Release."

11. Buttu, "How to Crush Palestinian NGOs," 59.

12. In February 2022, the director of the Union of Palestinian Women's Committees was put on trial in a military court based on secret evidence and sentenced to sixteen months in prison and fined. On March 7, Salah Hamouri, a lawyer with Addameer, was arrested and placed under house arrest. These cases, Susan Power of Al-Haq argues, are directly linked to Israel's designation.

13. See B'Tselem, "B'tselem's Response to MoD Gantz's Declaration"; B'Tselem, "Joint Statement"; Amnesty International, "Israel/OPT"; Human Rights Watch, "Israel/Palestine"; UNHCR, "Counter-Terrorism Legislation"; UNHCR, "UN High Commissioner."

14. Al-Haq, "Side Event."

15. Research took place from November to December in 2021, shortly after the ministry's classification, but before Israel officially shut down the six organizations (in addition to the Health Work Committees) in August 2022.

16. This would block any financial flows moving through institutions affiliated with a state that accepts the designation, even if tacitly—the implications of which would be massive if the United States were to silently endorse Israel's position. Any financial transaction converted into USD runs through US banks, just as any transaction converted into NIS runs through Israeli financial institutions and so on.

17. See Marieke de Goede, *Speculative Security*.

18. A Finnish Christian missionary group cut ties with Defence for Children International in May 2022, as did the Dutch government with UAWC for this very reason. See UNHCR, "Israel/Palestine."

19. Conversation with a policy analyst for Al Shabaka, Ramallah, November 2021. See also Ziv, "Israel Again Tries and Fails."

20. European countries have requested that the evidence on which Israel is basing its claim be provided; so far, no evidence has been released, leading many to speculate there is no evidence to provide. See Ziv, "Israel Again Tries and Fails."

21. UPWC had shut down when this research trip took place (November–December 2021).

22. Asphyxiatory violence underwrites the slogan of the Black Lives Matter movement: "I can't breathe," born of the murder of Eric Garner by police as they choked him to death. However, as Mayanthi Fernando asks, "Was Garner living or dying, not just in the minutes of his asphyxiation, but in the hours and days and years in which he and his body were slowly debilitated by a biopolitical state?" Death, Fernando suggests, is durational. See Fernando, "Temporality, Asphyxiation, Debilitation."

23. Puar, *The Right to Maim*.

24. Berlant, "Slow Death."

25. Khalili, *Time in the Shadows*.

26. Bhungalia, "Im/Mobilities"; Salamanca, "Unplug and Play"; Puar, *The Right to Maim*.

27. Salamanca, "Unplug and Play."

28. Salamanca, "Assembling the Fabric of Life," 30.

29. Puar, *The Right to Maim*.

30. Khalili, *Time in the Shadows*.

31. Interview at Al-Haq, Ramallah, December 2021.

32. UNHCR, "Counter-Terrorism Legislation."

33. The UN Human Rights Office in the occupied Palestinian territory critiqued the designation decision as published by the National Bureau for Counter Terror Financing of Israel as "extremely vague or irrelevant" and including legitimate activities such as the "promotion of steps against Israel in the international arena." This sentiment was also relayed in multiple interviews with staffers at the designated six organizations during a trip to Palestine undertaken in November and December 2021. See UNHCR, "Counter-Terrorism Legislation."

34. Interview with a staff member of UAWC, Ramallah, December 2021.

35. The United States had already largely curbed all of its civilian aid to the Palestinians under the Trump administration. Moreover, European donors are the primary funders of human rights work in Palestine.

36. Abraham, Ziv, and Rapoport, "Secret Israeli Document."

37. See Abraham, Ziv, and Rapoport, "Secret Israeli Document." The testimonies of Abdat and Hamuda were allegedly extracted under torture—a tactic commonly used in Israeli interrogations—according to their lawyers.

38. According to +972 which obtained a copy of the documents, the dossier contained not a "single piece of evidence proving the six organizations diverted their funds to the PFLP or to violent activities." See Abraham, Ziv, and Rapaport, "Secret Israeli Dossier."

39. Cited in Abraham, Ziv, and Rapoport, "Secret Israeli Document." In a second attempt, Israel sent a delegation to Washington in October 2021 to distribute a similar dossier to that circulated months earlier in Europe to members of the US Congress and congressional staff. The State Department requested additional materials regarding Israel's designation. Senior European officials also reported that Israel has ignored their governments' requests for more information regarding its designation. Neither Washington, nor any other foreign government, has moved to formally recognize Israel's designation. See Abraham, Ziv, and Rapoport. "Secret Israeli Dossier" and Goldenberg, "Israel Envoy to Brief US."

40. Cited in Abraham, Ziv, and Rapoport, "Secret Israeli Document."

41. On December 20, 2019, former chief prosecutor of the International Criminal Court Fatou Bensouda concluded that "all the statutory criteria under the Rome Statute for the opening of an investigation have been met." Expressing satisfaction that "war crimes have been or are being committed in the West Bank, including East Jerusalem, and the Gaza Strip" and that "there are no substantial reasons to believe that an investigation would not serve the interests of justice," Bensouda called for an investigation to commence. Al-Haq, among other designated organizations, was providing data to the ICC prosecutor for the case. See ICC, "Statement of ICC Prosecutor."

42. Beaumont, "ICC Opens Investigation."

43. Beaumont, "Why Israel Fears the ICC."

44. Dakwar, "The Terrorism Smear."

45. Dakwar, "The Terrorism Smear."

46. Dakwar, "The Terrorism Smear."

47. Interview, Ramallah, December 2021.

48. Interview, Ramallah, December 2021.

49. FMEP, "Israel Declares War."

50. Shehadeh, "By Banning."

51. Dakwar, "The Terrorism Smear."

52. Francis, "Israel's Military Courts."

53. See D. Khalidi, "The Terrorism Smear."

54. The case of the Palestinian land movement composed of Palestinian citizens in Israel, Al-Ard, is but one example. Israel banned the organization and associations linked to it in 1964 using, as Dakwar notes, "some of the Mandate colonial era laws that allowed the ministry of interior and subsequently other ministries to place restrictions and banning on these organizations." See FMEP, "The Terrorism Smear."

55. UNGA, "Report of the United Nations Fact-Finding Mission."

56. Fisher-Ilan, "Israel's Netanyahu Vows Long Fight."

57. NGO Monitor charges that UN fact-finding mission chose "the most polit-icized and radical NGOs operating in Israel, Gaza, and the Palestinian Authority, many of which are funded by European governments" and lists the following along with their funding sources:

> Addameer—funded by Sweden; The Public Committee Against Torture in Israel (PCATI)—funded by New Israel Fund, Norway, Sweden, Ireland, the EU, and Oxfam-Novib; The Gaza Community Mental Health Program (GCMHP)—funding information unavailable; Alternative Information Center (AIC)—funded by Diakonia (Swedish government); Christian Aid (Irish government), and Sodepau (Catalan government in Spain); Al-Haq—funded by Ford Foundation, Christian Aid , the Netherlands, Irish Aid, Norway, and Diakonia; The Palestinian Center for Human Rights (PCHR) funded by EU, Norway, Ireland, and Denmark.

See NGO Monitor, "Goldstone."

58. NGO Monitor, "Goldstone." It is also exceptionally rich that NGO Monitor alleges that the commission "held secret hearings in Geneva and possibly in Gaza. The full extent of NGO participation, therefore, remains hidden, as do other aspects of this highly non-transparent process" when NGO Monitor itself remains behind a veil of secrecy and lack of transparency.

59. NGO Monitor, "Made in Europe."

60. NGO Monitor, "The Durban Strategy."

61. MSA, "The Money Trail," 5.

62. MSA, "The Money Trail," 6.

63. MSA, "Terrorists in Suits: The Ties Between NGOs Promoting BDS and Ter-rorist Organizations."

64. MSA, "Terrorists in Suits: Blood Money," 4.

65. Interview with a staff member of Addameer, Ramallah, November 2021.

66. FMEP, "Israel Declares War."

67. At the same time, it remains crucial to hold at the center of any analysis of NGOs in Palestine or human rights work more broadly, acknowledgement of the role and function that NGOs have played historically in fragmenting and undermining Palestinian liberatory politics. In offering an analysis of the asphyxiatory violence the TO classification unleashes onto the designated entities, I do not intend to posit an uncritical defense of NGOs or posit NGOs as vehicles of Palestinian liberation. Instead, I hope to hold two threads together—to both acknowledge the violence of Israel's designation while also keeping at the fore an analysis of how processes of NGOization has invariably stymied Palestinian collective, national struggle. Thus,

the important question at hand for decolonial politics in Palestine is *how* NGOiza-tion and the infrastructure of foreign aid is to be undone—a process, I would argue, that should come about through decolonial practice and broad-based struggle, not ever-morphing technologies of war and colonial pacification. I am indebted to Neve Gordon on this point.

68. Palestinians have long pointed to how the discourse of terrorism has been used expansively by Israel to criminalize and prohibit any act that challenges their subjugated position.

69. I met with the directors and staff of all the organizations but the Union of Pal-estinian Women's Committees, which at the time of this fieldwork had closed down.

70. Each of the designated six fit one, if not both, categories, including the pro-vision of support to Palestinian farmers and rural Palestinian communities to resist processes of dispossession and remain on their land, primarily in Area C amid set-tler encroachment backed with the full force of the Israeli state, and the collection and sharing of data of human rights violations and war crimes with international tribunals and fora, including the International Criminal Court. The designation di-rectly targets the international networks of financial support on which these orga-nizations rely.

71. NGO Monitor, "The Road Not Taken," 6.

72. D. Khalidi, "The Terrorism Smear."

73. It was at this time that the IDF arrested Walid Hanatshah, the organization's deputy director, on suspicion of his involvement in a 2019 plot to murder Israeli cit-izen Rina Shnerb.

74. Abraham, Ziv, and Rapoport, "Secret Israeli Document."

75. Conversation with a Palestinian policy analyst, Ramallah, November 2021.

76. Interview with a high-level staffer of DCI–P, Ramallah, November 2021.

77. See No Way to Treat a Child Campaign, "New Bill Prohibits Israel."

78. Asad, "Reflections on Violence," 412.

79. Asad, "Reflections on Violence," 412.

80. Çubukçu, "Liberal Violence," np.

81. Buttu, "How to Crush Palestinian NGOs."

82. MSA, "Terrorists in Suits: The Ties Between NGOs Promoting BDS and Terror-ist Organizations"; see also NGO Monitor, "The Road Not Taken."

83. When Shawan Jabarin was an Al-Haq researcher, he was arrested by Israel and held in administrative detention for eight years without charge. As Diana Buttu, who worked as an Al-Haq intern at the time points out, "It is this very arrest that or-ganizations such as NGO Monitor invoke to assert that he is a member of the PFLP"; see Buttu, "How to Crush Palestinian NGOs," 59

84. Interview with legal researcher at Al-Haq, Ramallah, December 2021.

85. The lawyer representing Al-Haq in the ICC, Nada Kiswanson, received death threats, threats to her family, intimidation, harassment, interference in her communications, and defamation.

86. Interview at Al-Haq, Ramallah, December 2021.

87. Amnesty International, "Israel's Apartheid."

88. Charity & Security Network, "What Donors Should Know."

89. Lehto and Ayyub, "Finnish Christian Charity."

90. UNHCR, "Israel/Palestine."

91. Interview in Ramallah, December 2021.

92. The contemporary global financial system is governed by extensive surveillance mechanisms, sanctions databases, and regulatory instruments, including SWIFT, World-Check, and SafeWatch and Know Your Customer protocols, among others.

93. In 2014 a US federal court in New York found the bank liable for maintaining the accounts of Hamas members. While the Arab Bank conceded it did allow the transfer of funds through the accounts, it maintained it had undertaken the required screening provisions of the account holders and did not maintain any connection with the US-designated FTO. The case was later thrown out by a US appeals court that argued that the Brooklyn jury was incorrectly instructed by the trial judge that "under federal law, Arab Bank committed an 'act of international terrorism' by knowingly providing material support to Hamas." Following the verdict, Arab Bank reached a confidential settlement with victims of terrorist attacks that had occurred during the second *intifada* amounting to roughly $1 billion. See Stempel, "Arab Bank Terrorism Case."

94. See NYU Paris EU Public Interest Clinic, *Bank De-Risking*.

95. Charity & Security Network, "Financial Access."

96. NYU Paris EU Public Interest Clinic, *Bank De-Risking*.

97. Interviews with Addameer and DCI–P, Ramallah, 2019.

98. Interview with a senior-level staffer at Applied Research Institution, Bethlehem, September 2019.

99. Interview in Ramallah, November 2021.

100. NYU Paris EU Public Interest Clinic, *Bank De-Risking*, 10.

101. NYU Paris EU Public Interest Clinic, *Bank De-Risking*, 10.

102. Interview in Ramallah, November 2021.

103. Interview in Ramallah, November 2021.

104. Buttu, "How to Crush Palestinian NGOs," 57.

105. Khalili, "The Location of Palestine"; Bhungalia, "Managing Violence"; Turner, "Peacebuilding as Counterinsurgency."

106. Jabotinsky, "The Iron Wall"; Khalili, "Collective Interventions."

107. Interview at Al-Haq, Ramallah, December 2021.

108. Interview with an Al-Haq staffer, Ramallah, December 2021.

109. Interview with a director of a designated organization, Ramallah, December 2021.

110. Interview in Ramallah, December 2021.

111. Taraki, "Urban Modernity." See also Ferguson, *The Anti-Politics Machine.* The connections between restructuring of the aid industry in the 1990s and the rise of "new normal politics" marked by an "individualistic ethos, leisure, self-enhancement, and social mobility," which steadily replaced and devalued the old-style, pre-Oslo nationalist politics predicated on broad-based, grassroots organizing and popular mobilization, is now well documented. See Taraki, "Urban Modernity," 65; Hajjar, "Human Rights in Israel/Palestine"; Hanafi and Tabar. *Emergence of Palestinian Globalized Elite*; Khan, Giacaman, and Amundsen, *State Formation in Palestine*; Le More, *International Assistance.*

112. Tamari, "The Palestinian Movement"; Hammami, "NGOs."

113. A. Simpson, *Mohawk Interruptus.*

114. B'Tselem, "B'Tselem's Response to MoD Gantz's Declaration"; see also Amnesty International, "Israel/OPT"; Human Rights Watch, "Israel/Palestine"; UNHCR, "Counter-Terrorism Legislation"; UNHCR, "UN High Commissioner."

115. B'Tselem, "B'Tselem's Response to MoD Gantz's Declaration."

116. Human Rights Watch, "Israel/Palestine."

117. It is notable that Israel has long turned to law to facilitate its expansionist project from legal treaties under the British Mandate for Palestine, which enabled Jewish settlement, to the use of international legal frameworks to gain Jewish sovereignty in the wake of World War II, to the meticulous use of war lawyers in drone warfare, to its use of military and occupied law to rule Palestinians; see Erakat, *Justice for Some;* and Jones, *The War Lawyers.* In this case, however, and tracking within the now well-trodden path of powerful states claiming that less-powerful adversaries manipulate law and especially international law to achieve a military objective (lawfare), Israel is invoking its executive decisionism to block Palestinian access to the law.

118. Interview with a legal researcher at Al-Haq, Ramallah, December 2021.

119. Interview in Ramallah, December 2021.

120. Interview with an Al-Haq staffer, December 2021.

121. Mulder, *The Economic Weapon,* 2–4.

122. Mulder, *The Economic Weapon,* 4.

123. Wilson, *Case for the League of Nations.*

124. Wilson, *Case for the League of Nations,* 71–72.

125. Mulder, *The Economic Weapon*, 4–5.

126. Mulder, *The Economic Weapon*.

Conclusion

1. Biden, "Remarks on End of the War in Afghanistan."

2. Quoted in Savage, "Biden Seeks Update."

3. Tahir, "The Distributed Empire."

4. As Asma Khalid points out, "the full span of the war on terror is unknown to the U.S. public, in part, because the complete list of groups that the United States is at war with is classified." See Khalid, "Biden Pledged."

5. Landler, "20 Years On."

6. Hilal, "Ayman al-Zawahiri."

7. This is of course not to somehow suggest that liberalism is somehow outside of or ameliorative to violence. Rather liberalism, as Talal Asad, Ayça Çubukçu, and Eyal Weizman among others have demonstrated, enables violence.

8. W. Said, *Crimes of Terror*.

9. Stoler, "Imperial Formations," 60; italics in original.

10. One such proposed bill was HR 350, the Domestic Terrorism Prevention Act of 2021, a bipartisan bill to strengthen policing and intelligence efforts to prevent, monitor, and respond to threats of domestic terrorism. While the legal designation of foreign terrorist organizations has existed since the passage of the Antiterrorism and Effective Death Penalty Act of 1996, no such corollary designation exists for organizations operating within the United States.

11. Miller and Bhungalia, "The Fungible Terrorist."

12. Feldman, "Trump's Full Spectrum Assault."

13. Following the termination of US funds to the agency in 2018, UNRWA had attempted, unsuccessfully, to fill the gap created by the US withdrawal with donations from Gulf and European countries. Between 2018 and 2022, Gulf funding to UNRWA, and from the UAE and Bahrain, in particular, declined significantly. Emirati donations dropped from $20 million in 2018 to $1 million two years later. The decline in Gulf funding is arguably directly related to the Abraham Accords, an agreement brokered by the Trump administration, which normalized relations and diplomatic ties between the United Arab Emirates, Bahrain, Sudan, Morocco, and Israel. European funding to the agency during this period also declined significantly. In light of an ongoing budgetary crisis, UNRWA signed the agreement with Washington without consulting the Palestinian Authority or any other Palestinian leadership body. See Jebril, "UNRWA as a Proxy Site," and Humaid, "Palestinian Factions in Gaza."

14. United Nations Relief and Works Agency, "Additional Support for Palestinian Refugees."

15. United States and the United Nations Relief and Works Agency for Palestinian Refugees in the Near East, "Framework," 2.

16. As the Palestinian refugee rights organization BADIL notes, UNRWA has "its own processes and mechanisms regardless of donors to make sure it respects United Nations as well as international regulations on use of funds and the prohibition to support terrorist activities through international funding." As per these legally binding mechanisms, the agency undertakes routine checks on "staff names, suppliers, registered Palestine refugees, and micro-finance recipients," which it screens against Security Council Resolution 1267 lists. UNRWA furthermore checks suppliers against United Nations Suspect Vendor reports and complies with internal reporting mechanisms. See BADIL, "USA–UNRWA Framework Agreement," 5.

17. See BADIL, "USA–UNRWA Framework Agreement," 8. United Nations entities and organizations are theoretically only permitted to vet against the Security Council Resolution 1267 list. UN Secretary General for Legal Affairs noted in correspondence to the US ambassador to the UN, John Bolton, in 2006, "it would not be appropriate for the United Nations to establish a verification regime that includes a list of possible contractors developed by one Member State" as "it would not be in a position to justify and defend its decision in respect to any individual or entity that is included in such lists," quoted in Mackintosh and Duplat, *Impact of Donor Counter-Terrorism*, 107.

18. Pantuliano and Metcalfe, *Neutrality Undermined*, np.

19. BADIL, "The GPRN," 7; see also Pantuliano and Metcalfe, *Neutrality Undermined.*

20. BADIL, "USA–UNRWA Framework Agreement."

21. BADIL, "USA–UNRWA Framework Agreement," 15.

22. BADIL, "USA–UNRWA Framework Agreement," 11. The framework's annex moreover stipulates that in addition to being responsible for undertaking periodic security checks of UNRWA staff, refugees, and other persons against the Consolidated United Nations Security Council Sanctions List every six months and reporting to the United States the results of these checks, UNRWA must also hold monthly meetings with State Department officials to ensure conformance with section 301(c); see United States and the United Nations Relief and Works Agency for Palestinian Refugees in the Near East, "Framework," 8.

23. Humaid, "Palestinian Factions in Gaza."

24. See Al-Monitor, "Gaza Factions Increase Calls"; Humaid, "Palestinian Factions in Gaza"; Jebril, "UNRWA as a Proxy Site."

25. Al-Monitor, "Gaza Factions Increase Calls"; see also Humaid, ""Palestinian Factions in Gaza."

26. Friedman, "Anatomy of the ATCA."

27. Interview conducted in Ramallah, August 2018. Some of the specific security and counterterrorism instruments and practices being referenced here are the anti-terrorism certification, introduced by USAID in 2003, rigorous vetting of recipient entities, and prohibitions on relations with entities not cleared by donor intelligence systems.

28. Lutz, "Empire Is in the Details."

29. Engelhardt, "Is America Hooked on War?"

30. Al-Bulushi, Ghosh, and Tahir, "American Anthropology, Decolonization."

31. McGranahan and Collins, "Introduction: Ethnography and U.S. Empire," 4.

Bibliography

Abraham, Yuval, Oren Ziv, and Meron Rapoport. "Secret Israeli Document Offers No Proof to Justify Terror Label for Palestinian Froups." *Intercept.* November 3, 2021. https://theintercept.com/2021/11/04/secret-israel-dossier-palestinian-rights-terrorist/?utm_source=General+Mailing+List&utm_campaign=71d7d40b74-EMAIL_CAMPAIGN_2021_11_04_12_20&utm_medium=email&utm_term=0_586030c60d-71d7d40b74-82761927

———. "Secret Israeli Dossier Provides No Proof for Declaring Palestinian NGOs 'Terrorists.'" *+972.* November 4, 2021. https://www.972mag.com/shin-bet-dossier-palestinian-ngos/

ACLU. *Blocking Faith, Freezing Charity: Chilling Muslim Charitable Giving in the "War on Terrorism Financing."* American Civil Liberties Union. 2009. http://www.aclu.org/pdfs/humanrights/blockingfaith.pdf

———. *Establishing a New Normal: National Security, Civil Liberties, and Human Rights Under the Obama Administration: An 18-Month Review.* July 2010. https://www.aclu.org/files/assets/EstablishingNewNormal.pdf

Agamben, Giorgio. *Homo Sacer: Sovereign Power and Bare Life.* Stanford: Stanford University Press, 1998.

———. *State of Exception.* Translated by Kevin Attell. Chicago: University of Chicago Press, 2005.

Agnew, John. "Sovereignty Regimes: Territoriality and State Authority in Contemporary World Politics." *Annals of the Association of American Geographers* 95, no. 2 (2005): 437–461.

———. "The Territorial Trap: The Geographical Assumptions of International Relations Theory." *Review of International Political Economy* 1, no. 1 (1994): 53–80.

Akbar, Amna. "Policing 'Radicalization.'" *UC Irvine Law Review* 3, no. 4 (2013): 809–883.

Al-Haq. (2021). "Israel Takes Alarming Steps to Enforce its Persecution of Six Palestinian Organisations in the West Bank, International Community Must Intervene." November 7, 2021.

———. "Side Event Parallel to UNHRC 49th Calling for Rescinding the Designation of the 6 Organizations and the Protection of Human Rights Work in Palestine." News release. *Al-Haq.* March 24, 2022. https://www.alhaq.org/advocacy/19767.html

Al-Arian, Abudllah. "Political Islam and the Endurance of American Empire." *JadMag* 6, no. 4 (2018): 7–11.

Al-Bulushi, Samar, Sahana Ghosh, and Madiha Tahir. "American Anthropology, Decolonization, and the Politics of Location." *American Anthropologist.* 2020. https://www.americananthropologist.org/commentaries/al-bulushi-ghosh-and-tahir

Al-Monitor. "Gaza Factions Increase Calls to Revoke US-UNRWA Agreement." September 23, 2021. https://www.al-monitor.com/originals/2021/09/gaza-factions-increase-calls-revoke-us-unrwa-agreement#ixzz7aSjOHKBG

Alfred, Gerald Taiaiake. *Heeding the Voices of Our Ancestors: Kahnawake Mohawk Politics and the Rise of Native Nationalism.* Don Mills, ON: Oxford University Press, 1995.

Allen, John. "A More Than Relational Geography?" *Dialogues in Human Geography* 2, no. 2 (2012): 190–193.

———. "Powerful Assemblages?" *Area* 43, no. 2 (2011): 154–157.

———. "Three Spaces of Power: Territory, Networks, Plus a Topological Twist in the Tale of Domination and Authority." *Journal of Power* 2, no. 2 (2009): 197–212.

———. "Topological Twists: Power's Shifting Geographies." *Dialogues in Human Geography* 1, no. 3 (2011): 283–298.

———. *Topologies of Power: Beyond Territory and Networks.* New York: Routledge, 2016.

Amar, Paul. "Turning the Gendered Politics of the Security State Inside Out? Charging the Police with Sexual Harassment in Egypt." *International Feminist Journal of Politics* 13, no. 3 (2011): 299–328.

Amicelle, Anthony, and Elida Jacobsen. "The Cross-Colonization of Finance and Security Through Lists: Banking Policing in the UK and India." *Environment and Planning D: Society and Space* 34, no. 1 (2016): 89–106.

Amnesty International. *Israel/Gaza: Operation "Cast Lead": 22 Days of Death and Destruction.* July 2, 2009. https://www.amnesty.org/download/Documents/48000/mde150152009en.pdf

———. "Israel/OPT: Designation of Palestinian Civil Society Groups as Terrorists a Brazen Attack on Human Rights." October 22, 2021. https://www.amnesty.org/en/latest/news/2021/10/israel-opt-designation-of-palestinian-civil-society-groups-as-terrorists-a-brazen-attack-on-human-rights/

———. "Israel's Apartheid Against Palestinians." 2022. https://www.amnestyusa.org/wp-content/uploads/2022/01/Full-Report.pdf

Amoore, Louise. *The Politics of Possibility: Risk and Security Beyond Probability.* Durham: Duke University Press, 2013.

ARIJ. "PPI & Palestinian Local Authorities: A Special Study." *Applied Research Institute—Jerusalem.* July 15, 2009. http://www.arij.org/files/admin/specialreports/PPI%20%26%20Palestinian%20Local%20Authorities.pdf

Asad, Talal. "Reflections on Violence, Law, and Humanitarianism." *Critical Inquiry* 41, no. 2 (2015): 390–427.

Atia, Mona. "In Whose Interest? Financial Surveillance and the Circuits of Exception in the War on Terror." *Environment & Planning D: Society & Space* 25, no. 3 (2007).

Atshan, Sa'ed Adel. "Prolonged Humanitarianism: The Social Life of Aid in the Palestinian Territories." PhD dissertation, anthropology. Harvard University, 2013.

Aziz, Sahar F. "Countering Religion or Terrorism? Selective Enforcement of Material Support Laws Against Muslim Charities." *Institute for Social Policy and Understanding.* 2011. https://www.ispu.org/wp-content/uploads/2011/03/2011_Countering-Religion-or-Terrorism.pdf?x46312

Bachmann, Jan, Colleen Bell, and Caroline Holmqvist, eds. *War, Police and Assemblages of Intervention.* London: Routledge, 2014.

BADIL. *European Union Conditional Funding: Its Illegality and Political Implications.* April 2020. https://www.badil.org/phocadownloadpap/badil-new/publications/research/in-focus/EuropeanUnionConditionalFunding(PositionPaper-April2020).pdf

———. "The GPRN Calls on the International Donor Community to Rescind the Anti-Terrorism Clauses and Conditions in Their Granting Contracts." December 2021. https://www.badil.org/press-releases/12749.html

———. *PNGO & PHROC Position Paper on the Ongoing Campaign to Silence, Delegitimize, and De-fund Palestinian Civil Society Organizations and Human Rights Defenders.* March 22, 2018.

———. "Statement Issued by the Popular Committees in the Palestinian Refugee Camps—West Bank, 26 April 2002." News release. 2002.

———. "USA–UNRWA Framework Agreement: Assistance or Securitization?" January 2022. https://badil.org/cached_uploads/view/2022/02/21/wp-29-unrwa-eng-1645448404.pdf

Balawi, Hassan. "Palestinian Municipal Elections: A Gradual Change." European Institute of the Mediterranean. 2006. https://www.iemed.org/anuari/2006/aarti
cles/aBalawi.pdf

Barkawi, Tarak. "On the Pedagogy of 'Small Wars.'" *International Affairs* 80, no. 1
(2004): 19–37.

Beaumont, Peter. "ICC Opens Investigation into War Crimes in Palestinian Territories." *The Guardian*. March 3, 2021. https://www.theguardian.com/law/2021/mar
/03/icc-open-formal-investigation-war-crimes-palestine

———. "Why Israel Fears the ICC War Crimes Investigation." *The Guardian*. March
3, 2021. https://www.theguardian.com/law/2021/mar/03/israeli-officials-start
-to-feel-the-impact-of-icc-investigation

Bedford, Kate. "Letting the Right Ones in: Whitelists, Jurisdictional Reputation, and
the Racial Dynamics of Online Gambling Regulation." *Environment and Planning D: Society and Space* 34, no. 1 (2015): 30–47.

Belcher, Oliver Christian. "The Afterlives of Counterinsurgency: Postcolonialism,
Military Social Science, and Afghanistan 2006–2012." PhD dissertation, geography. University of British Columbia, 2013.

Bell, Colleen. "Civilianising Warfare: Ways of War and Peace in Modern Counterinsurgency." *Journal of International Relations and Development* 14, no. 3 (2011):
309–332.

Benton, Lauren A. *A Search for Sovereignty: Law and Geography in European Empires,
1400–1900*. Cambridge: Cambridge University Press, 2010.

Berlant, Lauren. "Slow Death (Sovereignty, Obesity, Lateral Agency)." *Critical Inquiry*
33, no. 4 (2007): 754–780.

Bhungalia, Lisa. "Im/Mobilities in a 'Hostile Territory': Managing the Red Line." *Geopolitics* 17, no. 2 (2012): 256–275.

———. "Managing Violence: Aid, Counterinsurgency, and the Humanitarian Present in Palestine." *Environment and Planning A* 47 (2015): 2308–2323.

Bhungalia, Lisa, Jeannette Greven, and Tahani Mustafa. "The Shifting Contours of US
Power and Intervention in Palestine." *Middle East Report* 290 (Spring 2019): 13–19.

Bialasiewicz, Luiza. "Off-Shoring and Out-Sourcing the Borders of Europe: Libya and
EU Border Work in the Mediterranean." *Geopolitics* 17 (2012): 843–866.

Biden, Joseph. "Remarks by President Biden on the End of the War in Afghanistan."
The White House. August 31, 2021.

Bigo, Didier. "Globalized (in)Security: The Field and the Ban-Opticon." In *Terror, Insecurity and Liberty: Illiberal Practices of Liberal Regimes After 9/11*, edited by
Didier Bigo and Anastassia Tsoukala, 10–48. Abingdon: Routledge, 2008.

———. "The Möbius Ribbon of Internal and External Security(ies)." In *Identities,
Borders, Orders: Rethinking International Relations Theory*, edited by Mathias

Albert, David Jacobson, and Yosef Lapid, 91–116. Minneapolis: University of Minnesota Press, 2001.

Bowker, Geoffrey C., and Susan Leigh Star. *Sorting Things Out: Classification and Its Consequences*. Cambridge, MA: MIT Press, 1999.

Browne, Simone. *Dark Matters: On the Surveillance of Blackness*. Durham: Duke University Press, 2015.

Brulin, Rémi. "Compartmentalization, Contexts of Speech and the Israeli Origins of the American Discourse on 'Terrorism.'" *Dialectical Anthropology* 39, no. 1 (2015): 69–119.

———. "Defining 'Terrorism': The 1972 General Assembly Debates on 'International Terrorism' and Their Coverage by the *New York Times*." In *If It Was Not for Terrorism: Crisis, Compromise and Elite Discourse in the Age of "War on Terror,"* edited by Banu Baybars-Hawks and Lemi Baruh, 12–30. Newcastle upon Tyne: Cambridge Scholars Publishing, 2011.

———. "Distorting Justice? Israel/Palestine & US 'Terrorism' Law." Center for Palestine Studies, Columbia University. May 6, 2013.

B'Tselem. "B'Tselem's Response to MoD Gantz's Declaration of Palestinian Human Rights Organizations as Terrorist Organizations." Press release. October 22, 2021.

———. "Joint Statement: Draconian Measure Against Human Rights." Press release. October 25, 2021. https://www.btselem.org/press_releases/20211025_draconian _measure_against_human_rights

———. "The Mass Deportation of 1992." January 1, 2011. https://www.btselem.org/ deportation/1992_mass_deportation

Bush, George W. "Fact Sheet on Terrorist Financing Executive Order." The White House. September 24, 2001. https://georgewbush-whitehouse.archives.gov/news/ releases/2001/09/20010924-2.html

———. "President Freezes Terrorists' Assets." The White House. September 24, 2001. https://georgewbush-whitehouse.archives.gov/news/releases/2001/09/200109 24-4.html

———. "Remarks by the President in Address to the Nation." Office of the Press Secretary. March 17, 2003.

Butler, Judith. *Frames of War: When Is Life Grievable?* London: Verso, 2009.

Buttu, Diana. "How to Crush Palestinian NGOs: Just Use the 'T' Word." *Journal of Palestine Studies* 51, no. 2 (2022): 57–61.

Callon, Michel, and John Law. "Introduction: Absence—Presence, Circulation, and Encountering in Complex Space." *Environment and Planning D: Society and Space* 22, no. 1 (2004): 3–11.

Certification Regarding Terrorist Financing, USAID Acquisition and Assistance Policy Directive (AAPD) 02–19. December 31, 2002.

Challand, Benoît. "The Evolution of Western Aid for Palestinian Civil Society: By-passing Local Knowledge and Resources." *Middle Eastern Studies* 44, no. 3 (2008): 397–417.

Charity & Security Network. "Congress Enacts Partial Fix to Anti-Terrorism Clarification Act." February 4, 2020. https://charityandsecurity.org/news/sres_171_aid_palestine/

———. "Financial Access and De-Risking: Moving Toward Solutions for Nonprofit Organizations." October, 2017. https://charityandsecurity.org/system/files/2017%20Fin%20Access%20Issue%20Briefdocx_0.pdf

———. "USA v Holy Land Foundation for Relief and Development." August 24, 2020. https://charityandsecurity.org/litigation/holy-land-foundation/

———. "What Donors Should Know Following the Dutch Government's Decision to Cut Funding for UAWC." January 2022.

———. "World-Check: The Dangers of Privatizing Terrorist Lists." *Security & Charity Network.* February 11, 2016. https://charityandsecurity.org/financial-access/worldcheck_private_databases_raise_concerns/

CHE Project. "Partner Vetting in Humanitarian Assistance: An Overview of Pilot USAID and State Department Programs." *Research and Policy Paper.* November 2013. http://blogs.harvard.edu/cheproject/files/2013/10/CHE-Project-Partner-Vetting-in-Humanitarian-Assistance-November-2013.pdf

Chesney, Robert. M. "The Sleeper Scenario: Terrorism-Support Laws and the Demands of Prevention." *Harvard Journal on Legislation* 42, no. 1 (2005): 1–89.

Clarno, Andy. *Neoliberal Apartheid: Palestine/Israel and South Africa After 1994.* Chicago: University of Chicago Press, 2017.

———. "Securing Oslo: The Dynamics of Security Coordination in the West Bank." *Middle East Report* 269 (2013): 35–39.

Cockayne, Daniel, Derek Ruez, and Anna Secor. "Thinking Space Differently: Deleuze's Möbius Topology for a Theorisation of the Encounter." *Transactions of the Institute of British Geographers* 45, no. 1 (2019): 194–207.

Coleman, Mat. "A Geopolitics of Engagement: Neoliberalism, the War on Terrorism, and the Reconfiguration of US Immigration Enforcement." *Geopolitics* 12, no. 4 (2007): 607–634.

———. "Immigration Geopolitics Beyond the Mexico–US Border." *Antipode* 39, no. 1 (2007): 54–76.

———. "Immigrant Il-Legality: Geopolitical and Legal Borders in the US, 1882–Present." *Geopolitics* 17, no. 2 (2012): 402–422.

———. "Topologies of Practice." *Dialogues in Human Geography* 1, no. 3 (2011): 308–311.

———. "U.S. Statecraft and the U.S.–Mexico Border as Security/Economy Nexus." *Political Geography* 24, no. 2 (2005): 185–209.

Coulthard, Glen. *Red Skin, White Masks: Rejecting the Colonial Politics of Recognition.* Minneapolis: University of Minnesota Press, 2014.

Çubukçu, Ayça. "Liberal Violence." Paper presented at "Resistance, Justice, Liberation: Critical Approaches to Knowledge Production on War, Violence and Colonization." Trinity Public Seminar Series, University of Oxford. 2022. https://www.rsc.ox.ac.uk/events/liberal-violence

Daily Star. "Lebanese Electoral Law 2017." May 5, 2018.

Dakwar, Jamil. "The Terrorism Smear: Israel's Move to Shut Down Palestinian Human Rights Work." Podcast Audio. *Occupied Thoughts.* Foundation for Middle East Peace. November 5, 2021.

Dana, Tariq. "Criminalizing Palestinian Resistance: The EU's Additional Condition on Aid to Palestine." *Al-Shabaka.* February 2, 2020. https://al-shabaka.org/commentaries/criminalizing-palestinian-resistance-the-eu-new-conditions-on-aid-to-palestine/

DCI–P. "Israeli Forces Raid DCI–P Office." July 29, 2021. https://www.dci-palestine.org/israeli_forces_raid_dcip_office_confiscate_computers_and_client_files

———. "UK Lawyers for Israel Recants Allegations of DCI–P Material Support to Designated Terror Group." 2020. https://www.dci-palestine.org/uk_lawyers_for_israel_recants_allegations_of_dcip_material_support_to_terror_group

de Goede, Marieke. *Speculative Security: The Politics of Pursuing Terrorist Monies.* Minneapolis: University of Minnesota Press, 2012.

de Goede, Marieke, Anna Leander, and Gavin Sullivan. "Introduction: The Politics of the List." *Environment and Planning D: Society and Space* 34, no. 1 (2016): 3–13.

de Goede, Marieke, and Gavin Sullivan. "The Politics of Security Lists." *Environment and Planning D: Society and Space* 34, no. 1 (2016): 67–88.

Deleuze, Gilles. *The Fold: Leibniz and the Baroque,* translated by Tom Conley. Minneapolis: University of Minnesota Press, 1993.

———. *Foucault.* Minneapolis: University of Minnesota Press, 1988.

Department of Justice. "Federal Officials Close Investigation into the Death of Sergio Hernandez-Guereca." April 27, 2012. https://www.justice.gov/opa/pr/federal-officials-close-investigation-death-sergio-hernandez-guereca

Deutsch, Michael E., and Erica Thompson. "Secrets and Lies: The Persecution of Muhammad Salah (Part I)." *Journal of Palestine Studies* 37, no. 4 (2008): 38–58.

———. "Secrets and Lies: The Persecution of Muhammad Salah (Part II)." *Journal of Palestine Studies* 38, no. 1 (2008): 25–53.

Devereaux, Ryan. (2019). "Secret Terrorism Watchlist Found Unconstitutional in

Historic Decision." *Intercept.* December 6, 2019. https://theintercept.com/2019/09/06/terrorism-watchlist-lawsuit-ruling/

Devereaux, Ryan, and Alex Emmons. "Obama Worries Future Presidents Will Wage Perpetual, Covert Drone War." *The Intercept.* October 3, 2016. https://theintercept.com/2016/10/03/obama-worries-future-presidents-will-wage-perpetual-covert-drone-war/

Dixon, Deborah, and John Paul Jones III. "The Tactile Topologies of Contagion." *Transactions of the Institute of British Geographers* 40, no. 2 (2015): 223–234.

Dodge, Martin, and Rob Kitchen. "Code and the Transduction of Space." *Annals of the Association of American Geographers* 95, no. 1 (2005): 162–180.

Duffield, Mark. *Global Governance and the New Wars: The Merging of Development and Security.* London: Zed Books, 2001.

Eaton, Leslie. "U.S. Prosecution of Muslim Group Ends in Mistrial." *New York Times.* October 23, 2007. https://www.nytimes.com/2007/10/23/us/23charity.html

Eid, Haidar. "Why I Marched on May 14 in Gaza Near the Israeli Fence." *Al Jazeera.* May 16, 2018. https://www.aljazeera.com/opinions/2018/5/16/why-i-marched-on-may-14-in-gaza-near-the-israeli-fence

Elden, Stuart. *The Birth of Territory.* Chicago: University of Chicago Press, 2013.

———. *Terror and Territory: The Spatial Extent of Sovereignty.* Minneapolis: University of Minnesota Press, 2009.

———. "What's Shifting?" *Dialogues in Human Geography* 1, no. 3 (2011): 304–307.

Elgindy, Khaled. *Blind Spot: America and the Palestinians, from Balfour to Trump.* Washington, DC: Brookings Institute Press, 2019.

Engelhardt, Tom. "Is America Hooked on War?" *The Nation.* September 17, 2009. https://www.thenation.com/article/archive/america-hooked-war/

Erakat, Noura. *Justice for Some: Law and the Question of Palestine.* Stanford: Stanford University Press, 2019.

Estrin, Daniel. "Palestinian School and Sewage Projects Unfinished as US Cuts Final Bit of Aid." *NPR.* January 17, 2019.

Fassin, Didier. "Humanitarianism as a Politics of Life." *Public Culture* 19, no. 3 (2007): 499.

Fassin, Didier, and Mariella Pandolfi, eds. *Contemporary States of Emergency: The Politics of Military and Humanitarian Interventions.* New York: Zone Books, 2010.

Feldman, Ilana. "Gaza's Humanitarian Problem." *Journal of Palestine Studies* 38, no. 3 (2008): 22–37.

———. "The Humanitarian Condition: Palestinian Refugees and the Politics of Living." *Humanity: An International Journal of Human Rights, Humanitarianism, and Development* 3, no. 2 (2012): 155–172.

———. *Life Lived in Relief: Humanitarian Predicaments and Palestinian Refugee Politics*. Oakland: University of California Press, 2018.

———. *Police Encounters: Security and Surveillance in Gaza Under Egyptian Rule*. Stanford: Stanford University Press, 2015.

———. "Trump's Full Spectrum Assault on Palestinian Politics." *Middle East Report Online*. December 2, 2018. https://merip.org/2018/12/trumps-full-spectrum-assault-on-palestinian-politics/

Feldman, Ilana, and Miriam Ticktin, eds. *In the Name of Humanity: The Government of Threat and Care*. Durham: Duke University Press, 2010.

Ferguson, James. *The Anti-Politics Machine: Development, Depoliticization, and Bureaucratic Power in Lesotho*. Minneapolis: University of Minnessota Press, 1994.

Fernando, Mayanthi. "Temporality, Asphyxiation, Debilitation." *Political Theology Network*. May 27, 2021. https://politicaltheology.com/temporality-asphyxiation-debilitation/

Fisher-Ilan, Allyn. "Israel's Netanyahu Vows Long Fight Against U.N. Report." *Reuters*. October 17, 2009. https://www.reuters.com/article/uk-israel-palestinians-un/israels-netanyahu-vows-long-fight-against-u-n-report-idUKTRE59G0Z32 0091017

FMEP. "Israel Declares War on Palestinian Human Rights Defenders." Podcast Audio. *Occupied Thoughts*. Foundation for Middle East Peace. October 22, 2021.

———. "The Terrorism Smear: Israel's Move to Shut Down Palestinian Human Rights Work." Podcast Audio. *Occupied Thoughts*. Foundation for Middle East Peace. November 5, 2021.

Foucault, Michel. *Security, Territory, Population: Lectures at the Collège de France, 1977–1978*, edited by Michel Senellart, translated by Graham Burchell. Basingstoke: Palgrave Macmillan, 2007.

Francis, Sahar. "Israel's Military Courts for Palestinians Are a Stain on International Justice." *The Guardian*. March 6, 2021. https://www.theguardian.com/commentisfree/2021/mar/06/israel-military-courts-palestinians-law-uk

Friedman, Lara. "The Anatomy of the ATCA." *PeaceCast*. Podcast Audio. February 8, 2019. https://peacenow.libsyn.com/71-the-anatomy-of-atca

———. "FMEP Legislative Round-Up." March 22, 2019. https://fmep.org/resource/fmep-legislative-round-march-22-2019/

———. "The Surprising New Battleground in the War Against Palestinian Rights: Your Local Courthouse." *The Forward*. January 7, 2019.

Front Line Defenders. "Press Release—Front Line Defenders Investigation Finds Pegasus Spyware on 6 Palestinian HRD Phones." *Front Line Defenders*. November 8, 2021.

———. "Six Palestinian Human Rights Defenders Hacked with NSO Group's Pegasus Spyware." November 8, 2021. https://www.frontlinedefenders.org/en/statement -report/statement-targeting-palestinian-hrds-pegasus

Gilbert, Emily. "Elasticity at the Canada–US Border: Jurisdiction, Rights, Accountability." *Environment and Planning C: Politics and Space* 37, no. 3 (2019): 424–441.

Gisha. *Red Lines Crossed: Destruction of Gaza's Infrastructure.* August 2009. https:// gisha.org/UserFiles/File/publications_/Infrastructures_Report_Aug09_Eng.pdf

Goldenberg, Tia. "Israel Envoy to Brief US over Ban on Palestinian Groups." *Associated Press.* October 26, 2021. https://apnews.com/article/middle-east-israel -united-states-tel-aviv-697d72bbf2e8dbf8147ffa0c361674d3

Gordon, Avery. *Ghostly Matters: Haunting and the Sociological Imagination.* Minneapolis: University of Minnesota Press, 2008.

Gordon, Neve, and Moriel Ram. "Ethnic Cleansing and the Formation of Settler Colonial Geographies." *Political Geography* 53 (2016): 20–29.

Gregory, Derek. *The Colonial Present: Afghanistan, Palestine, Iraq.* Oxford: Blackwell, 2004.

———. "The Everywhere War." *Geographical Journal* 177, no. 3 (2011): 238–250.

———. "War and Peace." *Transactions of the Institute of British Geographers* 35, no. 2 (2010): 154–186.

Griffiths, Mark. "The Geontological Time-Spaces of Late Modern War." *Progress in Human Geography* 46, no. 2 (2022): 282–298.

Grove, Jairus Victor. *Savage Ecology: War and Geopolitics at the End of the World.* Durham: Duke University Press, 2019.

Guinane, Kay. "19 Years Later EO 13224 Continues to Block Humanitarian Aid. It's Time for an Update." *Charity & Security Network.* 2020. https://charityandsecurity .org/blog/19-years-later-eo-13224-continues-to-block-humanitarian-aid-its -time-for-an-update/

Gyeney, Michelle. "US Aid Freeze Designed to Further Punish Palestinians." *Electronic Intifada.* October 11, 2011. https://electronicintifada.net/content/us-aid -freeze-designed-further-punish-palestinians/10473

Haddad, Toufic. *Palestine Ltd: Neoliberalism and Nationalism in the Occupied Territory.* London: I. B. Tauris, 2016.

Hajjar, Lisa. "The Afterlives of Torture: The Global Implications of Reactionary US Politics." *State Crime Journal* 8, no. 2 (2019): 164–174.

———. "The Afterlives of Torture: Putting the US War on Terror in Historical and Global Context." *Middle East Report* 47, no. 283 (2017): 16–22.

———. "The Counterterrorism War Paradigm Versus International Humanitarian Law: The Legal Contradictions and Global Consequences of the US War on Terror." *Law and Social Inquiry* 44, no. 4 (2019): 922–956.

———. "Grave Injustice: Maher Arar and Unaccountable America." *Middle East Report Online.* June 24, 2010. https://merip.org/2010/06/grave-injustice/

———. "Human Rights in Israel/Palestine: The History and Politics of a Movement." *Journal of Palestine Studies* 30, no. 4 (2001): 21–38.

———. *Torture: A Sociology of Violence and Human Rights.* New York: Routledge, 2013.

Hammami, Rema. "NGOs: The Professionalisation of Politics." *Race & Class* 37, no. 2 (1995): 51–63.

Hanafi, Sari, and Linda Tabar. *The Emergence of a Palestinian Globalized Elite: Donors, International Organizations and Local NGOs.* Jerusalem: Institute of Jerusalem Studies & Muwatin, 2005.

Harker, Christopher. "Debt Space: Topologies, Ecologies and Ramallah, Palestine." *Environment and Planning D: Society and Space* 35, no. 4 (2017): 600–619.

———. *Spacing Debt: Obligations, Violence, and Endurance in Ramallah, Palestine.* Durham: Duke University Press, 2020.

Hilal, Maha. "Ayman al-Zawahiri Killing Proves the 'War on Terror' Was Never Over." *Middle East Eye.* August 4, 2022. https://www.middleeasteye.net/opinion/ayman-zawahiri-killing-war-on-terror-never-over?mc_cid=5326a82971&mc_eid=38b457be6e

Hoffman, Bruce. *Inside Terrorism,* 3rd ed. New York: Columbia University Press, 2017 [1998].

Hoffman, David. "Israel Holds U.S. Men Said to Aid Hamas; Arab-Americans Said to Pass Funds to Group." *Washington Post.* February 1, 1993.

Howell, Alison, and Melanie Richter-Montpetit. "Is Securitization Theory Racist? Civilizationism, Methodological Whiteness, and Antiblack Thought in the Copenhagen School." *Security Dialogue.* 2019. https://doi.org/10.1177/0967010619862921

Humaid, Maram. "Palestinian Factions in Gaza Call to End Latest UNRWA-US Deal." *Al Jazeera.* October 5, 2021. https://www.aljazeera.com/news/2021/10/5/palestinian-factions-call-to-cancel-unrwa-us-agreement

Human Rights Watch. "Israel/Palestine: Designation of Palestinian Rights Groups as Terrorists: Attack on the Human Rights Movement." *HRW.* October 22, 2021. https://www.hrw.org/news/2021/10/22/israel/palestine-designation-palestinian-rights-groups-terrorists

Hussain, Murtaza. "One Man's No-Fly List Nightmare." *The Intercept.* May 30, 2021. https://theintercept.com/2021/05/30/no-fly-list-terrorism-watchlist/?utm_source=R%26I+Clips+%28Coalition%29&utm_campaign=6297fdba01-EMAIL_CAMPAIGN_2018_08_15_02_10_COPY_01&utm_medium=email&utm_term=0_3a915757be-6297fdba01-391722642&mc_cid=fe61bbd12a&mc_eid=38b457be6e

ICC. "Statement of ICC Prosecutor, Fatou Bensouda, on the Conclusion of the Preliminary Examination of the Situation in Palestine, and Seeking a Ruling on the Scope of the Court's Territorial Jurisdiction." *International Criminal Court*. December 20, 2019. https://www.icc-cpi.int/news/statement-icc-prosecutor-fatou-bensouda-conclusion-preliminary-examination-situation-palestine

Ismail, Tarek Z. "Palestine and the US 'War on Terror.'" Episode 29 [Webinar]. Coalition for Civil Freedoms. May 21, 2021.

Jabotinsky, Vladimir. "The Iron Wall." *The Jewish Herald*. November 26, 1937. http://www.marxists.de/middleast/ironwall/ironwall.htm

Jabri, Vivienne. "Global War and the Government of Populations." *Brown Journal of World Affairs* 24, no. 1 (2017): 89–104.

———. *The Postcolonial Subject: Claiming Politics/Governing Others in Late Modernity*. London: Routledge, 2012.

———. *War and the Transformation of Global Politics*. Basingstoke and New York: Palgrave Macmillan, 2007.

———. "War, Government, Politics: A Critical Response to the Hegemony of the Liberal Peace." In *Palgrave Advances in Peacebuilding: Critical Developments and Approaches*, edited by Oliver P. Richmond, 41–57. New York: Palgrave Macmillan, 2010.

Jamal, Amal. *The Palestinian National Movement: Politics of Contention, 1967–2005*. Bloomington: Indiana University Press, 2005.

Jebril, Mona. "UNRWA as a Proxy Site of Conflict? The Case of the Gaza Strip." *Carnegie Endowment for International Peace*. 2021. https://carnegieendowment.org/sada/87161

Jones, Craig A. "Lawfare and the Juridification of Late Modern War." *Progress in Human Geography* (2015): 1–19.

———. *The War Lawyers: The United States, Israel, and Juridical Warfare*. Oxford: Oxford University Press, 2020.

Jones, Craig A., and Michael D. Smith. "War/Law/Space: Notes Toward a Legal Geography of War." *Environment and Planning D: Society and Space* 33, no. 4 (2015): 581–591.

Jones, Reece, Corey Johnson, Wendy Brown, Gabriel Popescu, Polly Pallister-Wilkins, Alison Mountz, and Emily Gilbert. "Interventions on the State of Sovereignty at the Border." *Political Geography Political Geography* 59, no. 1 (2017): 1–10.

Joronen, Mikko. "Politics of Being-Related: On Onto-Topologies and 'Coming Events.'" *Geografiska Annaler: Series B, Human Geography* 98, no. 2 (2016): 97–107.

Kane, Alex, and Mariam Barghouti. "How an Israeli Smear Campaign Is Ripping

Away Funds from Palestinian Farmers." *+972.* January 25, 2021. https://www.972
mag.com/palestinian-funding-uawc-israel-lobby/

Kaplan, Amy. "Where Is Guantánamo?" *American Quarterly* 57, no. 3 (2005): 831–858.

Keating, Michael, Anne Le More, and Robert Lowe, eds. *Aid, Diplomacy and Facts on
the Ground: The Case of Palestine.* London: Chatham House, 2005.

Khalid, Asma. "Biden Pledged to End the Forever Wars, but He Might Just Be Shrinking Them." *NPR.* September 8, 2021. https://www.npr.org/2021/09/08/1034140589
/afghanistan-biden-pledge-to-end-forever-wars

Khalidi, Dima. "The Terrorism Smear: Israel's Move to Shut Down Palestinian
Human Rights Work." Podcast Audio. *Occupied Thoughts.* November 5, 2021.
Foundation for Middle East Peace.

Khalidi, Rashid. *Resurrecting Empire: Western Footprints and America's Perilous Path
in the Middle East.* Boston: Beacon Press, 2004.

Khalil, Osamah. "At the Crossroads of Empire: The United States, the Middle East,
and the Politics of Knowledge, 1902–2002." PhD dissertation, history. University
of California, Berkeley, 2011.

———. "Pax Americana: The United States, the Palestinians, and the Peace Process,
1948–2008." *New Centennial Review* 8, no. 1 (2008): 1–41.

Khalili, Laleh. "Collective Interventions: The Iron Wall." *Feminist Review* 84 (2006):
2–4.

———. "The Location of Palestine in Global Counterinsurgencies." *International
Journal of Middle East Studies* 42 (2010): 413–433.

———. *Time in the Shadows: Confinement in Counterinsurgencies.* Stanford: Stanford
University Press, 2013.

———. "The Utility of Proxy Detention in Counterinsurgencies." In *War, Police and
Assemblages of Intervention,* edited by Jan Bachmann, Colleen Bell, and Caroline
Holmqvist, 92–108. London: Routledge, 2014.

Khalili, Laleh, and Lisa Hajjar. "Torture, Drones, and Detention: A Conversation Between Laleh Khalili and Lisa Hajjar." *Jadaliyya Reports.* 2013. http://www.jadaliyya
.com/pages/index/9600/torture-drones-and-detention_a-conversation-betwee

Khan, Mushtaq Husain, George Giacaman, and Inge Amundsen, eds. *State Formation in Palestine: Viability and Governance During a Social Transformation.* New
York: Routledge, 2004.

Kirchgaessner, Stephanie. "Israeli Spyware Company NSO Group Placed on US
Blacklist." *The Guardian.* November 3, 2021. https://www.theguardian.com/us
-news/2021/nov/03/nso-group-pegasus-spyware-us-blacklist

Kumar, Deepa. "Terrorcraft: Empire and the Making of the Racialised Terrorist
Threat." *Race & Class* 62, no. 2 (2020): 34–60.

Kurd, Dana El. *Polarized and Demobilized: Legacies of Authoritarianism in Palestine.* London: Oxford University Press, 2019.

Lahav, Gallya, and Virginie Guiraudon. "Comparative Perspectives on Border Control: Away from the Border and Outside the State." In *The Wall Around the West*, edited by Peter Andreas and Timothy Snyder, 55–77. Lanham: Rowman & Littlefield, 2000.

Lakatos, Alex, and Jan Blöchliger. "The Extraterritorial Reach of U.S. Anti-Terrorist Finance Laws." *GESKR* 344 (2009): 344–354.

Landler, Mark. "20 Years On, the War on Terror Grinds Along, with No End in Sight." *New York Times.* September 10, 2021. https://www.nytimes.com/2021/09/10/world/europe/war-on-terror-bush-biden-qaeda.html

Lansner, Ruth. *Testimony of Ruth Lansner, Anti-Defamation League, International Terrorism: Threats and Responses: Hearings on H.R. 1710, Comprehensive Antiterrorism Act of 1995.* 104th Congress. 1995.

Lata, Iulian, and Claudio Minca. "The Surface and the Abyss/Rethinking Topology." *Environment and Planning D: Society and Space* 34, no. 3 (2016): 438–455.

Latour, Bruno. *Reassembling the Social.* Oxford: Oxford University Press, 2005.

———. *Science in Action: How to Follow Scientists and Engineers Through Society.* Cambridge, MA: Harvard University Press, 1987.

———. "Visualization and Cognition: Drawing Things Together." *Knowledge and Society* 6 (1986): 1–40.

Law, John. "After ANT: Complexity, Naming and Topology." In *Actor Network Theory and After*, edited by John Law and John Hassard, 1–14. Oxford: Blackwell, 1999.

———. "Collateral Realities." In *The Politics of Knowledge*, edited by Fernando Domínguez Rubio and Patrick Baert, 156–178. London: Routledge, 2012.

Law, John, and Annemarie Mol. "Situating Technoscience: An Inquiry into Spatialities." *Environment and Planning D: Society and Space* 19 (2001): 609–621.

Leander, Anna. "The Politics of Whitelisting: Regulatory Work and Topologies in Commercial Security." *Environment and Planning D: Society and Space* 34, no. 1 (2016): 48–66.

Lehto, Essi, and Rami Ayyub. "Finnish Christian Charity Cuts Ties with Palestinian NGO Accused by Israel of Aiding Militants." *Reuters.* November 5, 2021. https://www.reuters.com/world/finnish-christian-charity-cuts-ties-with-palestinian-ngo-accused-by-israel-2021-11-05/

Le More, Anne. *International Assistance to the Palestinians After Oslo: Political Guilt, Wasted Money.* New York: Routledge, 2008.

Levin, Naomi. "Are Our Tax Dollars Funding Palestinian Terror?" *Australian Jewish News.* July 5, 2018. https://ajn.timesofisrael.com/are-our-tax-dollars-funding-palestinian-terror/

Li, Darryl. "From Exception to Empire: Sovereignty, Carceral Circulation, and the Global War on Terror.'" In *Ethnographies of U.S. Empire*, edited by Carole Mc-Granahan and John F. Collins, 456–475. Durham: Duke University Press, 2018.

———. "A Jihadism Anti-Primer." *Middle East Report Online*. 2015. https://merip.org /2015/12/a-jihadism-anti-primer/

———. "Khaled el-Masri and Empire's Oblivion." *Middle East Report Online*. December 13, 2012. https://merip.org/2012/12/khaled-el-masri-and-empires-oblivion/

———. *The Universal Enemy: Jihad, Empire, and the Challenge of Solidarity*. Stanford: Stanford University Press, 2019.

Liptak, Adam. "Justices Weigh Agent's Cross-Border Shooting of Mexican Teenager." *New York Times*. Feburary 21, 2017. https://www.nytimes.com/2017/02/21/us/ politics/justices-weigh-agents-cross-border-shooting-of-mexican-teenager.html

Litani, Yehuda. "'Village Leagues': What Kind of Carrot?" *Journal of Palestine Studies* 11, no. 3 (1982): 174–178.

Loyd, Jenna, Emily Mitchell-Eaton, and Alison Mountz. "The Militarization of Islands and Migration Control: Tracing American Empire Through Bases in the Caribbean and the Pacific." *Political Geography* 53 (2016): 65–75.

Loyd, Jenna M., and Alison Mountz. *Boats, Borders, and Bases: Race, the Cold War, and the Rise of Migration Detention in the United States*. Berkeley: University of California Press, 2018.

Lutz, Catherine. "Empire Is in the Details." *American Ethnologist* 33, no. 4 (2006): 593–611.

Machold, Rhys. "Reconsidering the Laboratory Thesis: Palestine/Israel and the Geopolitics of Representation." *Political Geography* 65 (2018): 88–97.

Mackintosh, Kate, and Patrick Duplat. *Study of the Impact of Donor Counter-Terrorism Measures on Principled Humanitarian Action*. United Nations Office for the Coordination of Humanitarian Affairs and the Norwegian Refugee Council. July 2013. https://www.nrc.no/globalassets/pdf/reports/study-of-the-impact-of-do nor-counterterrorism-measures-on-principled-humanitarian-action.pdf

Maillet, Pauline, Alison Mountz, and Kira Williams. "Exclusion Through Imperio: Entanglements of Law and Geography in the Waiting Zone, Excised Territory and Search and Rescue Region." *Social & Legal Studies* 27, no. 2 (2018): 142–163.

Makky, Abed-Alnaser. "The Role of Local Government Bodies in the Case of the PNA's Collapse or Dissolution." *Palestinian Center for Policy & Survey Research*. October 2013. https://www.pcpsr.org/sites/default/files/Local.pdf

Markson, Sharri. "Our West Bank Deposits." *Daily Telegraph* (Australia). June 28, 2018.

Martin, Lauren, and Anna Secor. "Towards a Post-Mathematical Topology." *Progress in Human Geography* 38, no. 3 (2014): 420–438.

Martínez, José C. *States of Subsistence: The Politics of Bread in Contemporary Jordan.* Stanford: Stanford University Press, 2022.

———. "Topological Twists in the Syrian Conflict: Re-Thinking Space Through Bread." *Review of International Studies* 46, no. 1 (2020): 121–136.

Massumi, Brian. *Ontopower: War, Powers, and the State of Perception.* Durham: Duke University Press, 2015.

McConnell, Fiona. "De Facto, Displaced, Tacit: The Sovereign Articulations of the Tibetan Government-in-Exile." *Political Geography* 28, no. 6 (2009): 343–352.

———. "Sovereignty." In *The Ashgate Research Companion to Critical Geopolitics,* edited by Klaus Dodds, Merje Kuus, and Joanne Sharp, 109–128. Aldershot: Ashgate, 2013.

McGranahan, Carole, and John F. Collins, eds. *Ethnographies of U.S. Empire.* Durham: Duke University Press, 2018.

———. "Introduction: Ethnography and U.S. Empire." In *Ethnographies of U.S. Empire,* edited by Carole McGranahan and John F. Collins, 1–24. Durham: Duke University Press, 2018.

Miller, Andrea. "(Im)Material Terror: Incitement to Violence Discourse as Racializing Technology in the War on Terror." In *Life in the Age of Drone Warfare,* edited by Lisa Parks and Caren Kaplan, 112–133. Durham: Duke University Press, 2017.

———. "Shadows of War, Traces of Policing: The Weaponization of Space and the Sensible in Preemption." In *Captivating Technology,* edited by Ruha Benjamin, 85–106. Durham: Duke University Press, 2019.

Miller, Andrea, and Lisa Bhungalia. "The Fungible Terrorist: Abject Whiteness, Domestic Terrorism, and the Multicultural Security State." *Small Wars & Insurgencies* 33, no. 4–5 (2022): 902–925.

"Mohammad El Halabi Trial Overview." *World Vision.* 2016. https://www.wvi.org/jerusalem-west-bank-gaza/mohammad-el-halabi-trial-overview

Moreira, Tiago. (2004). "Surgical Monads: A Social Topology of the Operating Room." *Environment and Planning D: Society and Space* 22 (2004): 53–69.

Mountz, Alison. "The Enforcement Archipelago: Detention, Haunting, and Asylum on Islands." *Political Geography* 30, no. 3 (2011): 118–128.

———. "Political Geography I: Reconfiguring Geographies of Sovereignty." *Progress in Human Geography* 37, no. 6 (2013).

———. "Where Asylum-Seekers Wait: Feminist Counter-Topographies of Sites Between States." *Gender, Place & Culture* 18, no. 3 (2011): 381–399.

Mountz, Alison, and Nancy Hiemstra. "Spatial Strategies for Rebordering Human Migration at Sea." In *A Companion to Border Studies,* edited by Thomas M. Wilson and Hastings Donnan, 455–472. Hoboken: Wiley-Blackwell, 2012.

MSA. "The Money Trail: European Union Financing of Organizations Promoting Boycotts Against the State of Israel." State of Israel Ministry of Strategic Affairs and Public Diplomacy. January 2019.

———. "Terrorists in Suits: Blood Money." State of Israel Ministry of Strategic Affairs and Public Diplomacy. May 2020.

———. "Terrorists in Suits: The Ties Between NGOs Promoting BDS and Terrorist Organizations." State of Israel Ministry of Strategic Affairs and Public Diplomacy. February 2019.

Mukhimer, Tariq. *State Building Process: The Case of Palestine.* Berlin: Humboldt-Universität zu Berlin, Philosophische Fakultät III, 2005.

Mulder, Nicholas. *The Economic Weapon: The Rise of Sanctions as a Tool of Modern War.* New Haven: Yale University Press, 2022.

Murphy, Alexander B. "The Sovereign State System as Political-Territorial Ideal: Historical and Contemporary Considerations." In *State Sovereignty as Social Construct,* edited by Thomas J. Biersteker and Cynthia Weber, 81–120. Cambridge: Cambridge University Press, 1996.

Mustafa, Tahani. "Damming the Palestinian Spring: Security Sector Reform and Entrenched Repression." *Journal of Intervention and Statebuilding* 9 (2015): 1–19.

Nabulsi, Karma. "The State-Building Project: What Went Wrong?" In *Aid, Diplomacy and Facts on the Ground: The Case of Palestine,* edited by Michael Keating, Anne Le More, and Robert Lowe, 117–128. London: Chatham House, 2005.

Naftali, Timothy. *Blind Spot: The Secret History of American Counterterrorism.* New York: Basic Books, 2005.

National Bureau for Counter Terror Financing of Israel. "The Minister of Defense Designated Six Organizations of the 'Popular Front for the Liberation of Palestine' as Terror Organizations." *NBCTF.* 2021. https://nbctf.mod.gov.il/en/Pages/211021EN.aspx

National Counterterrorism Center. "March 2013: Watchlisting Guidance." https://assets.documentcloud.org/documents/1227228/2013-watchlist-guidance.pdf

———. *Terrorist Identities Datamart Environment.* 2017. https://www.dni.gov/files/Tide_Fact_Sheet.pdf

Netanyahu, Benjamin, ed. *International Terrorism: Challenge and Response.* New York: Routledge, 2017 [1981].

———, ed. *Terrorism: How the West Can Win.* New York: Farrar, Straus and Giroux, 1986.

9/11 Commission Report: Identifying and Preventing Terrorist Financing. Hearing Before the Committee on Financial Services, U.S. House of Representatives, 108th Congress, Second Session, August 23, 2004.

NGO Monitor. "The Durban Strategy." September 11, 2005. https://www.ngo-monitor
.org/in-the-media/_the_durban_strategy_/

———. "The Goldstone 'Fact Finding' Mission and the Role of Political NGOs." September 7, 2009. https://www.ngo-monitor.org/reports/the_goldstone_gaza_fact
_finding_committee_and_the_lund_london_guidelines_/

———. "Made in Europe: How Government Funded NGOs Shaped the Goldstone Report." October 1, 2009. https://www.ngo-monitor.org/reports/european_gov
ernment_funding_ngos_and_the_goldstone_report/

———. "NGO Monitoring Annual Report 2017." December 2017. https://www.annd
.org/data/file/files/PHROC%20and%20PNGO%20position%20paper%20
March%202018-pdf.pdf

———. "The Road Not Taken: Governmental Anti-Terror Regulations and NGO Funding." November 22, 2021. https://ngo-monitor.org/pdf/NGOMonitor_Terror
PolicyPaper_2021.pdf

No Way to Treat a Child Campaign. "New Bill Prohibits Israel from Using US Funds to Detain Palestinian Children." May 1, 2019. https://nwttac.dci-palestine.org/new_
bill_prohibits_israeli_military_from_using_u_s_funds_to_detain_and_ill_treat_
palestinian_children

NYU Paris EU Public Interest Clinic. *Bank De-Risking of Non-Profit Clients.* June 1, 2021. https://www.hscollective.org/assets/Uploads/NYU-HSC-Report_FINAL.pdf

OCHA. "Farming Without Land, Fishing Without Water: Gaza Agriculture Sector Struggles to Survive." Factsheet. United Nations Office for the Coordination of Humanitarian Affairs. May 2010. https://www.un.org/unispal/document/auto-insert
-205890/

OECD. "QWIDS: Query Wizard for International Development Statistics." OECD-DAC Aid Database. 2020. https://stats.oecd.org/qwids/

Oxfam. "Gaza Strip: A Humanitarian Implosion." March 6, 2008. https://unispal.un
.org/pdfs/GS_HumImplosion.pdf

Paasi, Anssi. "Geography, Space and the Re-Emergence of Topological Thinking." *Dialogues in Human Geography* 1, no. 3 (2011): 299–303.

Pantuliano, Sara, and Victoria Metcalfe. *Neutrality Undermined: The Impact of Counter-Terrorism Legislation on Humanitarian Action in Somalia.* Humanitarian Policy Group. March 20, 2012. https://odihpn.org/publication/neutrality-undermined
-the-impact-of-counter-terrorism-legislation-on-humanitarian-action-in-so
malia/

Parks, Lisa, and Caren Kaplan, eds. *Life in the Age of Drone Warfare.* Durham: Duke University Press, 2018.

Peterson, Andrew. "Addressing Tomorrow's Terrorists." *Journal of National Security Law & Policy* 2, no. 2 (2008): 297–354.

Petraeus, David H. "Learning Counterinsurgency: Observations from Soldiering in Iraq." *Military Review* (January–February 2006): 2–11.

Petti, Alessandro, Sandi Hilal, and Eyal Weizman. *Architecture After Revolution.* Berlin: Sternberg Press, 2013.

Plitnick, Michael, and Chris Toensing. " 'The Israel Lobby' in Perspective." *Middle East Report* (2007): 42–47.

PNCRCF. "Against Terrorism and Against Conditional Funding: Statement of the Palestinian National Campaign to Reject Conditional Funding." Palestinian National Campaign to Reject Conditional Funding. December 30, 2019. https://www.badil.org/en/publication/press-releases/90-2019/5033-pr-en-301219-65.html

———. "All You Need to Know About the EU's Counter-Terrorism Clause and Its Destructive Impact on Palestinian Civil Society." August 2020. https://www.badil.org/phocadownloadpap/badil-new/campaining-tools/brochures/2020/Q&A-eu-campaign-en.pdf

PNGO. "The Palestinian Non-Governmental Organizations Call for the Halting of Conditional Support." Palestinian NGO Network. July 12, 2003.

Policy Working Group. *NGO Monitor: Shrinking Space.* 2018. http://policyworkinggroup.org.il/report_en.pdf

"The President's New Counterterrorism Initiative [Cable]." *WikiLeaks.* January 25, 1995. https://search.wikileaks.org/plusd/cables/95STATE19130_a.html

Priest, Dana, and William M. Arkin. "Top Secret America: A Look at the Military's Joint Special Operations Command." *Washington Post.* September 2, 2011. https://www.washingtonpost.com/world/national-security/top-secret-america-a-look-at-the-militarys-joint-special-operations-command/2011/08/30/gIQAvYuAxJ_story.html

———. *Top Secret America: The Rise of the New American Security State.* New York: Little, Brown and Company, 2011.

Puar, Jasbir K. *The Right to Maim: Debility, Capacity, Disability.* Durham: Duke University Press, 2017.

Quandt, William B. *Peace Process: American Diplomacy and the Arab–Israeli Conflict Since 1967.* Berkeley: University of California Press, 2005.

Qutami, Loubie. "Palestine and the US 'War on Terror.' " Episode 29 [Webinar]. Coalition for Civil Freedoms. May 21, 2021.

Rabbani, Mouin. "Quick Thoughts: Mouin Rabbani on Israeli Annexation." *Jadaliyya.* July 4, 2020. https://www.jadaliyya.com/Details/41380/Quick-Thoughts-Mouin-Rabbani-on-Israeli-Annexation

———. "Team Trump's Magical Thinking on Palestine." *The Nation.* September 14, 2018. https://www.thenation.com/article/archive/team-trumps-magical-thinking-on-palestine/

Rabie, Kareem. *Palestine Is Throwing a Party and the Whole World Is Invited: Capital and State Building in the West Bank*. Durham: Duke University Press, 2021.

Rankin, Jennifer. "One Million Face Hunger in Gaza After US Cut to Palestine Aid." *The Guardian*. May 15, 2019. https://www.theguardian.com/world/2019/may/15/1-million-face-hunger-in-gaza-after-us-cut-to-palestine-aid#:~:text=More%20than%20a%20million%20people,a%20UN%20agency%20has%20said.

Reid-Henry, Simon. "On the Politics of Our Humanitarian Present." *Environment and Planning D, Society & Space* 31, no. 4 (2013): 753–760.

Roy, Sara. "De-Development Revisited: Palestinian Economy and Society Since Oslo." *Journal of Palestine Studies* 28, no. 3 (1999): 64–82.

Rubaii, Kali. "Birth Defects and the Toxic Legacy of War in Iraq." *Middle East Report* 296 (2020): 1–11.

———. "Counterinsurgency and the Ethical Life of Material Things in Iraq's Anbar Province." PhD dissertation, anthropology. University of California, Santa Cruz, 2018.

Ruff, Kathryn A. "Scared to Donate: An Examination of the Effects of Designating Muslim Charities as Terrorist Organizations on the First Amendment Rights of Muslim Donors." *New York University Journal of Legislation and Public Policy* 9 (2006): 447–502.

Sabin, Barry. *The 9/11 Commission Report: Identifying and Preventing Terrorist Financing*. Hearing Before the Committee on Financial Services, U.S. House of Representatives, 108th Congress, Second Session, August 23, 2004. US Government Printing Office, 2004.

Said, Edward. "The Essential Terrorist." *The Nation*. August 15, 2006 [1986]. https://www.thenation.com/article/archive/essential-terrorist/

———. "The Morning After." *London Review of Books* 15, no. 21 (1993): 3–5.

Said, Wadie E. "Coercing Voluntariness." *Indiana Law Journal* 85, no. 1 (2010): 1–48.

———. *Crimes of Terror: The Legal and Political Implications of Federal Terrorism Prosecutions*. Oxford: Oxford University Press, 2015.

———. "The Material Support Prosecution and Foreign Policy." *Indiana Law Journal* 86, no. 2 (2011): 543–594.

———. "Sentencing Terrorist Crimes." *Ohio State Law Journal* 75, no. 3 (2014): 477–528.

Salamanca, Omar J. "Assembling the Fabric of Life: When Settler Colonialism Becomes Development." *Journal of Palestine Studies* 45, no. 4 (2016): 64–80.

———. "Unplug and Play: Manufacturing Collapse in Gaza." *Human Geography* 4, no. 1 (2011): 22–37.

Savage, Charlie. "Biden Seeks Update for a Much-Stretched Law That Authorizes the

War on Terrorism." *New York Times.* March 5, 2021. https://www.nytimes.com/ 2021/03/05/us/politics/biden-war-powers.html

Scahill, Jeremy. "The Assassination Complex: Secret Military Documents Expose the Inner Workings of Obama's Drone Wars." *The Intercept.* October 15, 2015. https:// theintercept.com/drone-papers/the-assassination-complex/

Scahill, Jeremy, and Ryan Devereaux. "Blacklisted: The Secret Government Rule-book for Labeling You a Terrorist." *The Intercept.* July 23, 2014. https://theintercept .com/2014/07/23/blacklisted/

Secor, Anna. "Topological City." *Urban Geography* 34, no. 4 (2013): 430–444.

Serres, Michel, and Bruno Latour. *Conversations on Science, Culture and Time.* Ann Arbor: University of Michigan Press, 1995.

Shamas, Diala, and Nermeen Arastu. *Mapping Muslims: NYPD Spying and Its Impact on American Muslims.* Creating Law Enforcement Accountability & Responsibility Project, CUNY School of Law. 2013. http://www.law.cuny.edu/academics/ clinics/immigration/clear/Mapping-Muslims.pdf

Sharma, Aradhana, and Akhil Gupta, eds. *The Anthropology of the State: A Reader.* Malden: Blackwell Publishing, 2006.

Sharp, Jeremy. "U.S. Foreign Aid to Israel." Congressional Research Service. February 18, 2022. https://sgp.fas.org/crs/mideast/RL33222.pdf

Sharp, Jeremy, and Christopher M. Blanchard. "U.S. Foreign Aid to the Palestinians: CRS Report for Congress." Congressional Research Service, Library of Congress. June 27, 2006. https://www.everycrsreport.com/files/20060627_RS22370_f7436 0b59d356335a3184dfa6d0d8f4648324b7d.pdf

Shehadeh, Raja. "By Banning Six Palestinian NGOs, Israel Has Entered a New Era of Impunity." *The Guardian.* October 28, 2021. https://www.theguardian.com/ commentisfree/2021/oct/28/ngo-israel-human-rights-al-haq-palestinians

Shezaf, Hagar. "The NGOs Israel Designated as Terror Groups Remain Legal in the West Bank." *Haaretz.* November 1, 2021. https://www.haaretz.com/israel-news/ .premium-the-ngos-israel-designated-as-terror-groups-remain-legal-in-the -west-bank-1.10345231?v=1649010714063

Shushan, Debra. "Congress Must Move Quickly to Fix the Anti-Terrorism Clarification Act." *The Hill.* January 28, 2019. https://thehill.com/opinion/national-secur ity/427213-congress-must-move-quickly-to-fix-the-anti-terrorism-clarification

Signoles, Aude. "Local Government in Palestine." *Agence Française de Développement.* April 6, 2018. https://issuu.com/objectif-developpement/docs/02-va-fo cales

Silver, Charlotte. "The Unjust Fate of an American 'Terrorist.'" *Al-Jazeera.* September 22, 2012. http://www.aljazeera.com/indepth/opinion/2012/09/201291179187486

92.html

Simpson, Audra. *Mohawk Interruptus: Political Life Across the Borders of Settler States*. Durham: Duke University Press, 2014.

———. "On Ethnographic Refusal: Indigeneity, 'Voice' and Colonial Citizenship." *Junctures* 9, no. 1 (2007): 67–80.

Simpson, Leanne B. "The Misery of Settler Colonialism: Roundtable on Glen Coulthard's *Red Skin, White Masks* and Audra Simpson's *Mohawk Interruptus*." Paper presented at the American Studies Association Annual Meeting. 2015.

Sinnar, Shirin. "Separate and Unequal: The Law of 'Domestic' and 'International' Terrorism." *Michigan Law Review* 117, no. 7 (2019): 1333–1404.

Slim, Hugo. "With or Against? Humanitarian Agencies and Coalition Counter-Insurgency." *Refugee Survey Quarterly* 23, no. 4 (2004): 23–47.

Stäheli, Urs. "Indexing—The Politics of Invisibility." *Environment and Planning D: Society and Space* 34, no. 1 (2016): 14–29.

Stamatopoulou-Robbins, Sophia. "In Colonial Shoes: Notes on the Material Afterlife in Post-Oslo Palestine." *Jerusalem Quarterly* 48, no. Winter (2011): 54–77.

———. *Waste Siege: The Life of Infrastructure in Palestine*. Stanford: Stanford University Press, 2019.

Stampnitzky, Lisa. *Disciplining Terror: How Experts Invented "Terrorism."* Cambridge: Cambridge University Press, 2013.

Stempel, Jonathan. "Arab Bank Terrorism Case Ends as U.S. Court Voids Jury Verdict." *Reuters*. Feburary 9, 2018. https://www.reuters.com/article/us-arab-bank-decision/arab-bank-terrorism-case-ends-as-u-s-court-voids-jury-verdict-idUS KBN1FT26Z

Stoler, Ann L. "Imperial Formations and the Opacities of Rule." In *Lessons of Empire: Imperial Histories and American Power*, edited by Craig Calhoun, Frederick Cooper, and Kevin W. Moore, 48–60. New York: New Press, 2006.

———, ed. *Imperial Debris: On Ruins and Ruination*. Durham: Duke University Press, 2013.

———. "Introduction: 'The Rot Remains': From Ruins to Ruination." In *Imperial Debris: On Ruins and Ruination*, edited by Ann L. Stoler, 1–35. Durham: Duke University Press, 2013.

———. "On Degrees of Imperial Sovereignty." *Public Culture* 18, no. 1 (2006): 125–146.

Stoler, Ann Laura, with David Bond. "Refractions Off Empire: Untimely Comparisons in Harsh Times." *Radical History Review* 95 (Spring 2006): 93–107.

Strachan, Hew, and Sibylle Scheipers. "The Changing Character of War." In *The Changing Character of War*, edited by Hew Strachan and Sibylle Scheipers, 1–24. Oxford: Oxford University Press, 2011.

Sullivan, Gavin. *The Law of the List: UN Counterterrorism Sanctions and the Politics of Global Security Law.* Cambridge: Cambridge University Press, 2020.

Szulc, Tad. "US Moves for World Campaign to Counter Political Terrorists." *New York Times.* September 7, 1972.

Tabar, Linda. "The 'Urban Redesign' of Jenin Refugee Camp: Humanitarian Intervention and Rational Violence." *Journal of Palestine Studies* 41, no. 2 (2012): 44–61.

Tahir, Madiha. "The Distributed Empire of the War on Terror." *Boston Review.* September 10, 2021. https://bostonreview.net/global-justice/madiha-tahir-war-on-terror-empire-pakistan

———. "Life in the Age of Drone Warfare." In *Life in the Age of Drone Warfare,* edited by Lisa Parks and Caren Kaplan, 220–240. Durham: Duke University Press, 2017.

Tamari, Salim. "In League with Zion: Israel's Search for a Native Pillar." *Journal of Palestine Studies* 12, no. 4 (1983): 41–56.

———. "The Palestinian Movement in Transition: Historical Reversals and the Uprising." *Journal of Palestine Studies* 20, no. 2 (1991): 57–70.

Taraki, Lisa. "Enclave Micropolis: The Paradoxical Case of Ramallah/Al-Bireh." *Journal of Palestine Studies* 37, no. 4 (2008): 6–20.

———. "Urban Modernity on the Periphery: A New Middle Class Reinvents the Palestinian City." *Social Text* 26, no. 2 (2008): 61–81.

Tartir, Alaa. "Criminalizing Resistance: The Cases of Balata and Jenin Refugee Camps." *Journal of Palestine Studies* 46, no. 2 (2017): 7–22.

———. "Securitised Development and Palestinian Authoritarianism Under Fayyadism." *Conflict, Security & Development* 15, no. 5 (2015): 479–502.

Tartir, Alaa, Ṭariq Dana, and Timothy Seidel, eds. *Political Economy of Palestine: Critical, Interdisciplinary, and Decolonial Perspectives.* Cham: Palgrave Macmillan, 2021.

Tartir, Alaa, and Timothy Seidel, eds. *Palestine and Rule of Power: Local Dissent vs. International Governance.* Cham: Palgrave Macmillan, 2019.

Ticktin, Miriam. "Where Ethics and Politics Meet: The Violence of Humanitarianism in France." *American Ethnologist* 33, no. 1 (2006): 33–49.

Toensing, Chris. "A Dishonest Umpire." *Jacobin.* April 20, 2013. http://jacobinmag.com/2013/04/a-dishonest-umpire/

Touré, Madina. "CUNY Investigates Allegations That Partner Group Is Tied to Terrorism." *Politico.* March 3, 2019. Retrieved from https://www.politico.com/states/new-york/albany/story/2019/03/03/cuny-investigates-allegations-that-partner-group-is-tied-to-terrorism-885061

Trouillot, Michel-Rolph. "The Anthropology of the State in the Age of Globalization:

Close Encounters of the Deceptive Kind." *Current Anthropology* 42, no. 1 (2001): 125–138.

Turner, Mandy. "Peacebuilding as Counterinsurgency in the Occupied Palestinian Territory." *Review of International Studies* 41, no. 1 (2015): 73–98.

Turner, Mandy, and Omar Shweiki, eds. *Decolonizing Palestinian Political Economy: De-Development and Beyond.* New York: Palgrave Macmillan, 2014.

Turse, Nick. "America's Secret War in 134 Countries." *The Nation.* January 16, 2014. https://www.thenation.com/article/archive/americas-secret-war-134-countries/

UNGA. "A/HRC/34/70: Report of the Special Rapporteur on the Situation of Human Rights in the Palestinian Territories Occupied Since 1967." United Nations General Assembly, Human Rights Council. April 13, 2017.

———. "Report of the United Nations Fact-Finding Mission on the Gaza Conflict." United Nations General Assembly, Human Rights Council, 12th Session. September 25, 2009. https://documents-dds-ny.un.org/doc/UNDOC/GEN/G09/158/66/PDF/G0915866.pdf?OpenElement

UNHCR. "Counter-Terrorism Legislation Must Not Be Used to Constrain Legitimate Human Rights and Humanitarian Work." UN Office of the High Commissioner for Human Rights in the OPT. 2021.

———. "Israel/Palestine: UN Experts Call on Governments to Resume Funding for Six Palestinian CSOs Designated by Israel as 'Terrorist Organisations.'" April 25, 2022.

———. "UN High Commissioner for Human Rights Bachelet Calls Israel's 'Terrorism' Designation an Unjustified Attack on Palestinian Civil Society." Press release. October 26, 2021.

United Nations. "Two Years On: People Injured and Traumatized During the 'Great March of Return' Are Still Struggling." December 4, 2020. https://www.un.org/unispal/document/two-years-on-people-injured-and-traumatized-during-the-great-march-of-return-are-still-struggling/

United Nations Relief and Works Agency. "United States Announces Additional Support for Palestinian Refugees." July 17, 2021.

United Nations Security Council. *Letter from the Permanent Representative of Israel to the United Nations Addressed to the President of the Security Council 1972.* September 17, 1972. https://digitallibrary.un.org/record/588819?ln=en

United States and the United Nations Relief and Works Agency for Palestinian Refugees in the Near East. "Framework for Cooperation Between the United Nations Relief and Works Agency for Palestinian Refugees in the Near East and the United States of America 2021–2022." July 2021. https://www.state.gov/wp-content/uploads/2021/07/2021-2022-US-UNRWA-Framework-Signed.pdf

Unsleber, Steffi. "Destroying Belief in the Resistance?—The USAID Funded Palestinian Youth Summit." *Palestine Monitor.* September 14, 2011.

USAID. "ADS Chapter 319 Partner Vetting." January 15, 2021. https://www.usaid.gov/about-us/agency-policy/series-300/319

———. "Supporting the USAID Mission: Staffing and Activities from Inception to Present Day." 2007.

Usher, Graham. "The Politics of Internal Security: The PA's New Intelligence Services." *Journal of Palestine Studies* 25, no. 2 (1996): 21–34.

Wagner-Pacifici, Robin. *Discourse and Destruction: The City of Philadelphia Versus MOVE.* Chicago: University of Chicago Press, 1995.

———. *The Moro Morality Play: Terrorism as Social Drama.* Chicago: University of Chicago Press, 1986.

Weizman, Eyal. *Hollow Land: Israel's Architecture of Occupation.* London: Verso, 2007.

———. *The Least of All Possible Evils: Humanitarian Violence from Arendt to Gaza.* New York: Verso, 2011.

———. "Military Operations as Urban Planning." Interviewer: P. Misselwitz. *Mute Magazine.* August 28, 2003. http://www.metamute.org/editorial/articles/military-operations-urban-planning

Whidden, Michael. J. "Unequal Justice: Arabs in America and United States Antiterrorism Legislation." *Fordham Law Review* 69, no. 6 (2001): 2825–2888.

Whittall, Jonathan. "Treating Terrorists." *MSF Analysis.* August 5, 2016. http://msf-analysis.org/new-treating-terrorists/

Wilcox, Philip Jr. *Testimony of Philip Wilcox Jr., Counterterrorism Legislation.* Hearing on S. 390, A Bill to Improve the Ability of the United States to Respond to the International Terrorist Threat, and S.735, A Bill to Combat Terrorism. 104th Congress. 1995.

Wildeman, Jeremy, and Alaa Tartir. "Can Oslo's Failed Aid Model Be Laid to Rest?" *Al-Shabaka.* September 18, 2013. https://al-shabaka.org/briefs/can-oslos-failed-aid-model-be-laid-rest/

———. "Political Economy of Foreign Aid in the Occupied Palestinian Territories: A Conceptual Framing." In *Political Economy of Palestine: Critical, Interdisciplinary, and Decolonial Perspectives*, edited by Alaa Tartir, Tariq Dana, and Timothy Seidel, 223–247. Cham: Palgrave Macmillan, 2021.

Wilson, Woodrow. *Woodrow Wilson's Case for the League of Nations.* Princeton: Princeton University Press, 1923.

World Bank. "West Bank and Gaza: Local Government Performance Assessment." June 14, 2017. https://www.un.org/unispal/wp-content/uploads/2017/10/WBRPT_140717.pdf

Zanotti, Jim. "U.S. Foreign Aid to the Palestinians." Library of Congress. May 18, 2018. https://crsreports.congress.gov/product/pdf/RS/RS22967/59

Ziv, Oren. "Israel Again Tries and Fails to Connect Palestinian NGOs to Terrorism." Podcast Audio. *Occupied Thoughts.* 2021.

Index

Note: Page numbers in italics denote figures.

| Stanford Studies in Middle Eastern and
| Islamic Societies and Cultures

Laleh Khalili and Sherene Seikaly, editors
Joel Beinin, founding editor

For a complete listing of titles in this series, visit the
Stanford University Press website, www.sup.org.

The authorized representative in the EU for product safety and compliance is:
Mare Nostrum Group
B.V Doelen 72
4831 GR Breda
The Netherlands

www.ingramcontent.com/pod-product-compliance
Lightning Source LLC
Chambersburg PA
CBHW020658270326
41928CB00005B/172